# PUBLIC INVESTMENT, THE RATE OF RETURN, AND OPTIMAL FISCAL POLICY

# PUBLIC INVESTMENT, THE RATE OF RETURN, AND OPTIMAL FISCAL POLICY

KENNETH J. ARROW
and
MORDECAI KURZ

PUBLISHED FOR RESOURCES FOR THE FUTURE, INC.
by The Johns Hopkins Press
Baltimore and London

RESOURCES FOR THE FUTURE, INC.

*1755 Massachusetts Avenue N.W., Washington, D.C. 20036*



Resources for the Future is a nonprofit corporation for research and education in the development, conservation, and use of natural resources and the improvement of the quality of the environment. It was established in 1952 with the cooperation of the Ford Foundation. Part of the work of Resources for the Future is carried out by its resident staff; part supported by grants to universities and other nonprofit organizations. Unless otherwise stated, interpretations and conclusions in RFF publications are those of the authors; the organization takes responsibility for the selection of significant subjects for study, the competence of the researchers, and their freedom of inquiry.

This book is one of RFF's studies on water resources, which are directed by Charles W. Howe. Kenneth J. Arrow is Professor of Economics at Harvard University. Mordecai Kurz is Professor of Economics at Stanford University. Charts were drawn by Clare and Frank Ford.

*RFF Staff editors:* Henry Jarrett, Vera W. Dodds, Nora E. Roots, Sheila Barrows


Manufactured in the United States of America

The Johns Hopkins Press, Baltimore, Maryland 21218
The Johns Hopkins Press Ltd., London

Library of Congress Catalog Card Number 73–108380
Standard Book Number 8018–1124–4

# FOREWORD

Much of the work supported by RFF aims to provide a better factual and analytical basis for weighing the merits of alternative policies. These endeavors may take the form of the description of an emerging problem area, such as Herfindahl and Kneese's *Quality of the Environment;* the formulation of an analytical framework for a major problem of resource management, such as Krutilla and Eckstein's *Multiple Purpose River Development;* or the development of new theoretical structures required for the analysis of a general problem, such as that presented in Ayres and Kneese's article, "Production, Consumption, and Externalities."[1] From time to time, a specific need is uncovered for an extension of basic economic or social theory. It was a mutual awareness of the inadequacy of the existing theory of intertemporal criteria for resource allocation that first brought Professor Arrow and later Professor Kurz together with RFF.

The static theory of optimal resource allocation characterizes intertemporal value differences by one sole parameter: the discount rate. The selection of the optimum discount rate in a static setting itself poses many conceptual problems which have been discussed by leading economists, among them Baumol, Eckstein, Harberger, and Marglin. Professor Arrow made an earlier contribution in this field in "Discounting and Public Investment Criteria," published in *Water Research*,[2] which concerned the handling of risk by government.

[1] Orris C. Herfindahl and Allen V. Kneese, *Quality of the Environment: An Economic Approach to Some Problems in Using Land, Water, and Air* (Resources for the Future, 1965). John V. Krutilla and Otto Eckstein, *Multiple Purpose River Development: Studies in Applied Economic Analysis* (The Johns Hopkins Press for Resources for the Future, 1958). Robert U. Ayres and Allen V. Kneese, "Production, Consumption, and Externalities," *American Economic Review*, June 1969.

[2] Allen V. Kneese and Stephen C. Smith, eds., *Water Research* (The Johns Hopkins Press for Resources for the Future, 1966).

It has become increasingly clear with the passage of time that the criteria used in the allocation of resources must be derived from dynamic rather than static notions of efficiency. It has also become clear that these criteria have not been adequately related to the macroeconomic problems of stability and growth.

Professors Arrow and Kurz in this book have produced a pathbreaking formulation of the problems of public expenditure in the context of modern economic growth theory. Their work ties the determination of the allocation of resources between public and private sectors to the goal of getting the economic system onto an efficient growth path. While the models utilized are highly abstract, there are provocative implications for the determination of the appropriate discount rate and, indeed, the entire process of economic planning.

The authors first present a clear but rigorous analysis of optimal growth, distinguishing public and private capital as separate decision variables. This section of the book (chapters I–IV) constitutes an exceptionally fine exposition of modern growth theory.

Following this exposition, the authors develop an entirely new body of theory, a theory of "controllability." This seminal work systematically explores the question of whether or not the instruments of general fiscal control which the government has available (taxation, expenditure, and debt management) are sufficient to bring about an optimal intertemporal allocation of resources in the presence of the constraints imposed by private sector behavior. Private decisions may not lead to the optimum implied by the government's social welfare function even when there is no conflict between public and private objectives. The injection of the question of "controllability" into the fields of public finance and growth theory constitutes a major theoretical advance.

The findings of this study promise to influence the theoretical developments in the public expenditure field for a long time to come.

JOSEPH L. FISHER, *President,*
Resources for the Future, Inc.

September 1969

# CONTENTS

# ACKNOWLEDGMENTS

This research was supported primarily by a grant from Resources for the Future, Inc. to the Stanford Institute for Mathematical Studies in the Social Sciences; we have also received some support from National Science Foundation Grant GS-1440. The work was carried out at Serra House, Stanford University.

The early part of Mordecai Kurz's research was supported by a grant from Stanford Research Institute, for which special thanks are due to John Condliffe.

Stephen Marglin, Harvard University, was kind enough to read the entire manuscript, and we are indebted to him for some perceptive comments.

Finally, we wish to thank the secretary of Serra House, Laura Staggers, for her dedicated and patient help during all phases of our work.

Some of the material in the following volume has appeared or will appear in somewhat different form in the following articles by one or both of the authors: "Criteria for Social Investment," *Water Resources Research*, Vol. 1, No. 1 (1965); "Discounting and Public Investment Criteria," in *Water Research*, ed. Allen V. Kneese and Stephen C. Smith (Baltimore: The Johns Hopkins Press, 1966); "Optimal Consumer Allocation over an Infinite Horizon," *Journal of Economic Theory*, Vol. 1, No. 1 (1969); "Optimal Public Investment Policy and Controllability with Fixed Private Savings Ratio," *Journal of Economic Theory*, Vol. 1, No. 2 (1969); and "The Social Discount Rate," paper presented at the North American Seminar on Cost-Benefit Analysis of Manpower Programs, held at the University of Wisconsin (May 1969).

# THE FORMAT OF THE BOOK

The basic format has been selected to facilitate cross references.

*Chapters* are designated by roman numerals. Within each chapter we designate sections, propositions, theorems, and lemmas in numerical sequence. Thus,

"section II.3" means section 3 of chapter II;

"Proposition III.2" means Proposition 2 of chapter III.

*Equations* appear in parentheses in numerical order which begins again in each section. Thus,

"III.2.(5)" means equation (5) in section 2 of chapter III.

Equations appearing *within* a proposition use lower case letters. Thus,

"Proposition III.2.(b)" means equation (b), which appears in Proposition 2 of chapter III.

*Assumptions* are in numerical sequence within each section preceded by the letter A. Thus,

"Assumption IV.3.A.2" means Assumption 2, section 3, chapter IV.

If a reference in a chapter is made to any material in that chapter, the chapter designation will be dropped. Thus, in chapter VI we refer to section 2, not section VI.2.

When a reference in a section is made to an equation within the same chapter but in a different section, the chapter designation is omitted although the section designation is maintained. Thus, for example, in section 8 of a chapter we might refer to "equation 2.(17)" to mean equation (17) in section 2 of the same chapter. Similarly, within each section a reference to an equation will be designated by a number in parentheses. Thus, in section 3, for example, we might refer to equation (12), and not to equation 3.(12).

# SUMMARY

In view of the lengthy and technical nature of the following discussion, it seems worthwhile to expose the leading points of view in a more informal manner. In a short compass, the recapitulation is necessarily very incomplete. This summary is intended to be a self-contained statement of the ground covered in the book and draws in some cases on the exact words of the subsequent text which, in turn, depends in no way on the summary. The reader may therefore feel a certain jarring discontinuity, for which we apologize, if he passes immediately from this summary to the beginning of chapter I.

References in parentheses are to chapters and sections of the text.

## 1. The Basic Issues

In the social evaluation of a competitive economy, it is customary and proper to start by using market prices as an estimate of social costs. Why, then, are many of us not content to use the market rate of return on capital as the measure of its opportunity cost? Several related difficulties have long been pointed out or can be abstracted from economic theory (I.1–2, V.1–2).

a) There is not one but a whole spectrum of market rates of return. Which is the appropriate rate to use? Indeed, the spectrum is even greater than is apparent, for the prevalence of credit rationing means that numerous shadow rates exist that are unobserved on the market.

b) Since there are very few futures or other forward markets, the welfare-theoretical argument for the allocative role of market prices, and in particular for the interest rate, is gravely undermined. Only if price anticipations were reasonably accurate would the classical case remain valid.

c) The future is risky, and existing risk-bearing markets are not, in principle, sufficiently complex and differentiated for optimal allocation. This raises the question of how uncertainty is to be introduced into the evaluation of future income streams from government investment, possibly by adjustments in the discount factor.

d) We take it that government investment is primarily investment in public or collective goods; i.e., in goods that, because of inappropriability or increasing returns, cannot suitably be left to the market. Hence, the costs of these goods and, by implication, the returns to public investment cannot be fully recaptured. The problem of financing those investments (through taxes or borrowing) then arises and its solution may in turn have repercussions on the appropriate rate of discount.

e) There is a widespread feeling that the government, or the general public for which it is a trustee, has a special responsibility for the future above and beyond that expressed by actors in the current market. In formal economic-theoretical terms, a full optimization over time would require obviously impossible trading between unborn and living generations. The government is then thought of as acting implicitly on behalf of the unrepresented.

The first three factors are undoubtedly very closely interrelated. Since risk bearing is complementary to investment, the paucity of risk-bearing markets inhibits the making of forward contracts. The multiplicity of interest rates and the wide extent of credit rationing are clearly also substitutes for nonexistent separate markets for insuring credit risks. There is, strictly speaking, no single risk-free rate of interest, so long as there is uncertainty about price movements and about the future of the rate of interest itself (variations in the rate of interest give rise to capital gains and losses). The latter source of uncertainty is absent from time deposits and very nearly so from short-term bills, but long-term rates are, unfortunately, most natural for discounting projects of long duration. Even if there were some interest rate that could be regarded as essentially risk free, it would not necessarily follow that it measured the time preference of individuals. Such an interest rate would clearly be inappropriate for an individual who neither held nor issued any of the riskless security. Further, if an individual planning over an extended period of time knows that in the future he cannot borrow at the riskless rate, his current consumption and portfolio decisions will be affected in complicated and not easily understood ways. There is a presumption that the riskless rate would understate the true marginal time preference.

There seem, then, to be three basic problems in identifying the social discount rate with market rates: (a) the divergence between private values and market behavior because of capital market imperfections; (b) the divergence between social values and private costs in the products of government investment activity; (c) the divergence between social and private values with regard to perspectives for the future. A fourth, more specific, problem has been mentioned prominently: the imperfections of the capital market that are a direct result of the corporate income tax.

## 2. Economic Policy in a Mixed Economy (V)

In a perfectly and ideally centralized economy, the divergences just listed would be irrelevant; the central planning board could produce an optimum investment policy and enforce it. In the course of computing this policy, it might be useful to determine some Lagrange multipliers that can be interpreted as discount rates.

In a world in which both a government and a private sector are involved in economic decision making, the problem is in principle more complicated. After all, the decisions on public investment should be made in light of those on consumption and private investment, and vice versa, both because all these activities compete for the same resources and because there are complementarity relations between public and private investment and between investment of either type today and consumption tomorrow. The government cannot directly control private investment or consumption, but it can influence them through its *instruments,* such as taxes and creation or retirement of debt. Hence, the government decision on public investment should be made jointly with a choice of instruments. Since a decision on the volume of public investment is implicitly a decision on its marginal productivity—i.e., on its rate of discount—this position is equivalent to the more usual formulation that the social rate of discount depends on the mode of financing.

The clearest way of posing the issues is to regard them as the dynamic analogue of Tinbergen's theory of economic policy. The government is assumed to have certain ends and to be endowed with a given set of instruments for their accomplishment. It is possible to calculate what may be termed the *publicly optimal policy,* the policy with regard to all variables (in this case, public investment, private investment, and consumption) that would be adopted by a perfectly altruistic government with unlimited powers. Then the first question that might be asked is whether or not the publicly optimal policy can be achieved by a suitable choice of values of the instruments by the government. Formally and more generally, we will say that a given allocation policy is *controllable* by a given set of instruments if there exist values of the instruments, varying over time in general, which cause the private and government sectors together to realize that policy (V.0, V.3).

The controllability of the publicly optimal policy will of course depend on the number and power of the instruments available. When the specified instruments are insufficient to control the publicly optimal policy, it is necessary to seek a "second-best" policy, the best that can be achieved with the given set of instruments (V.4).

## 3. Investment Policy as Optimization over Time (I.3)

Some problems encountered in understanding the question of the social rate of discount are common to all problems of investment policy. They inhere in the stock-flow relations between capital, which determines output, and investment, which is that part of output that goes to the increase of capital. Capital is a stock, measured in quantity units; investment, like consumption and output, is a flow, measured in quantity per unit time. If there were only one commodity and one kind of capital, we would have, in the absence of depreciation, the basic relation of capital accumulation,

$$\dot{K} = I, \tag{1}$$

where $K$ is the stock of capital, $I$ is the rate of investment, and the dot denotes the rate of change of $K$ over time. If $Y$ is output and $C$ is consumption, we then supplement (1) with the identity,

$$Y = C + I, \tag{2}$$

and with some production relation linking $Y$ to $K$. In a perfectly centralized economy, the instruments of the government at any moment of time are $C$ and $I$, to be chosen subject to (2) to maximize some appropriately chosen utility functional which evaluates the entire consumption path.

This simple formulation has significant implications for analysis. Many previous analyses have simply evaluated the direct return from government investment. More recent writers have recognized that the return to government investment (the so-called throw-off) is available for future consumption, private investment, or government investment. However, even these writers have assumed an undue rigidity in future allocations. In particular, it is sometimes assumed that the proportion of the throw-off devoted to further government investment in the future will be fixed. But this reflects an inconsistency of viewpoint. The whole purpose of investment policy is to determine optimal decisions at a given moment; but then it should also be assumed that future investment is optimal.

A consistent simultaneous optimization of present and future investment decisions requires the use of mathematical techniques which, in their modern form, are known as "dynamic programming" and "optimal control theory" (II).

## 4. The Production and Valuation Assumptions

We assume now that there are two types of capital—private and government—and that output, $Y$, at any moment is a function of the quantities of these two types of capital, $K_p$ and $K_g$, respectively, and of the labor force, $L$. We assume further that the labor force is growing at a constant rate, $\pi$. First, suppose that constant returns to all variables prevail and that technological progress is labor-augmenting at a constant rate, $\tau$.

$$Y = F(K_p, K_g, e^{\tau t}L), \tag{1}$$

where $t$ is time. The function $F$ is concave and homogeneous of degree 1. If we define the natural rate of growth, $\gamma = \pi + \tau$, and let

$$y = e^{-\gamma t}Y, \qquad k_p = e^{-\gamma t}K_p, \qquad k_g = e^{-\gamma t}K_g, \tag{2}$$

then we can write

$$y = f(k_p, k_g), \tag{3}$$

where $f(k_p, k_g)$ is strictly concave (I.5, III.1, IV.1–2).

What may not be so well known is that certain cases of increasing returns can be written the same way. Basically, it is assumed that government capital is labor-augmenting, a case which certainly covers manpower programs very well. Assume that government capital and labor cooperate, with possible increasing returns, to produce an intermediate good, which might be termed "trained labor," which, in turn, cooperates with private capital under constant returns to produce output. The production function for trained labor is in particular taken to be of the form, $H(K_g, L^\delta)$, where $H$ is concave and homogeneous of degree 1. The case $\delta > 1$ displays increasing returns.

We may generalize this formulation by assuming in addition labor-augmenting technological progress at a rate $\tau'$. The production assumptions now take the form

$$Y = G[K_p, H(K_g, L_E^\delta)] \tag{4}$$

for some $\delta > 0$, where $G$ and $H$ are both homogeneous of degree 1 and concave, and $L_E = Le^{\tau' t}$. (This form is the most general which admits the possibility of balanced growth.) If we now define $\gamma = \delta(\pi + \tau')$, $\tau = \gamma - \pi$, and use the definitions (2), we can again arrive at (3), together with the relation, $\gamma = \pi + \tau$. (I.5, III.5, IV.8).

The criterion function that evaluates alternative policies is here taken to be

$$\int_0^\infty e^{-\rho t}P(t)U[\tilde{c}(t)]dt, \tag{5}$$

where $\rho$ is a discount factor for utilities (not necessarily for commodities), $P$ is population, $\tilde{c}$ is per capita consumption, and $U$ is the current flow of utility (or *felicity*). A detailed defense of this criterion function will not be attempted here but we hope that it will be accepted as plausible and will add a few remarks. (a) Expression (5) does ignore distributional considerations, from which we are abstracting. (b) The additivity over time and the stationarity of the discounting process seems eminently reasonable in the analysis of long-run consequences. (c) The infinite horizon is an idealization of the fundamental point that the consequences of investment are very long-lived; any short horizon requires some method of evaluating end-of-period capital stocks, and the only proper evaluation is their value in use in the subsequent future. (d) Utility attaches to per capita consumption, since that is what the representative individual receives, but if different generations have different numbers of individuals, society should maximize the sum of discounted total utilities for all generations; otherwise, the more numerous generations are discriminated against. (e) Some government capital contributes directly to consumer satisfaction, and it would be more general to let $U$ depend on $\tilde{k}_g$, per capita government capital, as well as $\tilde{c}$. The more general assumption is made in the following text; only the simpler assumption is made in this summary (I.4).

Assume in addition that $U(\tilde{c})$ is homogeneous of degree $1 - \sigma (\sigma > 0)$; the family of such functions is broad and flexible. If we define

$$c = P(t)\tilde{c}e^{-\gamma t} = P(0)\tilde{c}e^{-\tau t} \tag{6}$$

(i.e., total consumption adjusted for the natural rate of growth), then some elementary manipulation shows that

$$e^{-\rho t}P(t)U(\tilde{c}) = [P(0)]^{\sigma}e^{-\gamma t}U(c),$$

where

$$\omega = \rho + \sigma\tau, \qquad \lambda = \omega - \gamma. \tag{7}$$

The constant, $[P(0)]^{\sigma}$, can be ignored in maximization problems, so that the criterion function can be written

$$\int_0^{\infty} e^{-\lambda t}U[c(t)]dt. \tag{8}$$

We assume $\lambda > 0$.

By definition, we have

$$Y = C + I_p + I_g, \qquad \dot{K}_p = I_p, \qquad \dot{K}_g = I_g,$$

where $I_p$ and $I_g$ are the rates of investment in private and government capital, respectively, and the dot over a symbol denotes its derivative with respect to time. If we now introduce the growth-normalized investment rates,

$$i_p = e^{-\gamma t} I_p, \qquad i_g = e^{-\gamma t} I_g, \tag{9}$$

then from (2) and (6) we can say,

$$y = c + i_p + i_g, \qquad \dot{k}_p = i_p - \gamma k_p, \qquad \dot{k}_g = i_g - \gamma k_g. \tag{10}$$

It is probably easiest, after these reductions, to assume that we are dealing with a stationary population and technology, with future utilities discounted at $\lambda$ and both kinds of capital depreciating at a rate $\gamma$. From the preceding discussion and, in particular, formulas (8), (2), and (10), such a static model is completely isomorphic to the dynamic one we are primarily concerned with (III.1–2, IV.1–2).

## 5. The Publicly Optimal Policy (IV)

It is useful as a starting point to consider the intertemporal allocation policies that would be followed by a fully centralized economy which can choose consumption and both kinds of investment. We start from some initially given quantities of the two kinds of capital. The problem then is to choose the instruments—consumption, $c$, and the two kinds of investment, $i_p$ and $i_g$—as functions of time so as to maximize the criterion function, (8) or (5). Notice that at any moment of time the future from then on has the same structure; it is therefore clear that the choice of instruments is a function only of $k_p$ and $k_g$.

An optimal policy will, under the hypotheses made, tend to a stationary equilibrium, a pair of values for $k_p$ and $k_g$ (the growth-adjusted stocks of the two kinds of capital); call them $k_p^\infty$ and $k_g^\infty$, respectively. Under the hypotheses made, if the initial values of $k_p$ and $k_g$ are $k_p^\infty$ and $k_g^\infty$, respectively, the optimal policy calls for keeping these constant; then the growth-adjusted values of consumption and the two kinds of investment, $c$, $i_p$ and $i_g$, respectively, are also constant. However, the following discussion is not necessarily confined to balanced growth paths; the initial conditions may be arbitrary.

If the two kinds of capital are freely transferable between the two sectors, then a publicly optimal policy would regard the two kinds of capital as one. Specifically, let $k = k_p + k_g$; then at any given moment of time, the total $k$ should be reallocated between the two sectors so as to maximize output. (Under the assumption made, capital can be reallocated in the future as desired; hence, maximization of current output clearly dominates any other policy.) Maximization of output requires that

$$f_g = f_p; \tag{11}$$

i.e., the familiar doctrine that the rate of return on government capital should equal that on private capital.

However, it is important to note that even when this position holds, it is not a complete description of policy; by itself it does not in any way determine the volume of investment to be undertaken. We need a complete description of the optimal policy.

In this case, the process is fairly simple. Since we are choosing $k_p$, $k_g$, to maximize output for given $k$, the output is now determined, from (3), by

$$y = g(k) = \max_{k_p + k_g = k} f(k_p, k_g). \tag{12}$$

From (10), we note,

$$\dot{k} = i - \gamma k, \qquad y = c + i, \tag{13}$$

where $i = i_p + i_g$ is total growth-adjusted investment. We choose instruments, $c$, $i$, as functions of time, or, better, of $k$, so as to maximize the criterion function (5) subject to the constraints (12) and (13) for a specified initial value of $k = k_0$.

Associated with any proposed consumption stream, there is an implicit rate of interest, as will be shown in the next paragraph; then an optimal accumulation policy is one for which the marginal product of capital [the same for both kinds according to (11)] equals the consumption rate of interest (III.1–2, IV.1–2).

For a given consumption stream, the consumption discount factor for time $t$ is simply the marginal rate of substitution between future and present consumption; in view of (5) or (8) it is the ratio of their marginal felicities, modified by the discount on future felicities.

$$\text{Consumption discount factor} = (\text{felicity discount factor}) \times \left(\frac{\text{marginal felicity of future consumption}}{\text{marginal felicity of present consumption}}\right).$$

Since the (proportional) rate of change of a product is the sum of the rates of change of the factors and an interest rate is the negative of the rate of change of a discount factor,

$$\text{consumption rate of interest} = (\text{felicity rate of interest}) - (\text{rate of change of marginal felicity of consumption}).$$

Let us apply this statement to (8),

rate of change of marginal felicity of (growth-adjusted) consumption

$$= \frac{1}{U'(c)} \frac{dU'(c)}{dt} = \frac{U''(c)}{U'(c)} \dot{c} = \frac{U''(c)c}{U'(c)} \frac{\dot{c}}{c} = -\sigma \frac{\dot{c}}{c}.$$

Thus, the rate of interest appropriate to growth-adjusted consumption is $\lambda + \sigma(\dot{c}/c)$. Since growth-adjusted consumption increases at a rate that is lower than that of consumption itself by $\gamma$,

$$\text{consumption rate of interest} = r_c = \omega + \sigma(\dot{c}/c)\,, \tag{14}$$

from (7).

Then by the usual arguments, optimality demands that

$$f_p = f_g = g' = r_c\ ; \tag{15}$$

i.e., the rate of interest used in evaluating either kind of investment should be that implicit in the individuals' evaluations of their changing consumption stream.

A very important and not always understood implication of these elementary remarks is that the rate of investment (in this case, either type of investment) is not determined merely by the rate of interest. What (15) tells us is that the stock of capital is at any moment related to the rate of interest. Changes in the growth-adjusted capital stock (i.e., investment other than that needed to maintain the normal growth of the capital stock) require changes in the rate of interest.

Indeed, in (15), the line of causation in the short run goes from the existing capital stock to the rate of interest rather than vice versa. The latter in turn determines not consumption (and therefore investment) but the rate of change of consumption. From (14) and (15),

$$\dot{c}/c = [g'(k) - \omega]/\sigma\,. \tag{16}$$

This equation, together with

$$\dot{k} = g(k) - c - \gamma k\,, \tag{17}$$

deducible from (13) and (12), constitute a pair of differential equations governing the evolution over time of the capital stock and the consumption level. The initial stock of capital is given, but that of consumption is not, since it is an instrument.

In fact, the initial value of consumption has to be determined by the condition that the two time paths must converge to their stationary values. These in turn are found by setting $\dot{c}$ and $\dot{k}$ both equal to 0 in (16) and (17).

$$f_p^{\infty} = f_g^{\infty} = g'(k^{\infty}) = \omega\,, \tag{18}$$

$$c^{\infty} = y^{\infty} - \gamma k^{\infty}\,. \tag{19}$$

That is, in the long run the marginal productivities of the two kinds of capital have to equal the subjective time preference parameter; investment is that needed to increase the stocks of capital at the natural rate of growth; and consumption is whatever is left out of output.

From (16) it follows that consumption is increasing so long as the rate of interest is above long-run subjective time preference; i.e., if the initial stock of capital is low, then consumption is low and gradually increases to its steady-state value as capital increases to its steady-state value. The relation between investment and present and future rates of return is complex; it can be said that, to a first approximation, growth-adjusted investment is proportional to the discrepancy between the current rate of return and the steady-state time preference, $\omega$.

To repeat, the optimal level of investment, apart from normal growth, is not determined by the rate of interest but primarily by its future changes. An interest rate determination for optimal public investment policy makes sense only when joined to an appropriate level of investment activity.

## 6. Controllability with Fixed Savings Ratio in the Private Sector (VI)

We turn now to the controllability of the publicly optimal policy and to the possibility of being forced to seek second-best policies if the publicly optimal policy is not controllable in the sense of section 2. The possibility of controllability depends upon the workings of the private markets and upon the range of instruments open to the government.

We noted briefly in section 1 good reasons for believing that private savings behavior is not a decisive indicator of individual time preference. There is little evidence that savings are in fact responsive to rates of return, though it would be premature to say that the contrary is proved. For our purposes, the simple assumption is made that private savings are a fixed fraction, $s$, of disposable income.

$$s_p = sy_d, \tag{20}$$

where $s_p$ and $y_d$ are the growth-adjusted values of private savings and disposable income, respectively.

We consider several alternative hypotheses concerning the range of instruments available to the government. The first case most nearly reflects actual practice; financing of government investment is accomplished through the income tax alone. Borrowing, at least in peacetime, is relatively small compared with the total budget and is primarily motivated by considerations of employment, rather than allocation, policy. In this case, it is simplest to assume the absence of debt. Let $x$ be the rate of income tax. Then,

$$y_d = (1 - x)y, \tag{21}$$

$$c = (1 - s)y_d. \tag{22}$$

Private capital formation equals private saving; adjustment for growth yields

$$\dot{k}_p = sy_d - \gamma k_p, \tag{23}$$

while government capital formation equals taxes,

$$\dot{k}_g = xy - \gamma k_g. \tag{24}$$

The aim of an optimal policy is to maximize the criterion function, (8), subject to the above constraints. First, we observe that the publicly optimal policy is not controllable except by chance. From (23) and (22),

$$(\dot{k}_p + \gamma k_p)/c = s/(1 - s).$$

In the limit, then,

$$\gamma k_p^{\infty}/c^{\infty} = s/(1 - s).$$

If the publicly optimal policy could be achieved, the left-hand side would have a certain value which would not depend on $s$; hence, equality could hold only by accident.

Since the publicly optimal policy is not in general controllable, the optimal policy sought for is a "second-best" policy. We proceed heuristically as follows. For any given initial values of $k_p$ and $k_g$, there is an optimal policy which yields a value of total discounted utility, (8); call this value $W(k_p, k_g)$. Then the shadow price in utility terms of $k_p$ is

$$p_p = \partial W/\partial k_p$$

and similarly, for government capital,

$$p_g = \partial W/\partial k_g.$$

Any point of time could be regarded as the initial point; so two functions of time—$p_p(t)$ and $p_g(t)$, termed auxiliary variables in control theory—are associated with the optimal policy. Hence, an addition to either kind of capital (growth-adjusted) can be valued at these rates. At the same time, a consumption, $c$, yields a current utility return, $U(c)$, so that total national income in utility terms can be written

$$H = U(c) + p_p\dot{k}_p + p_g\dot{k}_g,$$

or, from (23) and (24),

$$H = U(c) + p_p(sy_d - \gamma k_p) + p_g(xy - \gamma k_g). \tag{25}$$

Since it is always desirable to increase $H$, the sole instrument, $x$, is to be chosen to maximize $H$. (Recall that $c$ and $y_d$ both depend on $x$.) Then setting $\partial H/\partial x = 0$ yields

$$(1 - s)U'(c) + sp_p = p_g, \tag{26}$$

which can be thought of as an equation to determine $x$ in terms of $k_p$, $k_g$, $p_p$, and $p_g$. Note that the burden of an increment of government capital, financed by taxation, falls on consumption and private saving in the proportions $1 - s$ and $s$.

The evolution of the auxiliary variables over time remains to be determined. The equations used are the analogues in utilities and auxiliary variables to the usual equilibrium condition for the holding of an asset: the marginal productivity plus capital gains must equal the rate of interest times the price. Since we are dealing with utilities here, the "rate of interest" is simply $\lambda$. The "marginal productivity" is the contribution to $H$. Thus the equation for private capital is

$$(\partial H/\partial k_p) + \dot{p}_p = \lambda p_p$$

and a corresponding equation holds for government capital. From (25), we find, after some simplification,

$$\dot{p}_p = \omega p_p - p_g f_p, \qquad (27)$$

$$\dot{p}_g = \omega p_g - p_g f_g. \qquad (28)$$

These equations, together with (23), (24), and (26), form a complete dynamic system. The solution is then defined if the initial conditions are specified. The initial values of $k_p(0)$ and $k_g(0)$ are given historically; however, those of the auxiliary variables have to be so chosen that the solution converges to a stationary value.

It is not easy to give a simple interpretation of an interdependent system like this. For analysis we clearly need not only the rates of return, $f_p$ and $f_g$, but also the auxiliary variables and their rates of change. These solutions are computable, however.

Some insight can be found by looking at the stationary values, which, as before, we denote by superscript $\infty$. The stationarity of the capital stocks, whose motion is defined by (23) and (24), implies,

$$s y_d^\infty = \gamma k_p^\infty,$$
$$x^\infty y^\infty = \gamma k_g^\infty.$$

Multiply the second equation by $s$, and add to the first, while recalling the definition of $y_d$.

$$s f(k_p^\infty, k_g^\infty) = \gamma(k_p^\infty + s k_g^\infty), \qquad (29)$$

a form of the Harrod-Domar relation. The stationarity of the auxiliary variables, whose motion is defined by (27) and (28), implies

$$f_p(k_p^\infty, k_g^\infty) = (p_p^\infty/p_g^\infty)\omega, \qquad (30)$$

$$f_g(k_p^\infty, k_g^\infty) = \omega. \qquad (31)$$

Equations (29) and (31) involve only $k_p^\infty$ and $k_g^\infty$, which are therefore determined. Then the asymptotic ratio of the auxiliary variables is, from (30) and (31), in the same ratio as the marginal productivities of the two kinds of capital.

Equation (31) is a little surprising; the long-run rate of return on government capital is the social rate of time preference, even though the return on private capital may be quite different. This holds because the benefits from a government investment project increase national income and therefore are partly saved. Hence, indirectly, the returns from government investment include some benefit from private investment projects. It turns out that in balanced growth this benefit exactly offsets the loss of private investment due to the initial act of government investment.

The uncontrollability of the publicly optimal policy and the need to resort to a second-best policy in the above discussion arose from the restriction to a single financing instrument, the income tax. To illustrate the possibility of controllability with more instruments, suppose that the tax rates on consumption can differ from those on savings, but that a balanced budget is still required (no borrowing) (VI.7). We shall understand the hypothesis of a fixed savings ratio to mean that post-tax savings and post-tax consumption are fixed fractions of total personal income. Thus, expenditures on savings are $sY$, but the government takes a fraction $x_s$ of this so that private savings are reduced to $s(1 - x_s)Y$; similarly, consumption is $(1 - s)(1 - x_c)Y$. Government tax collections, and therefore government investment, are given by

$$[sx_s + (1 - s)x_c]Y.$$

Then,

$$\dot{k}_p = s(1 - x_s)y - \gamma k_p, \tag{32}$$

$$\dot{k}_g = [sx_s + (1 - s)x_c]y - \gamma k_g, \tag{33}$$

$$c = (1 - s)(1 - x_c)y. \tag{34}$$

Suppose the government wishes to control the publicly optimal or indeed any other feasible policy. Since

$$c + i_p + i_g = y,$$

where

$$\dot{k}_p = i_p - \gamma k_p, \qquad \dot{k}_g = i_g - \gamma k_g,$$

it is clear that if the government can choose its instruments—the two tax rates—to satisfy two of the three equations (32)–(34), the third is automatically satisfied. Given any policy determining consumption and the two kinds of capital as functions of time, it is then only necessary to solve (34) for $x_c$, the consumption tax, and $x_s$, the tax on savings. The consumption tax thus insures that the correct amount of aggregate investment is forthcoming, while the tax on savings allocates it between the two forms of capital formation.

Controllability is also achieved if the government can both borrow and impose either an income tax or a consumption tax. It may be worth noting that merely counting instruments is not a sufficient condition for controllability; borrowing plus a tax on savings will not achieve controllability (VI.8).

Thus, the rule that the rate of discount for government investment should equal that in the private sector requires not only that the appropriate level of investment be forthcoming, as argued in section 5, but also, in a mixed economy, that the financing be accomplished by the unique appropriate mixture of taxes (or of borrowing and taxes).

## 7. Controllability with Perfectly Rational Consumers (VII, VIII)

The fixed savings ratio assumption is perhaps extreme in emphasizing the shortsightedness of the consumer. The opposite extreme hypothesis is that the consumer chooses his consumption pattern over time to maximize the sum of discounted utilities in full knowledge of all future interest rates and wage levels. We can then ask under what conditions the publicly optimal policy is controllable.

Although more general cases can be analyzed, we confine ourselves here to the case in which there is no divergence between public and private values. It is assumed, that is, that the consumer is seeking to maximize the same criterion function, (5) or (8), as the government.

We will assume here that the government borrows (or lends) and can impose one kind of tax. We also assume that bonds are a perfect substitute for private capital from the viewpoint of the consumer, so that the rate of interest on government bonds equals the marginal productivity of private capital. (Government bonds are assumed to be short-term bonds, so that capital gains may be ignored.)

We only summarize the results here. The fact that there may be an initial debt is important, because the interest on it must be financed in any case, in addition to subsequent government investment. Actually, if the initial debt has an appropriate initial value, then choosing government investment according to the publicly optimal policy and financing it out of borrowing alone is optimal (VIII.2). An income tax in the ordinary sense cannot be used; it destroys optimality through the well-known double taxation of savings. But if the initial debt differs from the critical initial value just described, then an initial capital levy (which has no incentive effects) can be used to change the debt to the appropriate level, after which financing is again done only by borrowing. The initial capital levy might be thought of as a limiting form of the income tax (VIII.3).

The most interesting case is the one in which the sole tax is the consumption tax (VIII.4). It turns out that the publicly optimal policy can be carried out with a consumption tax whose rate is constant over time; the remainder of the government investment is financed by borrowing. Of course, this remainder might be negative, in which case the government retires debt or even lends to the private sector. Incidentally, the constant rate of the consumption tax has a simple interpretation. If *private wealth* is defined as the sum of government debt, private capital, and future wages discounted to the present according to the wages and interest rates implicit in the publicly optimal policy (wages equal to marginal product of labor), the consumption tax is then the ratio of private wealth to the total of future consumption discounted to the present. The consumption tax rate will thus depend, among other things, on the initial level of debt.

## 8. Risk and the Rate of Return

The analysis so far has been based on the implicit assumption that the returns to government investment are riskless. If they are not, then it is contended here that as a general rule the uncertain benefits and costs should be evaluated at their expected value and discounted at the rate of return appropriate to riskless investments. This statement is not applicable to all circumstances but is a proposition which follows from certain hypotheses that are approximately fulfilled, with some exceptions.

First, suppose that: (a) an optimal allocation of risk bearing occurs before the government investment in question, and (b) the random returns on the government investment are statistically independent of those in the economy before the investment takes place. Then it can be shown that the proposed new investment should be introduced if and only if its expected net return is positive (I.2).

The assumption of statistical independence appears not unreasonable as a first approximation. However, that of the optimality of risk bearing in the private sector is more dubious. But much the same result still holds if the assumption is dropped, for the allocation of risks among all taxpayers implies not only that the risk to any one is negligible but more strongly that the total of all risk premiums tends to zero as the number of individuals grows indefinitely large. If the government adopts an expected value criterion, while private industry does not, then a government investment may indeed displace a private investment of higher expected value; however, this is correct in the context, because the government is supplying a valuable complementary activity of risk bearing which is not being supplied by the private sector.

We do note, however, the possibility that the benefits accruing to an individual as a result of government investment may increase his uncertainty. An example of this is the introduction of irrigation with an uncertain water supply into a predictably dry climate. Then, indeed, the benefits should be discounted at a rate higher than the riskless rate; but the preceding analysis shows that it would be still better for the government to offer insurance against failure of the irrigated water and then evaluate the total package of water and insurance at the riskless rate.

Note that no contention has been made that the government uses a riskless rate because it can spread its risks over a great many projects; Hirshleifer (1966, pp. 270–75) is certainly right in asserting that each project should be evaluated separately if the appropriate discount factors are used.

## 9. Some Loose Ends

Some aspects have been considered in the literature that have not been taken into account here. In effect, we have been assuming that, apart from divergence between private and social time preferences, the problem of determining the social discount rate arises from a particular set of imperfections in the market structure, the inappropriability of the products of government investment, the existence of an initial debt which needs financing, and, in section 6, the imperfection of private capital markets as reflected in the fixed savings ratio hypothesis. Implicitly, it has been assumed that the market structure is otherwise perfect. If, however, there are imperfections elsewhere in the market structure—such as monopolistic price distortions, excise taxes, or the corporate income tax that falls on the fruits of some but not all private investment—then the analysis becomes far more complicated. Any suggested policy must be evaluated in terms of all sorts of cross-effects.

Another neglected aspect is the relation between government bond rates and return on private capital. In the preceding discussion and indeed in virtually all analysis, the two are assumed equal, whenever government borrowing is considered as a possible means of financing. In fact, this is very far from the case. This raises the possibility that if public investment is financed by bonds, the government is in effect producing a joint product; the investment creates the opportunity to produce bonds, which are preferred to private capital. This suggests the appropriateness of discounting by the government bond rate rather than by the average observed rate of return.

# PUBLIC INVESTMENT, THE RATE OF RETURN, AND OPTIMAL FISCAL POLICY

# I

# BASIC CONCEPTS FOR THE THEORY OF PUBLIC INVESTMENT

## 0. Introduction

One of the major economic phenomena of the twentieth century has been the emergence of the public sector as the most powerful economic agent in all modern societies. The economic strength of this sector varies from complete control, as is the case in Communist societies, to subtle and indirect power, as is the case in the more decentralized economics of the West.

The economic-theoretical analysis that has dealt with the functioning of the government sector has mostly been focused on two major aspects: on one hand, fiscal and monetary policies directed toward stability and growth and, on the other, the theory of public finance dealing with the welfare implications of alternative ways of financing the public sector. A limited amount of theoretical work has been done in the area of the behavior of the public sector as an investing agent. It may be contended that this behavior ought not to differ from the behavior of any private firm; we shall argue that this is not the case and that specialized criteria are needed to guide the investment decisions of the public sector.

Faced with a lack of conceptual development, the various agencies of the government have developed rules of thumb for their decision-making procedures. Under pressure from Congress and the public, the administration has sought to unify these criteria in order to have objective methods of evaluating alternative public projects. These efforts have resulted in what has come to be known as cost-benefit analysis. This analysis aims at measuring the cost of and evaluating the benefits from public projects so that they can be ranked according to their "desirability." The application of cost-benefit analysis is usually difficult since it involves quantities that have no market price. Thus, only further theoretical developments in these areas will clarify the issues and enable us to establish more reliable estimates of social returns from investments.

Most discussion of the nature of public goods has focused attention on the static allocation problem. The only serious work on criteria for public investments has been done in connection with the development of water resources (see Eckstein 1958; Hirshleifer, De Haven, and Milliman 1960). We shall not review this work but rather reconsider the problems afresh from a more fundamental point of view.

In the following sections of this chapter we shall consider several basic conceptual and technical matters that will serve to guide our investigation into the determination of the volume of public investments, with particular reference to its rate of return. In sections 1 and 2, the special nature of social investments is stressed, particularly those aspects relevant to the choice of the discount rate. In section 3, the general optimization principles of investment policy are discussed briefly, and some indication is given of how our approach differs from that of those who have already studied the field. In section 4, the criteria by which the optimality of alternative public investment programs is to be judged are discussed. Finally, in section 5, some of the basic ideas of the so-called neoclassical growth theory are summarized.

## 1. The Special Nature of Social Investments

### *Appropriability*

Most investments yield their benefits in the form of identifiable goods that can be marketed or withheld. These benefits are in a very natural way *appropriable* in the sense that the organization producing them can without difficulty charge individual consumers for them, so that those who want and need the product can buy, and others can refrain. The production of food and clothing provides, perhaps, the purest example of appropriable benefits. The future benefits from such an investment can be fairly measured by the output evaluated at the price at which it can all be sold, less, of course, all current production costs (wages and materials).

But a wide and important class of investments yields benefits which, in their very act of production, inure to a wide class of individuals. These people cannot be excluded from the benefits and, hence, a price cannot be charged that will effectively discriminate between those who want the service and those who do not. Water purification provides a simple example: if it is decided to install equipment that will improve the purity of the water, all users will receive the benefits over the lifetime of the equipment whether or not they would be willing to bear the cost in a free choice. (This choice is not only a matter of individual taste for pure water; some of the uses of household water, such as gardening, have much lower purity requirements than others, so that some individual consumers may, in fact, derive very little additional benefit.) The price system is not operative, for it would require that each consumer be given the freedom to buy water at both the older and newer levels of purity or, at the very least, be given his option between the two, with price differences reflecting cost differences. Water purification is really of the same order as the general run of collective services provided by the government. In this context it is differentiated from the rest only in that there is an investment component; i.e., the benefits and costs do not accrue at the same point of time.

The example of water purification indicates the common nature of all public investments: they generate a great many benefits which inure to individual consumers and firms in such a way that the normal market mechanism would not price these benefits correctly, and this leads to the incorrect allocation of resources to their production. This does not mean that one cannot design methods for pricing these benefits. In the example of water purification, it is possible to construct two water systems and let each consumer have two water outlets; in this way he can be offered each kind of water at a different price. However, in fact, there is generally only one water system, not two; thus, neither a competitive mechanism nor public decisions could lead to this double price structure for water.

There are other instances in which pricing of benefits would be technically feasible, but for other reasons it is not regarded as performing an appropriate social function. Elementary, secondary, and, to a considerable extent, higher education have begun to belong to this category. The public schools could charge pupils or their parents for the cost of education, but in the first place there may be a divergence of interest between the parents who are capable of paying and the children who are receiving the benefit. This is part of a wider class of cases in which the beneficiaries are incapable of appreciating the benefit, either because of natural limitations of understanding (as in children or mental patients) or because the benefits would not really be understood until they have been experienced. The second reason, in the case of education, is that the benefits of education accrue not merely to the students but to the society of which they are a part.

In general, the line between appropriability and inappropriability cannot be drawn very sharply. There are very few acts, even of private consumption, that do not have some direct effect on the welfare of others. It is a matter partly of empirical evaluation and partly of value judgment as to when the external effects of benefits are sufficiently widespread to set aside the principle that the individual is the best judge of his own welfare.

Another and very important reason, rooted in the facts of technology, exists for the treatment of wide-scale classes of benefits as inappropriable, even though it would be technically feasible to set prices; namely, in cases where there are increasing returns to the scale of operation. In that circumstance, a collective agreement to undertake a productive enterprise and to share the costs in some way may benefit everyone, yet any ordinary pricing system would fail. For example, competition among electricity systems would certainly not ensure an optimal allocation of resources but instead would probably reduce the supply of electricity to small proportions. It is, to be sure, often possible (for example, in irrigation) to determine the benefits through a pricing calculation, but the supply must nevertheless be arranged through a monopoly; because of the dangers of monopoly in certain circumstances, the investment must actually be provided socially.

For our present purposes it is not useful to examine in detail either the problem of measuring benefits or the use of pricing of government services to increase efficiency in their use. The main point to be made here is that the services derived from government investment may not be charged for at all, or, if they are, the rate need not correspond to their marginal usefulness to society.

### *Divergence between Social and Private Benefits*

A classic in economic theory is the case in which there is a direct beneficiary from whom the product can be withheld, but his act of consumption, or the act of production in order to achieve this consumption, yields benefits to other parties against whom no exclusion is possible. The water purification example cited above is an extreme case. To supply pure water to even one individual, it is necessary to supply it to everyone. Milder interactions are very common. Thus, treatment of infectious diseases is beneficial to the patient but, in addition, the possibility that other individuals may be infected is also reduced. Under these conditions it would be necessary to take into account the fact that the aggregate benefits are greater than the part that can be allocated privately with ease. Hence, to be justified, it is not necessary for an investment in public health, including medical care of infectious diseases, to be fully repaid from fees charged to patients.

A special possibility of this divergence may arise from the relation between successive generations; this point is discussed briefly in the following section.

*Production and Consumption Benefits*

Although, in the last analysis, all benefits accrue to individuals whom we may think of as consumers, the relation may be direct or it may be an indirect result of the facilitation of the production of goods desired by consumers. Most social investment activities yield benefits of both types. A highway increases the convenience of private automobile travel, a direct benefit to consumers; it also decreases the cost of trucking operations, thus ultimately decreasing the cost or increasing the supply of consumers' goods.

Consumption benefits are those whose immediate beneficiaries are individuals in their capacities as consumers; production benefits are those whose immediate beneficiaries are economic units engaged in production for a market. Thus, government investment may affect both the output of goods and the satisfactions of individual consumers.

## 2. Decentralization and the Discount Factor Appropriate for Public Investments

In a totally centralized society, the problem of optimal public investments is rather simply defined: The central planning board sets up its objectives and then seeks those investment criteria that will maximize these objectives subject to the technological constraints and resource availability. This kind of procedure will be discussed in chapters III and IV.

In a decentralized society, where individuals and firms are free to maximize their own objectives subject to their own private constraints, the investment and financing behavior of the public sector becomes a more delicate matter. Under these conditions, what can be said about the discount factor appropriate to public investment decisions?

One approach to this question is to ask: Why not use the market rate of interest?

*Social and Private Rates of Time Preference*

If the private capital market were perfect, and if there were no divergences between social and private benefits (in the static and intertemporal senses) on it, the discount rate on public investments would be the same as that found on the private market. The argument for this proposition is the standard one in welfare economics and need not be repeated in detail here: If the public investment program were determined by evaluating benefits according to some rate different from that of the market, then there would always be a way to increase total output by some reallocation of investment resources as between the public and private sectors.

It has been argued that the divergence between social and private benefits in the capital market is the consequence of a special responsibility for future generations considered collectively (see especially the view of Sen 1961 and Marglin 1963*b*, and the critical comments of Tullock 1964 and Lind 1964). According to this view, the government has an obligation to the future and, in particular, to unborn generations who are not represented in the current market. Each individual derives satisfaction from having wealth added to future generations. Each one can, by his own actions, add only infinitesimally to this wealth, but a collective agreement to do so will increase everyone's welfare. It should be made clear that this interest must be over and above the interest felt by individuals in the future welfare of their own heirs, born and unborn, for the latter is already reflected in individual time preference.

If this argument is accepted, it does not necessarily lead to a special rate of discount for social investment. Indeed, the optimal solution would be to lower the required rate of return on all investment, private and social (for example, by lending to private business at a lower rate than that of the market or by driving the rate of interest down through a budgetary surplus and debt retirement). More private investment would be undertaken so that the marginal investment would have a lower rate of return and the opportunity cost of capital would be lower. Then, without changing the rule of discounting the benefits of social investment at the opportunity cost, the interest rate would be lowered.

If, however, it is accepted that there is an institutional limit on the extent to which the government can engage in direct or indirect financing of private investment, the social rate of time preference may remain below the common value of the opportunity cost of capital and the individual rate of time preference. It would clearly not be socially advantageous to transfer resources from private investment to social investment with a lower rate of return, but it would be socially advantageous to transfer some resources from consumption to social investment because of the divergence between social and individual time preference. Under these assumptions, the appropriate rate of discount on future benefits from social investment will depend on the source of financing; it will be an average of the social rate of time preference and the opportunity cost of capital, with the weights depending on the extent to which resources are drawn from consumption or investment.

### *Imperfections of the Capital Market*

An additional argument against the appropriateness of using the market interest rate for discounting the returns on public investments is the well-known one of imperfections of the capital market. These are discussed further in section V.2.

*Risk and the Rate of Return*

Reference to *the* rate of return on government investment brings to mind the argument frequently advanced that the rate of return the government should require should vary from one project to another, according to its riskiness. This view hinges on the assumption that the government, like private individuals, should display risk aversion in its behavior. This assumption is disputed here; we hold that the government's choice should be risk neutral and that the proper procedure is to compute the expected values of benefits and costs, and discount them at a riskless rate, contrary to the view of Hirshleifer (1964, p. 85).

Suppose the future to be unknown; it is known that one of a set of states will prevail and their probabilities are known (or believed in). A given state is equivalent to a complete description of all production possibilities so that all uncertainties are resolved when the state is known. To summarize some earlier discussions (Arrow 1964*a*; Debreu 1959, chapter 7; Hirshleifer 1964, pp. 80–85; a further discussion of the points raised here will be found in Arrow and Lind, 1970), we can achieve an optimal allocation if we imagine markets in all possible commodity-options—a commodity-option being an obligation to deliver a fixed amount of a given commodity if, and only if, a given state prevails.

Suppose, for example, that there is only one commodity and, to make matters really simple, only one consumer (or all consumers are alike). The consumer or consumers start out owning claims on future production. The amount of the commodity they can claim is of course a random variable whose outcome depends on the state of nature. Thus, the representative individual is entitled, before trading, to an amount $\bar{y}_s$ if state $s$ occurs. Let $\Pi_s$ be the probability of state $s$, and let $p_s$ be the market price of a claim to one unit of the commodity if state $s$ occurs. Using the Ramsey–von Neumann–Morgenstern utility construction, the consumer chooses claim $y_s$ so as to maximize $\sum \Pi_s U(y_s)$, subject to a budget constraint, $\sum p_s y_s = \sum p_s \bar{y}_s$. Hence, by the usual Lagrangian techniques we have, for any two states $s$ and $t$,

$$p_s/p_t = (\Pi_s/\Pi_t)[U'(y_s)/U'(y_t)].$$

Equality of supply and demand on the market insures that $y_s = \bar{y}_s$, all $s$. Hence, the price of a claim in state $s$ is relatively higher than the actuarial value if the marginal utility of income is relatively higher. Under the assumption of risk aversion (diminishing marginal utility), the price is higher than the actuarial value for adverse conditions, and vice versa.

Consider now a small project that will yield a random variable, $h_s$, depending on the state $s$. It is worthwhile to introduce this project if

$\sum p_s h_s \geqq 0$. Since, as noted, the prices $p_s$ are not proportional to the probabilities, it might appear that something different from an expected value calculation is relevant. Indeed, in general this is so. But if we add a plausible condition we find the criterion reduces to the expected value. We suppose that the return to the new investment is independent of the variations in income before the investment is made. In the context of public investment, $y_s$ should be interpreted as the total national income considered as a random variable. The returns to a particular new project are apt to have little statistical relation to the previous national income. The criterion for introducing a new project can be written as

$$\sum_s \Pi_s U'(y_s) h_s \geqq 0,$$

the left-hand side being the expectation of the product of random variables, $U'(y_s)h_s$. If $h_s$ is independent of $y_s$, it is also independent of $U'(y_s)$, so that the expectation of the product is the product of the expectations. The criterion becomes

$$E[U'(y_s)]E(h_s) \geqq 0,$$

and since the first factor is necessarily positive, this is equivalent to the condition $E(h_s) \geqq 0$. Hence, for small investments uncorrelated with previous national income, the government should be risk neutral.

Indeed, in many cases (e.g., flood control), one would expect that there is a negative relation between $y_s$ and $h_s$, and hence a positive relation between $U'(y_s)$ and $h_s$, so that the new project may be justified even if its expected value is negative, since it reduces aggregate uncertainty.

Consider a private investment of comparable riskiness. In a perfect system of risk markets such as those suggested above, the firm can reinsure its risks in effect with the whole economy, and therefore would behave as the government should. But in fact these markets do not exist. Hence, the $y_s$ for the firm is basically only the firm's own other income, and this is apt to be positively related to the return on the new investment, so that the criterion for accepting the project becomes more rigid than the expected value criterion. Thus, the firm displays risk aversion, and the government should not be required to observe the same standards. Note that the difference between the expected returns in the private and public sectors is not evidence of inefficiency. The private investor does not value his uncertain return at its expected value but at something less. If the public sector can use the tax powers to spread risks widely, then it is appropriate for it to measure returns at the expected value. This should be equated to the certainty-equivalent of the private sector returns.

(As in all cases of imperfection, this raises the question of whether the important step might be the institution of risk markets. The trouble here is the difficulty of divorcing risk taking and responsibility. It is socially desirable to permit insurance against unavoidable risks, but not against a failure of the individual to optimize; and observation does not ordinarily permit a clear distinction, at least not costlessly.)

The argument given above extends readily from one consumer to many. That is, if either the benefits are so widely diffused that they are small for any individual, or there are adequate mechanisms by which possible beneficiaries may be insured against uncertainty in benefits, then the maximization of expected value is a Pareto efficient policy. Indeed, it is possible to make a stronger statement. The analysis to this point has been based on the assumption that the allocation of risk bearing before the public investment was optimal. But even if it were not, the cost of bearing the risks of a public investment would be negligible if the risks were spread over a large enough population and the investment itself was small on the scale of the national income. More precisely, let the *risk-premium* $k$ for the risk $h$ be defined by

$$E[U(y + h)] = E[U(y + E(h) - k)].$$

(Note that $y$, the preproject income, is in general itself a random variable.) We can apply this definition to each individual. If, for each individual, $h$ is defined as his share of the risk, spread more or less evenly over the population, then it can be shown that the total of the risk premiums for all individuals approaches zero as the size of the population becomes large.

However, it is important to remark that if benefits are uncertain, large in relation to other income of the beneficiaries, and uninsured, then the benefits are indeed valued by a risk-averting individual and should be valued by society at less than their expected value.

It can be argued that many markets, especially those in equities, do perform some of the functions of risk markets. This is correct, but their performance is far from perfect; as evidence, note that perfect risk markets would eliminate risk to the *firm*, and we know that this elimination has not occurred.

## 3. The General Nature of Optimal Investment Policy

Most previous analyses have simply evaluated the direct return from government investment. More recent writers have recognized that the cost of the investment may fall partly on consumption and partly on private investment, and that the return to the government investment is available for future consumption, private investment, or government investment (see Eckstein 1958 and Marglin 1963*c*). Of course, if rates of return were perfectly equalized in all directions, there would be no difference between these two points of view, but it is precisely the failure of equalization to work automatically that creates the need for a category of government investment, both in the real world and in economic theory.

However, those writers who have taken account of the future uses of the return to government investment (the so-called throw-off) have assumed an undue rigidity in future allocations; see, for example, Marglin (1963*c*), whose account is much the most complete. In particular, it is assumed that the proportion of the throw-off devoted to further government investment in the future will be fixed. But this reflects an inconsistency of viewpoint. The whole purpose of investment policy is to determine optimal decisions at a given moment; but then it should also be assumed that future government investment decisions are similarly optimal.

The implication is clear: *an investment policy is a simultaneous choice of present and future investments,* and the optimal choices at different times are interrelated. This point of view is of course the same as that applied to the theory of profit-maximizing private investment by Hicks (1946), but it has received little explicit recognition in analysis of the specific problems of public investment.

A consistent simultaneous optimization of present and future investment decisions requires the use of mathematical techniques which, in their modern form, are known as dynamic programming and optimal control theory. A heuristic exposition of these theories, and especially of the latter, is presented in chapter II. These techniques have been used increasingly extensively in the theory of economic planning but, to the best of our knowledge, the only application to the theory of public investment is that of Uzawa (1966). The model Uzawa discussed (especially on pp. 129–38) is similar to that discussed in chapter IV of this book. We differ, however, in our conception of the role of public capital in the economic system. He assumes that the output in each of the private and public sectors is determined by the amount of capital and labor invested in it, while we assume that private output depends on the amounts of both kinds of capital, as well as of labor. However, the analytic methods used are identical.

## 4. The Criterion Function

We have spoken of optimal investment policies; it is necessary to specify a criterion function by which optimality can be judged.

Since such judgments concern the welfare of a society of many individuals, some living, some not yet born, it will not surprise the reader that no definitive criterion can be given that will withstand all criticism. All that can be suggested here is an analytically manageable form of criterion function, or *utility functional*, which will (a) depend on the main factors determining the satisfaction derived by individuals from the entire economic system, including government investment, and (b) reflect value judgments about intertemporal distribution. We will not seek to represent the effects of government investment on income redistribution at a given period of time; this issue is assumed to be handled by government policies other than investment.

The criterion we propose is the following: Let $P(t)$ be population at time $t$. Then the utility we attach to a policy yielding per capita consumption, $\bar{c}(t)$, and per capita government capital, $\bar{k}_g(t)$, at time $t$, is given by

$$\int_0^{\infty} e^{-\rho t} P(t) U[\bar{c}(t), \bar{k}_g(t)] dt, \tag{1}$$

where $\rho$ is a positive constant, and $U$ a concave increasing function. In words, the flow of consumption and the services of government capital to each individual are assumed to yield a flow of what may be termed *felicity*[1] to each individual. The flow of felicity to society is the sum over individuals at a given time; the total utility from a policy is taken to be the sum over all time of the felicities of each time, discounted back to the present at a constant rate.

It is hoped that the form will strike the reader as reasonable. Some of the arguments leading to it will be reviewed here. We take up successively more complicated cases.

a) Suppose there is no extension in time and only one individual. Then the criterion is simply the maximization of $U(\bar{c}, \bar{k}_g)$; this form is the analytic representation of the observation that government capital yields direct consumption benefits in addition to influence on general productivity and therefore on consumption.

b) Now consider one individual who, however, lives forever. Then expression (1), with $P(t) = 1$, is based on the following hypotheses: (1) utilities are additive over time; (2) future felicities are to be discounted to the present at a constant positive rate.

Hypothesis (1) is equivalent to the statement that the marginal rate of substitution between consumption or government capital services at two distinct points of time is independent of their values at other time points. Over short periods of time this hypothesis cannot be asserted with confidence; there can easily be relations of complementarity or substitutability between satisfactions at nearby points of time. But our

[1] This term was first used by Gorman (1957, p. 43).

interest is, after all, in long-term investment policy. If we take units of time of the order of a year, the hypothesis seems much more reasonable. Losses or gains of satisfaction in one year are not likely to be much affected by what happens in the next year.

With regard to hypothesis (2), there are two possible objections. One is that the future ought not to be discounted at all; the other is that the discount rate may vary rather than be constant.

With regard to the first objection, it is not usually denied that individuals in fact behave as if they discounted future felicities; rather it is held, as for example by Pigou (1952, p. 25), that such behavior "implies only that our telescopic faculty is defective," and should not play a role in normative analysis. Ramsey (1928) similarly held that discounting is "ethically indefensible and arises merely from weakness of the imagination." But in an informal talk before congenial friends, his attitudes come through without being covered up by the Sunday-best clothes appropriate for a serious *Economic Journal* article; the passage is so charming that we cannot forebear from a lengthy quotation:

> My picture of the world is drawn in perspective, and not like a model to scale. The foreground is occupied by human beings and the stars are all as small as threepenny bits. I don't really believe in astronomy, except as a complicated description of part of the course of human and possibly animal sensation. *I apply my perspective* not merely to space but also *to time*. In time the world will cool and everything will die; but that is a long time off still, and *its present value at compound interest is almost nothing*. (Ramsey 1931, p. 291; italics added.)

It is hard to see why the revealed preference of individuals should be disregarded in the realm of time, where it is accepted, broadly speaking, in evaluating current commodity flows. Further, as Koopmans has brought out strongly, there is a fundamental difficulty with zero discounting; if consumption at all points of time is equally valuable, then total utility must be insensitive to changes at one point of time. (See Koopmans 1960; Koopmans, Diamond, and Williamson 1964; and Koopmans 1968.)

The second objection—that the discount rate may vary, for example, with the level of consumption—is precluded by the assumption of additivity over time plus an assumption of stationarity; i.e., the utility derived from the present and future should be the same function of present and future consumption (including services of government capital), whatever point is considered to be the present.

The above remarks are merely designed to make our choice of utility functional plausible; a much more rigorous examination is to be found in the above-cited works of Koopmans.

c) Let us revert to the case in which there is no extension in time, but there are many individuals. Since we seek to waive distributional considerations, we will make some heroic assumptions: (1) all individuals are alike; (2) the social welfare function is such that the optimal distribution is egalitarian. These conditions are satisfied by taking the social welfare function to be the sum of utilities. Given the quantities of consumption goods and government capital, the optimal allocation will be to give the same amount to everyone; hence, if there are $P$ individuals, the total social welfare achieved is

$$PU(\tilde{c}, \tilde{k}_g),$$

where, it will be recalled, $\tilde{c}$ and $\tilde{k}_g$ are per capita magnitudes.

d) Now suppose there is a constant population extended in infinite time. At each instant of time it is still assumed to be optimal to achieve an egalitarian distribution. Then combining the discussion under a) and b) leads to the maximization of

$$\int_0^\infty e^{-\rho t} PU[\tilde{c}(t), \tilde{k}_g(t)]dt, \tag{2}$$

where $P$ is the constant population.

e) So long as $P$ is a constant, it plays no role in the maximization of (2). Suppose now that population is growing so that $P$ is a function of time, $P(t)$. A number of authors who have studied analogous optimization problems in the theory of economic growth have used as a criterion function:

$$\int_0^\infty e^{-\rho t} U[\tilde{c}(t), \tilde{k}_g(t)]dt\,; \tag{3}$$

the felicity of a given generation is measured by that of any single individual, with no allowance for the numbers involved. This point of view seems incorrect to us; we agree rather with Meade (1955, chapter VI, especially pp. 87–89) that the social felicity is better measured by the sum of all the individual felicities in a given generation; if more people benefit, so much the better.

The difference between the approaches can best be described by the following analogy: Consider an economy consisting of two islands, with populations $N_1$ and $N_2$. The government is contemplating the allocation of an amount $\bar{C}$ among the members of the economy. Let $C_1$, $C_2$ be the total amounts of consumption goods distributed in the two islands;

within each island equal distribution is assumed. The criterion analogous to (1) is

$$N_1 U(C_1/N_1) + N_2 U(C_2/N_2),$$

to be maximized subject to $C_1 + C_2 = \bar{C}$. The solution satisfies the condition

$$U'(C_1/N_1) = U'(C_2/N_2);$$

i.e., consumption is equalized for all individuals in the two islands, which is obviously the correct solution since the geographical details are irrelevant economically. The criterion analogous to (3) is

$$U(C_1/N_1) + U(C_2/N_2),$$

and its constrained maximization implies

$$\frac{U'(C_1/N_1)}{U'(C_2/N_2)} = \frac{N_1}{N_2}.$$

Under this assumption, it is optimal to provide less consumption per head to the more populous island (if we assume that $U$ is concave so that $U'' < 0$). Analogously, the use of a criterion like (3) discriminates inequitably against more numerous generations.

## 5. Some Basic Propositions of Neoclassical Growth Theory

Public investment policy by definition involves commitment over time and, as modern economic theory makes clear, must be judged in the context of a growing economy. Fundamentally, growth here means increases in population and technological knowledge, though the course of capital accumulation enters as both cause and effect.

We shall present some of the basic principles of neoclassical growth theory as it has evolved over the past twenty years. This will serve as a background for the following chapters.

The growth theory which will be presented here originated in the work of Harrod (1939) and Domar (1946), and was further developed by Solow (1956) and Swan (1956). In the following exposition a few other contributions will be mentioned, but there is no intent to review the vast literature on the subject. For such a review article, the reader is referred to the work of Hahn and Matthews (1964).

### *Specification*

The theory at hand is aggregative in nature and deals with the broad tendencies of a growing economy. This economy is specified by three components; these are described first.

*Technology.* The technology of the economy is specified by a concave, twice differentiable production function of the type

$$Y(t) = F[K(t), L(t), t], \tag{1}$$

where $Y(t)$ is aggregate output at time $t$; $K(t)$ is aggregate capital stock at time $t$; $L(t)$ is aggregate labor employed at time $t$; $t$ is an index specifying the exogenous process of technological progress. The production function $F(K, L, t)$ is usually assumed to exhibit constant returns to scale in $K$ and $L$ so that

$$Y(t) = L(t)F\left[\frac{K(t)}{L(t)}, 1, t\right] = L(t)f[k(t), t],$$

where $k(t)$ is the capital-labor ratio; but we shall note later the possibility of treating certain cases of increasing returns. Output per man, $\frac{Y(t)}{L(t)} = y(t)$, is thus defined by a concave function of $k$,

$$y(t) = f[k(t), t]. \tag{2}$$

*Intertemporal choice.* Given the stock of capital and the size of the labor force, social output is determined. Society must decide now how much of this output to save and how much to consume. In the early development of the theory, writers assumed a constant savings ratio, $s$. Thus, if $S(t)$ is total savings, then it was assumed that

$$S(t) = sY(t). \tag{3}$$

In addition, it was assumed that there were no short-term economic fluctuations, so that full employment with equality between desired savings and desired investment was postulated. Hence, $\dot{K}(t)$, being the growth of the capital stock, was assumed to satisfy

$$\dot{K}(t) = S(t) = sY(t). \tag{4}$$

*Growth of exogenous resources.* The only exogenous resource in the model is labor, and in general it was assumed that the labor force grows at a constant proportional rate, $\pi$, such that if $L(0)$ is the labor force at time $t = 0$, then

$$L(t) = L(0)e^{\pi t}. \tag{5}$$

*Growth Without Technological Change*

We start with the analysis of the growth process under the condition of static technology so that the production function is written:

$$Y(t) = F[K(t), L(t)]. \tag{6}$$

Thus,

$$\dot{K}(t) = sF[K(t), L(t)], \tag{7}$$

and since

$$\dot{k}(t) = \frac{\dot{K}(t)L(t) - \dot{L}(t)K(t)}{L(t)^2} = \frac{\dot{K}(t)}{L(t)} - \frac{\dot{L}(t)}{L(t)} \cdot \frac{K(t)}{L(t)}, \tag{8}$$

it follows that

$$\dot{k}(t) = \frac{sF[K(t), L(t)]}{L(t)} - \pi\frac{K(t)}{L(t)} \tag{9}$$

or

$$\dot{k}(t) = sf[k(t)] - \pi k(t), \tag{9'}$$

and this is the fundamental differential equation which describes the evolution of the system.

In diagrammatic terms (from Solow 1956), the process is described in Figure 1, in which $sf(k)$ is a concave function which measures savings per

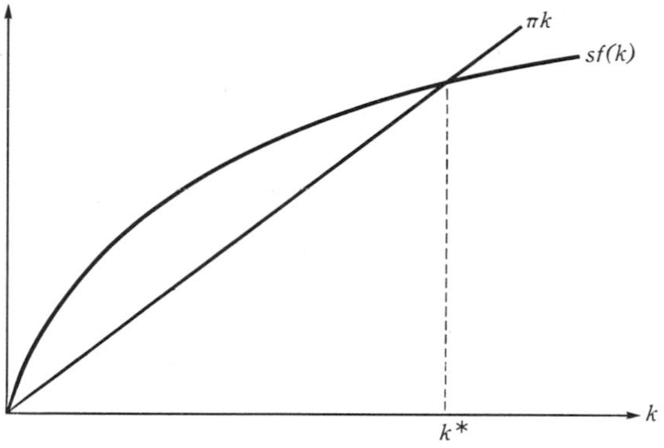


**Figure 1**

capita, while $\pi k$ measures the amount of per capita investments necessary to keep the capital-labor ratio constant. If $sf(k) > \pi k$, then $\dot{k} > 0$; and if $sf(k) < \pi k$, then $\dot{k} < 0$. It is seen that at $k^*$ we have $sf(k^*) = \pi k^*$ and $\dot{k} = 0$. This state is called balanced growth or long-run equilibrium of the system, and is characterized by the fact that at $k^*$ the capital-labor ratio and per capita income are constant. This means that *total* output and *total* capital are then growing at a constant percentage growth rate $\pi$, which is the growth rate of the labor force.

The existence of a value $k^*$ for which balanced growth occurs has not been guaranteed by our assumptions. Had we assumed, for example, that at $k = 0$, $f'(0) = +\infty$, and as $k \to \infty$, $f'(k) \to 0$, then the concavity of $f(k)$ with $\pi > 0$ would suffice to ensure the existence of a unique solution $k^*$. Okamoto and Inada (1962) have shown that much less is needed; if the marginal productivity of labor is positive, then $f(k)/k$ is decreasing as $k$ increases, so that the existence of a unique balanced growth is ensured.[2]

Note that in a competitive economy the interest rate, $r(t)$, is equal to the marginal productivity of capital. Hence, if $F(K, L) = Lf(K/L)$, we have

$$\frac{\partial F}{\partial K} = Lf'\left(\frac{K}{L}\right)\frac{1}{L} = f'(k)\,. \tag{10}$$

But from the concavity of the $f(k)$ function it follows that the behavior of the interest rate can be summarized as follows:

a) The interest rate depends on the capital-labor ratio only.

b) Since $f''(k) < 0$ (diminishing marginal productivity of capital), it follows that when $k$ is rising, then the interest rate is falling; when $k$ is falling, the interest rate is rising.

c) On the balanced growth path, the interest rate is constant and equals $f'(k^*)$. If $k(0) < k^*$, then over time $k(t)$ rises toward $k^*$ and the interest rate falls toward $f'(k^*)$; and if $k(0) > k^*$, then over time $k(t)$ falls toward $k^*$ and the interest rate rises toward $f'(k^*)$.

Finally, we note that $\pi$, the growth rate of the labor force, is defined to be the *natural rate of growth* and this is the rate of growth of the system in its long-run equilibrium. In this state $\dot{k} = 0$, thus $sf(k^*) = \pi k^*$; hence, the growth rate $\pi$ is nothing but $sf(k^*)/k^*$, which is the rate of

[2] In Okamoto and Inada (1962) the origin is accepted as a possible solution. Hence, the situation in the following diagram can occur; however, in this case the origin is the *unique* balanced growth solution.

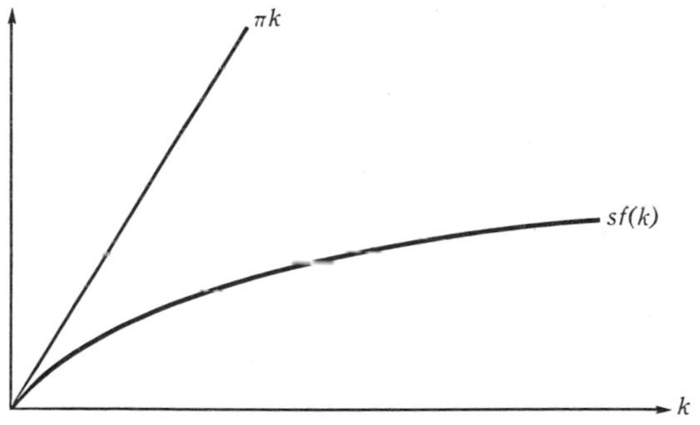

investment per unit of capital. Now we may wish to choose $s$ in such a way as to maximize the per capita level of consumption on the balanced growth path. This yields the quality $\pi = f'(k^*)$, which is the celebrated "Golden Rule of Accumulation" (see section III.2, footnote 4 and accompanying text).

*Growth with Technological Progress*

Once we introduce technological progress into the process of growth, the paths of accumulation change drastically. Naturally, the first question that comes to mind concerns the character of technological progress. In the abstract, the formulation $F(K, L, t)$, where $t$ stands for technological change, does not allow a great deal of theoretical development. The concept of "neutral technological progress" was defined in the literature in order to delineate one class of technological processes. However, two substantially different definitions were formulated: the first by Hicks (1932) and the second by Harrod (1937).

*Hicks neutrality: Technological progress in the function $F(K, L, t)$ is said to be* Hicks neutral *if the ratio of the marginal product of capital to the marginal product of labor remains unchanged at a constant capital-labor ratio.*

*Harrod neutrality: Technological progress in the function $F(K, L, t)$ is said to be* Harrod neutral *if the marginal product of capital remains undisturbed at a constant capital-output ratio.*

As we shall see below, these definitions lead to different restrictions on the function $F(K, L, t)$ but both have plausible motivations. Hicks's definition was motivated by the idea that technological progress ought to be called neutral if it does not change the relative prices of factors. Since, in a competitive economy, the ratio of the marginal products of labor and capital is equal to their relative prices, then it follows from Hicks neutrality that technological progress will not influence prices directly but only through its possible influence on the long-term capital-labor ratio.

Harrod's notion of neutral technological progress is based on the idea that, given the interest rate in the economy, the capital-labor ratio, and hence the capital-output ratio, is determined. Now, if technological progress leads to an autonomous change of the capital-output ratio without a change in the interest rate, it should not be regarded as neutral; conversely, if the capital-output ratio depends only on the interest rate, technological progress is neutral since its influence on the capital-output ratio is only the result of a change in the interest rate.

More recently, Robinson (1937–38) and Uzawa (1961) have shown that if technological progress is Harrod neutral, then the production function must be of the form

$$F(K, L, t) = F[K, A(t)L],$$

where $A(t)$ is a factor measuring the overall effectiveness of labor. In this case we say that technological progress is "labor-augmenting." Because of this it is often convenient to talk about the "effective" labor employed—the quantity $A(t)L(t)$—rather than the "actual" labor employed—$L(t)$.

On the other hand, it was shown that, if technological progress is Hicks neutral, the production function must be of the form

$$F(K, L, t) = A(t)F(K, L),$$

and $A(t)$ in this case measures the exogenous increase in the overall productivity of the economy.

Given the existence of technological change, we must alter our definition of balanced growth. Since we do not expect the capital-labor ratio to be constant along such a path, a balanced growth path can be defined as follows:

> *An economy is said to be on a path of balanced growth if the capital stock and total output are growing at a constant proportional rate; i.e.,* $\dot{Y}/Y = \dot{K}/K = \gamma$; $\gamma$ *is termed the natural growth rate of the system.*

Let us consider the case of Harrod neutral technological progress and evaluate the growth process. We shall consider a special case, commonly studied, in which the exogenous function $A(t)$ is an exponential of the form:

$$A(t) = e^{\tau t},$$

where $\tau$ is a constant called "the constant rate of Harrod neutral technological progress."

We shall then assume

$$Y(t) = F[K(t), e^{\tau t}L(t)];$$

thus, anticipating the fact that the capital-labor ratio is *not* going to be constant in the long run, we can consider the ratio between $K$ and the effective labor force $e^{\tau t}L(t)$, where the word "effective" refers to the impact of technological progress on the quality of labor. Defining

$$k(t) = \frac{K(t)}{e^{\tau t}L(t)}, \tag{11}$$

we have

$$y(t) = \frac{Y(t)}{e^{\tau t}L(t)} = f[k(t)] = F\left[\frac{K(t)}{e^{\tau t}L(t)}, 1\right]; \tag{12}$$

and since $\frac{\dot{L}(t)}{L(t)} = \pi$, we have

$$\dot{k}(t) = \frac{\dot{K}(t)}{e^{\tau t}L(t)} - \left[\frac{\dot{L}(t)}{L(t)} + \tau\right]k(t). \tag{13}$$

Hence,

$$\dot{k}(t) = sf[k(t)] - (\tau + \pi)k(t). \tag{14}$$

We see that this fundamental differential equation is identical in its character to equation (9′). A balanced growth here is characterized by the solution $k^*$ to the equation

$$sf(k^*) = (\tau + \pi)k^*. \tag{15}$$

Along the balanced growth path, $k^*$ is constant and the natural growth rate of the system is

$$\gamma = \tau + \pi. \tag{16}$$

This is seen from the fact that the constancy of $k^*$ implies the constancy of $y^*$, so that if $\frac{K(t)}{e^{\gamma t}}$ and $\frac{Y(t)}{e^{\gamma t}}$ are constant, then it follows that

$$\frac{\dot{K}(t)}{K(t)} = \frac{\dot{Y}(t)}{Y(t)} = \gamma = \pi + \tau. \tag{17}$$

Note that the fundamental differential equation (14) leads to the conclusion that if a balanced growth solution $k^*$ exists, then the behavior of $k(t)$ is similar to the one observed earlier without technical progress: if $k(0) > k^*$, then $k(t)$ declines to $k^*$, and if $k(0) < k^*$, then $k(t)$ rises to $k^*$. A similar argument applies to the interest rate. This is so since

$$Y(t) = F[K(t), e^{\tau t}L(t)] = e^{\tau t}L(t)f(k);$$

thus, the interest rate equals

$$r(t) = \frac{\partial Y}{\partial K} = e^{\tau t}L(t)f'(k)\frac{1}{e^{\tau t}L(t)} = f'(k).$$

And since $f(k)$ is concave, it follows that along the balanced growth path the interest rate is constant and equals $f'(k^*)$; when $k(t)$ rises the interest rate falls, and when $k(t)$ falls the interest rate rises.

It is crucial to note that if the system starts at time $t = 0$ with a capital stock $K(0)$, and labor supply $L(0)$ such that $\frac{K(0)}{L(0)} = k^*$, then the system is actually *on* the balanced growth path, and for all $t > 0$, $\frac{\dot{K}(t)}{K(t)} = \frac{\dot{Y}(t)}{Y(t)} = \gamma$. In the case of Harrod neutral technological progress, the existence of a balanced growth path is ensured by the same kind of conditions on $f(k)$ that operate without technological progress. For example, the condition $f'(0) = \infty$ and $f'(\infty) = 0$ is sufficient for existence.

In the general case of technological progress, the existence of a balanced growth path is more problematic. For example, if we have the same model as above except that technological progress is Hicks neutral, the production function is

$$Y(t) = e^{\tau t}F[K(t), L(t)]. \tag{18}$$

In this case, let $k(t) = \frac{K(t)}{L(t)}$; then

$$\dot{K} = sLe^{\tau t}F\left(\frac{K}{L}, 1\right). \tag{19}$$

Hence,

$$\dot{k}(t) = se^{\tau t}f(k) - \pi k. \tag{20}$$

A balanced growth path will require the existence of an initial value $k(0)$ such that for all $t > 0$, $\frac{\dot{k}}{k} = \gamma - \pi$ and the equation $\gamma = \frac{se^{\tau t}f[k(t)]}{k(t)}$ is satisfied. Hence,

$$\frac{e^{\tau t}f[k(t)]}{k(t)} = \text{constant}. \tag{21}$$

Differentiating logarithmically with respect to time, we find that

$$\tau + \left[\frac{f'(k)}{f(k)}k\right](\gamma - \pi) = (\gamma - \pi), \tag{22}$$

so that we have the condition

$$\frac{f'(k)}{f(k)}k = \frac{\gamma - \pi - \tau}{\gamma - \pi} = \text{constant}. \tag{23}$$

But (21) and (23) together imply

$$e^{\tau t}f'(k) = \text{constant}. \tag{24}$$

To interpret these results, we note the following:

a) Since the expression $\frac{e^{\tau t}f(k)}{k}$ is nothing but the output/capital ratio, equation (21) states the requirement of balanced growth.

b) Since $Y = e^{\tau t}F(K, L) = e^{\tau t}Lf(k)$, it follows that the interest rate, $r(t)$, is

$$r(t) = \frac{\partial Y}{\partial K} = e^{\tau t}Lf'\left(\frac{K}{L}\right)\frac{1}{L} = e^{\tau t}f'(k) ;$$

hence, $e^{\tau t}f'(k)$ is the interest rate. Thus equation (24) states the requirement that the interest rate be constant.

c) Since $e^{\tau t}f'(k)$ is the interest rate, and since $e^{\tau t}f(k)$ is the per capita output, it follows that

$$\frac{e^{\tau t}f'(k)}{e^{\tau t}f(k)}\,k = \frac{e^{\tau t}f'(k)(K/L)}{e^{\tau t}F(K, L)(1/L)} = \frac{e^{\tau t}f'(k)K}{e^{\tau t}F(K, L)}$$

$$= \text{relative capital share in output;}$$

thus, equation (23) requires that the relative capital share be a constant. It is clear, then, that the requirement that an economic system be capable of attaining a balanced growth path restricts the class of production functions and technological progress rather severely; in fact, we have the result by Kurz (1963, footnote 5) that if technological progress is Hicks neutral and the system is required to have a balanced growth path for all values of $\tau > 0$, $\pi > 0$, and $0 < s < 1$, then the only production function which satisfies these requirements is the Cobb-Douglas production function; i.e., $F(K, L) = AK^{\alpha}L^{1-\alpha}$.

*Increasing Returns*

We can, with little change in the analysis, introduce certain forms of increasing returns into our model. Just as labor-augmenting technological progress creates few major analytic problems but requires reinterpretation, so appropriate modifications of the way labor enters the production function introduce interpretative but not analytic difficulties. The following discussion is based on Levhari and Sheshinski (1969). For a first example, assume that the production function has the form:

$Y = F(K, L) = G(K, L^{\delta})$, where $G$ is concave and homogeneous of degree 1. (25)

If $\delta > 1$, then this is a model of increasing returns to scale. In the presence of labor-augmenting exponential technological progress, equation (25) becomes

$$Y = G(K, e^{\tau t}L^{\delta}) . \tag{26}$$

For example, the Cobb-Douglas production function, $Y = AK^{a}L^{b}$, with $a + b > 1$ but $a < 1$, can be written in the form of (25): $Y = AK^{a}(L^{\delta})^{1-a}$, $\delta = b/(1 - a) > 1$. Also, "learning-by-doing" production functions can, under suitable conditions, be written in this form (see Arrow 1962, p. 159; Levhari 1966, pp. 119–20).

It can easily be seen that a production function of the form of (26) can be fitted into the usual analysis under the assumption of exponential growth of the labor force.

$$\begin{aligned} e^{\tau t} L^{\delta} &= e^{\tau t}(L_0 e^{\pi t})^{\delta} \\ &= e^{[\tau + (\delta - 1)\pi] t}(L_0^{\delta} e^{\pi t}). \end{aligned}$$

If we replace $\tau$ by $\tau + (\delta - 1)\pi$ and $L_0$ by $L_0^{\delta}$, we have exactly the model just discussed. All the preceding analysis remains valid.

A form of increasing returns to scale that appears to be more complicated is represented by the production function

$Y = F(K, L) = G(K, K^{\epsilon}L)$, where $G$ is concave and homogeneous of degree 1 and strictly increasing in both variables, and $0 < \epsilon < 1$. (27)

A model that might account for a production function such as (27) is the following: Each act of investment is also an experience and produces "knowledge" as a by-product. The stock of knowledge increases the efficiency of each worker but, once formed, it is a public good in the Samuelson sense that the efficiency of any number of workers can be improved equally. On the other hand, the extent to which capital formation can, by its by-product of experience, increase the productivity of any one worker is subject to diminishing returns. A model such as this is more plausible when there is more than one type of investment, and will be so used in chapter IV and later chapters.

Suppose there were a balanced growth solution to (27), with a growth rate $\gamma$. With a constant savings ratio, $Y$ and $K$ must both grow at this rate, which might be considered the natural rate of growth of the system. Since $G$ is homogeneous of degree 1, it is possible for $Y$ and $K$ to grow at the rate $\gamma$ if and only if $K^{\epsilon}L$ is growing at that rate. But $K^{\epsilon}$ is growing at the rate $\gamma\epsilon$ and $L$ is growing, by assumption, at the rate $\pi$, so that $K^{\epsilon}L$ is growing at the rate $\gamma\epsilon + \pi$. Hence,

$$\gamma = \gamma\epsilon + \pi,$$

or

$$\gamma = \pi/(1 - \epsilon). \tag{28}$$

The previous transformations of variables will be useful here. Let

$$k = Ke^{-\gamma t}.$$

From the previous definitions and discussion,

$$e^{-\gamma t}K^{\epsilon}L = e^{-(\gamma\epsilon + \pi)t}K^{\epsilon}L = (e^{-\gamma t}K)^{\epsilon}e^{-\pi t}L = k^{\epsilon}L_0,$$

and

$$Y = G(K, K^\epsilon L) = e^{\gamma t} G(k, k^\epsilon L_0) = e^{\gamma t} f(k),$$

where

$$f(k) = G(k, k^\epsilon L_0).$$

From the assumed fixed savings ratio,

$$\dot{K} = sY,$$

it follows, by using the same manipulations as before, that

$$\dot{k} = se^{-\gamma t} Y - \gamma k = sf(k) - \gamma k,$$

which has the same form as (9′).

To show the existence of a unique balanced growth equilibrium, it is, as already seen, sufficient that $f(k)$ be strictly concave (with $f'$ varying from $+\infty$ to 0). To this end we recall the assumption that $G$ is concave and strictly increasing in $K^\epsilon L$, and note that $k^\epsilon L_0$ is a strictly concave function of $k$ when $\epsilon < 1$. Let $k_1$ and $k_2$ be any two values, $0 < t < 1$, and $k = tk_1 + (1 - t)k_2$. To prove the strict concavity of $f(k)$ means, by definition, to show that

$$f(k) > tf(k_1) + (1 - t)f(k_2). \tag{29}$$

Let

$$y = k^\epsilon L_0, \qquad y_1 = k_1^\epsilon L_0, \qquad y_2 = k_2^\epsilon L_0.$$

From the strict concavity of the function $k^\epsilon$,

$$y > ty_1 + (1 - t)y_2.$$

Then, since $G(k, y)$ is strictly increasing in $y$,

$$\begin{aligned} G(k, y) > G[k, ty_1 + (1 - t)y_2] &= G[tk_1 + (1 - t)k_2, ty_1 + (1 - t)y_2] \\ &\geqq tG(k_1, y_1) + (1 - t)G(k_2, y_2), \end{aligned}$$

the weak inequality following from the concavity of $G$. But by definition,

$$G(k, y) = f(k), \qquad G(k_1, y_1) = f(k_1), \qquad G(k_2, y_2) = f(k_2),$$

so that (29) has been shown to hold.

It is an easy generalization to permit both increasing returns of the type represented by (27) and labor-augmenting technological progress:

$$Y = G(K, e^{\tau' t} K^\epsilon L).$$

If we seek balanced growth paths at rate $\gamma$, the same analysis as that just given yields the relation $\gamma = \tau' + \gamma\epsilon + \pi$, or $\gamma = (\pi + \tau')/(1 - \epsilon)$.

The rest of the analysis proceeds as before. Note that the system tends toward a steady state when the variables have been normalized by the growth of the economy; hence, such magnitudes as total output or total consumption are eventually growing at the rate $\gamma$. Since population is growing at the rate $\pi$, per capita consumption is growing at the rate $\gamma - \pi$ and we might in this case define $\tau = \gamma - \pi$. This magnitude (and not the rate of labor-augmenting technological progress, $\tau'$) plays a role analogous to the rate $\tau$ for constant returns models.

It may finally be useful to remark that the two types of increasing returns are both special cases of the more general form

$$Y = F(K, L) = G[K, H(K, L^\delta)], \tag{30}$$

where $G$ and $H$ are both concave functions and both homogeneous of degree 1. Along the lines just used, we may interpret $H(K, L^\delta)$ as the production of "experienced labor" from capital and labor. The model (30) implies increasing returns if $\delta > 1$. To see that (25) and (27) are indeed special cases of (30), let $H(K, L^\delta) = L^\delta$ to derive (25), while $H = K^\epsilon(L^\delta)^{1-\epsilon}$, with $\delta = 1/(1 - \epsilon)$ in the second.

Suppose in (30) that $Y$ and $K$ are growing at some rate $\gamma$. Then $H$ must be growing at this rate since $G$ is homogeneous of degree 1. But again, since $H$ is growing at rate $\gamma$ and so is $K$, it must be that $L^\delta$ is growing at rate $\gamma$. We know that $L$ is growing at rate $\pi$ and therefore $L^\delta$ at rate $\delta\pi$, so that

$$\gamma = \delta\pi. \tag{31}$$

As before, if we define $\tau = \gamma - \pi$, all the results of the constant returns case are still valid with suitable reinterpretations. Also, labor-augmenting technological progress can be added to the model with no structural alteration. Finally, the strict concavity of

$$f(k) = G[k, H(k, L_0^\delta)] \tag{32}$$

can be demonstrated as before if $H$ is strictly concave in $K$ for fixed $L$.

# II

# METHODS OF OPTIMIZATION OVER TIME

## 0. Introduction

This chapter is designed as a heuristic introduction to modern methods of optimization over time. Investment planning, whether public or private, is, of course, a most important example of intertemporal optimization.

The exposition to be given here follows the modern techniques developed in the last twenty years—especially by the American mathematician, Richard Bellman (1957), and the Russian mathematician, L. S. Pontryagin (1962)—though they are a natural development of the calculus of variations studied since the seventeenth century and already used in an economic context by such writers as Frank P. Ramsey (1928), Harold Hotelling (1931), G. C. Evans (1930, chapters 14 and 15, and appendix 2), and Pierre Massé (1946).

It is not possible to give a rigorous derivation of the mathematical methods to be employed. Our intention here is simply to be suggestive and heuristic. The techniques to be used are especially those of Pontryagin and his associates, but they will be motivated from the viewpoint of Bellman's methods of "dynamic programming."

## 1. Dynamic Programming: Discrete Time, Finite Horizon

We imagine a system, economic or other, evolving in time. For the present assume that time is discrete; that is, it is divided into periods (days, months, years). At any moment of time, the system is in some *state*, which can be described by a finite number of coordinates. For an economic system, the amount of capital goods of each type might constitute a suitable state description. Let the values of the state variables at time $t$ be denoted by $x_1(t), \ldots, x_s(t)$.

In an optimization problem, there is some possibility of controlling the system. Thus, at any time $t$, there are some variables $v_1(t), \ldots, v_n(t)$, which can be chosen by a decision maker. The variables $v_i(t)$ are frequently referred to in the literature as control or decision variables; following the terminology of Tinbergen (1952, p. 7) in a static context, we here use the term *instruments*. In an economic system, the instruments are typically the allocations of resources to different productive uses and to consumption, or perhaps taxes and bond issues which at least partially determine allocations.

It is assumed that the state and the instrument variables at any point of time completely determine the state of the system at the next point of time. Thus, for a given technology and labor force, the outputs of all goods are determined by the capital structure (state variables) together with its allocation among different uses (by some of the instruments). The goods, in turn, are allocated between consumption and capital accumulation (through additional instruments). Thus the capital structure of the next period is determined. In symbols, the evolution of the state of the system is governed by the difference equations

$$x_i(t+1) = T_i[x_1(t), \ldots, x_s(t), v_1(t), \ldots, v_n(t), t], \qquad (i = 1, \ldots, s). \quad (1)$$

The time variable $t$ enters into the transition functions $T_i$ to allow for the possibility that they may vary over time as a result of technological progress, labor force growth, and possibly other exogenous factors.

Given, then, the state at some time, say 0, and the choice of instrument variables at each time point $t$ ($t = 0, \ldots, T$), the whole course of the system is determined. In this section, the analysis will be carried out only until a finite horizon is reached, after which the process ceases.

By suitable choices of the values of the instruments over time, alternative histories of the process can be achieved. As is usual in economic analysis, we assume that these histories can be valued in some way; i.e., we can express preferences as between alternative histories, and these preferences can be given numerical value. This is expressed in a *utility function* with variables $x_1(0), \ldots, x_s(0), v_1(0), \ldots, v_n(0), \ldots, x_1(t), \ldots, x_s(t), v_1(t), \ldots, v_n(t), \ldots, x_1(T), \ldots, x_s(T), v_1(T), \ldots, v_n(T)$. The optimization problem is to choose the values of the instrument variables so as to maximize the criterion function subject to the constraints implied by (1), the constraints on the choices of the instruments, and the initial values of the state variables.

More specifically, it will be assumed that the utility function is additive over time. That is, at each moment $t$ there is a return, or *felicity*, which depends only on the values of the state variables and the instruments at time $t$, such that the utility of a whole history is the sum of the values of the felicities at each moment of time. Let

$U(x_1, \ldots, x_s, v_1, \ldots, v_n, t) =$ felicity at time $t$ if the state variables have the values $x_1, \ldots, x_s$, and the instruments have the values $v_1, \ldots, v_n$. (2)

In what follows, the collection of instruments $v_1, \ldots, v_n$ will be abbreviated as $v$ and the collection of state variables, $x_1, \ldots, x_s$ as $x$; similarly, the values of the instruments at time $t$, $v_1(t), \ldots, v_n(t)$, will be abbreviated as $v(t)$, and the values of the state variables at time $t$, $x_1(t), \ldots, x_s(t)$ as $x(t)$.

In addition to the felicity generated at each moment of time during the process, the decision maker may also assign a value to the state achieved at the end of process, $T$. In an industrial application, the stock of machines may have a *scrap value*, and we will use this term generally. In a general economic context, if $T$ is not literally the end of the world, the capital stock left over at the end will have some use in the future. We denote the scrap value by $S[x_1(T), \ldots, x_s(T)] = S[x(T)]$.

The function $U$ will in general depend on time; because, among other reasons, of the phenomenon of time preference—future felicities being valued less if other things are equal.

The general form of a dynamic programming problem, then, is

Maximize $\sum_{t=0}^{T} U[x(t), v(t), t] + S[x(T)]$ with respect to $v_1(t), \ldots, v_n(t)$ $(t = 0, \ldots, T)$ subject to (1) and initial conditions $x_i(0) = x_i$. (3)

It will be convenient to introduce a notation for the maximum utility value realizable from some time $t_0$ on, given the state at time $t_0$. The *return function* is defined by

$$V(x, t_0) = \max\left\{\sum_{t=t_0}^{T} U[x(t), v(t), t] + S[x(T)]\right\},$$

where the maximum is with respect to the instruments $v_i(t)$ $(i = 1, \ldots, n; t = t_0, \ldots, T)$, and $x_i(t_0) = x_i$. (4)

Bellman's optimality principle is the observation that if, in the optimal solution to (3), the state at time $t_0$ is given by $x$, the optimal choices of instruments and state variables thereafter is identical with that implied by (4). In symbols, let $v_i^*(t)$ $(i = 1, \ldots, n; t = 0, \ldots, T)$ be values of the instrument variables which solve (3). From the laws of motion of the system (1) and the initial conditions, the successive states of the system are defined; denote them by $x_i^*(t)$ $(i = 1, \ldots, s; t = 0, \ldots, T)$. Now, for any $t_0$ and any $x$, there is an optimal set of instruments for $t = t_0$,

$\ldots, T$, when $x_i(t_0) = x_i$. In particular, let the instruments for time $t_0$ be designated as $v_i^*(x, t_0)$.

The functions $v_i^*(t)$ may be referred to as the optimal *strategy* or open loop control; the functions $v_i^*(x, t)$ are the optimal *policy* or feedback control. Then Bellman's optimality principle asserts, in this context, that $v_i^*(t) = v_i^*[x^*(t), t]$, where $x^*(t)$ is defined by (1), with $v(t) = v^*(t)$, and $x^*(0) = x(0)$.

This approach gives rise to a method of solving dynamic programming problems by backward recursion. Introduce the following notation: $\max_t$ means maximization with respect to the variables $v_i(t)$ $(i = 1, \ldots, n)$, holding all other variables constant. Then (4) can be written,

$$V(x, t_0) = \max_{t_0} \ldots \max_T \left\{\sum_{t=t_0}^{T} U[x(t), v(t), t] + S[x(T)]\right\}. \tag{5}$$

First, let $t_0 = T$ (i.e., consider the last stage of the process). Note that $S[x(T)]$ does not depend on $v(T)$. Then (5) reduces simply to choosing $v(T)$, so as to maximize $U[x(T), v(T), T]$.

Since $x(T) = x$,

$$V(x, T) = \max_T U[x, v(T), T] + S(x). \tag{6}$$

Now let $t_0 = T - 1$. Then,

$$\begin{aligned} V(x, T-1) = \max_{T-1} \max_T \{&U[x(T-1), v(T-1), T-1] \\ &+ U[x(T), v(T), T] + S[x(T)]\} \end{aligned}$$

But notice that the first term in the braces does not depend on the values of $v_i(T)$. Hence, when maximizing with respect to those variables, we need only consider the second term. We also require that $x(T-1) = x$.

$$\begin{aligned} V(x, T-1) &= \max_{T-1} \{U[x, v(T-1), T-1] \\ &\quad + \max_T U[x(T), v(T), T] + S[x(T)]\} \\ &= \max_{T-1} \{U[x, v(T-1), T-1] + V[x(T), T]\}, \end{aligned} \tag{7}$$

from (6). The maximization here is subject to the conditions that,

$$x_i(T) = T_i[x, v(T-1), T-1] \qquad (i = 1, \ldots, s),$$

or, in abbreviated form,

$$x(T) = T[x, v(T-1), \mathrm{T} - 1]$$

which is (1) with $t = T - 1$. Thus once the *function* $V(x, T)$ has been determined (in the sense that its values are known for all $x$), the function $V(x, T-1)$ can be determined by a straightforward maximization for any given $x$.

It is easy to see that this argument can be continued. For any $t_0$, with $x(t_0) = x$, we can write

$$
\begin{aligned}
V(x, t_0) &= \max_{t_0} \max_{t_0+1} \ldots \max_T \Big\{ U[x(t_0), v(t_0), t_0] \\
&\qquad + \sum_{t=t_0+1}^{T} U[x(t), v(t), t] + S[x(T)] \Big\} \\
&= \max_{t_0} \Big\{ U[x, v(t_0), t_0)] \\
&\qquad + \max_{t_0+1} \ldots \max_T \Big[ \sum_{t=t_0+1}^{T} Ux(t), v(t), t \Big] + S[x(T)] \Big\} \\
&= \max_{t_0} \{ U(x, v(t_0), t_0) + V[x(t_0+1), t_0+1] \} . \qquad (8)
\end{aligned}
$$

The maximization in (8) is subject to the constraint

$$x(t_0 + 1) = T[x, v(t_0), t_0] . \qquad (9)$$

Thus, if we can calculate the function $V(x, t_0 + 1)$, we can by maximization derive $V(x, t_0)$ for any $x$. Proceeding step by step from the easily calculable function $V(x, T)$ yields ultimately $V(x, 0)$, which is precisely the sought for optimum of the dynamic process (3).

## 2. Dynamic Programming: Discrete Time, Infinite Horizon

For many purposes it is more convenient to introduce the fiction that the horizon is infinite. Certainly processes of capital accumulation for the economy as a whole, of the kind that will be dealt with in this book, have no natural stopping place in the definable future. At any given date in the future, the state of the system (its capital structure) will have implications for the further future. If we choose to stop our analysis at any fixed date, it will be necessary, as we have noted, to include in our utility function some scrap value for the stock of capital at the end of the period. But the only logically consistent way of doing so is to determine the maximum utility attainable in the future beyond our given date starting with any given stock of capital.

Of course, astronomers assure us that the world as we know it will come to an end in some few billions of years. But, as elsewhere in mathematical approximations to the real world, it is frequently more convenient and more revealing to proceed to the limit and make a mathematical infinity in the model correspond to the vast futurity of the real world.

Formally, the only change in the dynamic programming model from the finite-horizon to the infinite-horizon case is to let $T = +\infty$ and to omit $S[x(T)]$ in 1.(3). However, going to the limit here, as usual, involves some risks. The utility function, being an infinite series, might not converge at all; and even if it does, an optimal policy might not exist. [Gale (1967, pp. 3–4) has given simple examples of cases in which such a policy does not exist.]

It is customary to assume that, in some relevant sense, future felicities are discounted relative to the present and increasingly so for more distant dates. Although the presence of a discount factor does not necessarily insure that either of the above problems is resolved, it does make their occurrence much less likely. We therefore assume the existence of a set of positive numbers, called *discount factors*, $\alpha_t$, with $\sum_{t=0}^{+\infty} \alpha_t < +\infty$, and we replace the felicity $U(x, v, t)$ by $\alpha_t U(x, v, t)$. Informally, we can interpret $U$ as the felicity considered at the moment it occurs and $\alpha_t U$ as the felicity considered from the viewpoint of the beginning of the process at time 0. With this interpretation, we can assume $\alpha_0 = 1$. Our problem now can be stated as:

$$\begin{aligned}&\text{maximize } \sum_{t=0}^{\infty} \alpha_t U[x(t),v(t),t] \text{ with respect to } v(t) \ (t \geqq 0)\\ &\text{subject to 1.(1) and the initial conditions } x(t) = x.\end{aligned} \tag{1}$$

The preceding arguments can be repeated, with $U$ everywhere replaced by $\alpha_t U$, and the basic recursion relation 1.(8) can be written (with $t_0$ replaced by $t$) as

$$V(x, t) = \max_t \{\alpha_t U[x, v(t), t] + V[x(t + 1), t + 1]\} \tag{2}$$

where

$$V(x, t_0) = \max \sum_{t=t_0}^{\infty} \alpha_t U[x(t), v(t), t], \tag{3}$$

the maximizations in (2) and (3) being subject to the constraints 1.(1) any additional constraints on the choices of the instruments $v(t)$, and initial conditions $x(t_0) = x$. From (3), we see that the return function $V$ is evaluated from the viewpoint of time 0 (since each felicity is multiplied by the corresponding discount factor $\alpha_t$). It is somewhat more illuminating to make evaluations as of time $t_0$ when maximizing over the future beginning at time $t_0$. Since one unit of felicity at time $t$ is equivalent to $\alpha_t$ units at time 0, it is necessary to divide $V(x, t)$ by $\alpha_t$. Let the *current-value return function* be

$$W(x, t) = \frac{V(x, t)}{\alpha_t} \tag{4}$$

Then

$$V(x, t) = \alpha_t W(x, t),$$
$$V[x(t+1), t+1] = \alpha_{t+1} W[x(t+1), t+1].$$

Substitute into (2), divide through everywhere by the positive constant $\alpha_t$ (an operation that does not affect maximization), and let

$$\beta_t = \alpha_{t+1}/\alpha_t. \tag{5}$$

$$W(x, t) = \max_t \{U[x, v(t), t] + \beta_t W[x(t+1), t+1]\}, \tag{6}$$

where, it will be recalled from 1.(9), the state variables at time $t+1$ are functions of the instruments at time $t$ through the relation

$$x(t+1) = T[x, v(t), t]. \tag{7}$$

It is frequently appropriate to make the important *Stationarity Assumption*:

$$\begin{aligned} U(x, v, t) &= U(x, v), \\ T(x, v, t) &= T(x, v), \\ \beta_t &= \beta, \end{aligned} \tag{8}$$

where the right-hand sides do not depend on $t$ for any given values of the instruments and state variables, and the domain from which the instruments can be chosen for any given values of the state variables is also independent of time.

Under the Stationarity Assumption, $\alpha_{t+1} = \beta\alpha_t$, so that $\alpha_t = \beta^t$ (since $\alpha_0 = 1$). The condition under which $\sum_{t=0}^{\infty} \alpha_t$ converges then becomes simply

$$\beta < 1. \tag{9}$$

From (3) and (4), and the Stationarity Assumption, (8),

$$W(x, t_0) = \max \sum_{t=t_0}^{\infty} \beta^{t-t_0} U[x(t), v(t)], \tag{10}$$

where the maximization satisfies the constraints

$$x(t+1) = T[x(t), v(t)], \qquad x(t_0) = x. \tag{11}$$

It is clear that the particular value of $t_0$ no longer enters essentially into the problem; if we replace $t_0$ by 0, say, the optimum policy from (10) would be identical. Under stationary conditions, calendar time, as such, would have no significance. Then the optimal policy at time $t_0$ would depend only on the value of the state variables then and not explicitly on $t_0$; and the value of the current value return function, $W(x, t_0)$, would in fact be independent of $t_0$.

> Under the Stationarity Assumption, the optimal policy is given by a function, $v_i^*(x)$ $(i = 1, \ldots, n)$, such that the optimal values of the instrument variables at time $t$ are $v_i^*[x^*(t)]$, where the states $x^*(t)$ are determined in turn by the previous values of the $v_i^*$'s through (11). (12)

The current-value return function, $W(x, t) = W(x)$, is independent of time. Under the Stationarity Assumption, the recursion relation (6) becomes

$$W(x) = \max_v \{U(x, v) + \beta W[T(x, v)]\}. \tag{13}$$

The notation $\max\limits_v$ is designed to emphasize that the form of the maximization now no longer depends on the time point; the domain of the instruments is independent of time (though it may depend on the state), and so is the maximand (in braces).

## 3. Continuous Time, Finite Horizon: The Pontryagin Necessary Conditions

Instead of assuming that time is discrete, we will take the point of view—both more realistic and analytically more convenient—of continuous time. As far as the utility function goes, it is simply a question of replacing a sum, as in 1.(3), with an integral, $\int_0^T U[x(t), v(t), t]dt$, provided that we are willing to maintain the additivity of felicities at different points of time. As before, scrap values, $S[x(T)]$, denote the value of the end-of-period state variables. As for the transition relations 1.(1), the analogue in continuous time may be approached by first writing them in terms of changes in the state variables:

$$x_i(t+1) - x_i(t) = T_i[x_1(t), \ldots, x_s(t), v_1(t), \ldots, v_n(t), t] - x_i(t).$$

Thus, the *change* in a state variable is a function of the state variables and instruments at a given moment of time. In continuous time, the analogous statement is that the *rate of change* of a state variable, which will be denoted by $\dot{x}_i(t)$ (dots denote derivatives with respect to time), is a function of the state variables and instruments. The equations of motion of a system in continuous time will then be written in an abbreviated form as

$$\dot{x}(t) = T[x(t), v(t), t]. \tag{1}$$

In an economic system, if $x_i(t)$ is the quantity of some form of capital, $\dot{x}_i(t)$ is the rate of investment in that form of capital and depends on the total capital resources of the society and the allocations made of them.

The decision maker makes a choice of functions $v_i(t)$, defined for $0 \leqq t \leqq T$, designating the values of each instrument as a function of time. Given a policy of this form and given the initial conditions $x(0)$, the values of the state variables $x(t)$ $(0 \leqq t \leqq T)$ are determined as the solution of the differential equations. The basic problem of optimization over time can then be written:

$$\text{Maximize} \int_0^T U[x(t), v(t), t]dt + S[x(T)] \text{ with respect to choice of the policy functions, } v_i(t) \text{ subject to (1) and the initial conditions } x(0) = x. \tag{2}$$

We now present a heuristic, nonrigorous account of the modern theory of the basic necessary conditions for solving (2), as given by Pontryagin et al. (1962). In this account we have drawn heavily on the expositions of Bellman and Dreyfus (1962, pp. 190–92), Kalman (1963), and Dreyfus (1965, chapters III–V). For a fully rigorous analysis, see Halkin (1964).

The basic reasoning of Bellman's optimality principle is still valid. Choose a small interval $t_0 \leqq t \leqq t_0 + h$. Given the values of the state variables $x$ at time $t_0$ and a choice of instruments $v(t)$ over this interval, the values of the state variables at time $t_0 + h$ are defined as the solution of (1). Beginning at $t_0 + h$, the decision maker certainly chooses an optimal policy given the state values then. The payoff (utility) is

$$\int_{t_0}^{t_0+h} U[x(t), v(t)]dt + V[x(t_0 + h), t_0 + h], \tag{3}$$

which, as noted, is completely determined by the choice of the instruments over the interval $\langle t_0, t_0 + h\rangle$. Hence, by definition (3),

$$V(x, t_0) = \max_{t_0, t_0+h} \left\{ \int_{t_0}^{t_0+h} U[x(t), v(t), t]dt + V[x(t_0 + h), t_0 + h] \right\}, \tag{4}$$

where $\max_{t_0, t_0+h}$ means maximization over policies $v(t)$, $t_0 \leqq t \leqq t_0 + h$, and it is understood that $x(t_0) = x$.

We now proceed to approximations. Basically, we assume for expository purposes that the optimal policy, $v(t)$, is a continuous function of time. In many real problems, this is not so (although it usually will be so in the problems treated in this book). However, the results to be obtained remain valid even though the optimal policy is not in fact continuous in time. Since $U$ is continuous in all its arguments and since, by assumption, each is a continuous function of time, we have approximately

$$U[x(t), v(t), t] \cong U[x, v(t_0), t_0] \quad \text{for} \quad t_0 \leqq t \leqq t_0 + h, \tag{5}$$

for $h$ small, where the symbol $\cong$ means "approximately equal."

Assume $V$ is a differentiable function of its arguments. Then Taylor's theorem assures us that

$$V[x(t_0 + h), t_0 + h] \cong V(x, t_0) + V_{x_1}[x_1(t_0 + h) - x_1] + \ldots + V_{x_s}[x_s(t_0 + h) - x_s] + V_t h,$$

where $V_{x_i}$ and $V_t$ are the partial derivatives of $V$ with respect to $x_i$ and $t$, respectively, evaluated at the point $(x_1, \ldots, x_s, t_0)$. [It will be recalled that $x(t_0) = x$.] Let

$$p_i = V_{x_i} \qquad (i = 1, \ldots, s). \tag{6}$$

Note that $p_i$ is the marginal contribution of the state variable $x_i$ to the utility function, and therefore it is a "price" in an economic sense. From (1),

$$x_i(t_0 + h) - x_i \cong T_i[x, v(t_0), t_0]h.$$

$$V[x(t_0 + h), t_0 + h] \cong V(x, t_0) + \sum_{i=1}^{s} p_i T_i[x, v(t_0), t_0]h + V_t h. \tag{7}$$

Substitute (5) and (7) into (4).

$$V(x, t_0) \cong \max_{t_0, t_0+h} \left\{ U[x, v(t_0), t_0]h + V(x, t_0) + \sum_{i=1}^{s} p_i T_i[x, v(t_0), t_0]h + V_t h \right\}$$

$$= h \max_{t_0} \left\{ U[x, v(t_0), t_0] + \sum_{i=1}^{s} p_i T_i[x, v(t_0), t_0] \right\} + V(x, t_0) + V_t h,$$

where the last step follows since only $v(t_0)$ [and not $v(t)$ for $t_0 < t \leqq t_0 + h$] enters into the right-hand maximization, the terms $V(x, t_0) + V_t h$ are independent of the maximizing variables, and the constant positive multiplier $h$ can be factored out of the maximization operation. Cancel $V(x, t_0)$ from both sides, divide through by $h$, and subtract $V_t$ from both sides. Also replace $t_0$ by $t$.

$$-V_t = \max_v H = H^0, \tag{8}$$

where

$$H = H(x, v, p, t) = U(x, v, t) + \sum_{i=1}^{s} p_i T_i(x, v, t), \tag{9}$$

and $p$ is an abbreviation for $p_1, \ldots, p_s$.

The function $H$ is known as the *Hamiltonian*. Because of the definitions of the prices $p_i$ in (6), (8) is a partial differential equation satisfied by the return function $V$; it is known as the Hamilton-Jacobi equation.

We now derive (nonrigorously) the rate of change of the "prices" (also called auxiliary or dual variables). From the definition (6) and the chain rule for differentiation,

$$\dot{p}_i = \sum_{j=1}^{s} V_{x_i x_j} \dot{x}_j + V_{x_i t}, \tag{10}$$

where $V_{x_i x_j} = \partial^2 V / \partial x_i \partial x_j$, and $V_{x_i t} = \partial^2 V / \partial x_i \partial t$.

Notice that $H^0$ in (8) is a function of $x$, $p$, and $t$; but $p_i$ is a function of $x$ and $t$ through its definition (6). Differentiate (8) with respect to $x_i$, holding other $x$'s and $t$ constant.

$$-V_{x_i t} = H^0_{x_i} + H^0_{p1} V_{x_i x_1} + \cdots + H^0_{p_s} V_{x_i x_s}. \tag{11}$$

Now recall a general principle in differentiating functions which are themselves derived by maximization, a general "envelope theorem" much used in economics (Samuelson 1947, p. 34). If $\phi(v, y)$ is a function of two variables (or more generally two sets of variables), let $v(y)$ be a stationary point of $\phi$ as a function of $v$ for fixed $y$; i.e., $\partial\phi/\partial v = 0$ (or $\partial\phi/\partial v_k = 0$, all $k$). Let $F(y) = \phi[v(y), y]$. Then $dF/dy = (\partial\phi/\partial v)(dv/dy) + (\partial\phi/\partial y) = \partial\phi/\partial y$, evaluated at the value of $v$ which makes $\phi$ stationary for given $y$ (it may but need not be a maximum or minimum). That is, to the first order, the variation of $\phi$ with respect to the other variable is the same whether the first variable is held constant or varied so as to keep $\phi$ stationary. This is, of course, because at a stationary point $\phi$ is locally constant with respect to variations in the first variable.

In the present context, denote the value of $v$ which maximizes $H$ for given $x$, $p$, $t$ as $v^0(x, p, t)$. For an interior maximum,

$$\partial H / \partial v_k = 0 \qquad (k = 1, \ldots, n) \qquad \text{when } v = v^0.$$

By definition,

$$H^0 = H(x, v^0, p, t).$$

Differentiate both sides with respect to $x_i$, holding other $x$'s, $p_1, \ldots, p_s$, and $t$ constant.

$$H^o_{x_i} = H_{x_i} + \sum_{k=1}^{n} (\partial H/\partial v_k)(\partial v^0_k / \partial x_i) = H_{x_i}. \tag{12}$$

Similarly,

$$H^o_{p_i} = H_{p_i} \qquad (i = 1, \ldots, s). \tag{13}$$

From (9), however, $H$ is linear in $p_i$ ($i = 1, \ldots, s$), and

$$H_{p_i} = T_i(x, v^0, t) = \dot{x}_i \qquad (i = 1, \ldots, s) \tag{14}$$

from (1). By substituting (12)–(14) into (11) and the result into (10), we derive the remarkably simple expression,

$$\dot{p}_i = -\partial H/\partial x_i \qquad (i = 1, \ldots, s), \tag{15}$$

where the instruments are chosen so that

$$v \text{ maximizes } H \text{ at each moment of time.} \tag{16}$$

At any given moment, given the state variables $x$ and the auxiliary variables $p$, the instruments are determined by the maximization of the Hamiltonian in (16). These, in turn, determine the derivatives of the state and auxiliary variables, by (1) and (15), and therefore the immediate future of the system. The whole history of the system is determined, provided we know how to start it.

PROPOSITION 1 (*Pontryagin Maximum Principle*). *Let* $v^*(t)$ *be a choice of instruments* $(0 \leqq t \leqq T)$ *which maximizes* $\int_0^T U[x(t), v(t), t]dt + s[x(T)]$, *subject to the conditions,*

(a) $$\dot{x} = T[x(t), v(t), t],$$

*some constraints on the choices of the instruments, and initial conditions on the state variables. Then there exist auxiliary variables, functions of time,* $p_i(t)$, *such that, for each* $t$,

(b) $v^*(t)$ *maximizes* $H[x(t), v, p(t), t]$ *where* $H(x, v, p, t) =$

$$U(x, v, t) + \sum_{i=1}^{s} p_i T_i(x, v, t),$$

*and the functions* $p_i$ *satisfy the differential equations*

(c) $\dot{p}_i = -\partial H/\partial x_i$, *evaluated at* $x = x(t)$, $v = v^*(t)$, $p = p(t)$.

Mathematically speaking, the optimal path is the solution of the differential equations (a) and (c), of which there are twice the number of state variables. The solution is determined only when we also specify an equal number of initial conditions. Usually, the values of the state variables at the beginning of the process, $x_i(0)$, are known, but these constitute only $s$ conditions. However, if we return to definition (3) of the return function, we see that

$$V(x, T) = S(x),$$

so that $\partial V(x, T)/\partial x_i = \partial S/\partial x_i = p_i(T)$ from definition (6).

PROPOSITION 2 (*Transversality Conditions*). *The solution to Proposition* 1 *also satisfies the condition,* $p_i(T) = S_{x_i}[x(T)]$.

The conditions of Proposition 2 supply the $s$ additional conditions needed to determine completely the solutions of the differential equations in Proposition 1(a) and (c).

In the sequel, we shall be interested in a slightly different formulation of the end-of-period conditions. Instead of a scrap value, suppose we require simply that the end-of-period values of the state variables be nonnegative. (Actually, the purpose of this discussion is to motivate the corresponding condition for the infinite-horizon case.) The nonnegativity condition can, however, be approximated by a scrap value function. Essentially, we can permit negative values but impose a very large penalty. Formally, let

$$S(x) = \sum_{i=1}^{s} P_i \min (x_i, 0),$$

where the $P_i$'s are large numbers. The symbol, $\min (x_i, 0)$, means the smaller of the two numbers $x_i$ and 0; it equals $x_i$ when $x_i < 0$, and 0 otherwise. For $x_i < 0$, $S_{x_i} = P_i$; for $x_i > 0$, $S_{x_i} = 0$. If $x_i = 0$, the right-hand derivative is zero and the left-hand derivative is $P_i$; this fact can be expressed loosely by the statement, $0 \leqq S_{x_i} \leqq P_i$.

Now, if $P_i$ is chosen to be very large, we may be sure that the optimal policy will never lead to a final negative value of $x_i(T)$, so we may assume that

$$x_i(T) \geqq 0.$$

From the preceding discussion we see that $S_{x_i}[x(T)] \geqq 0$ in any case, and $S_{x_i}[x(T)] = 0$ if $x_i(T) > 0$. In view of Proposition 2, this amounts to saying that

$$p_i(T) \geqq 0, \qquad p_i(T)x_i(T) = 0.$$

PROPOSITION 3. *Let* $v^*(t)$ *be a choice of instruments* $(0 \leqq t \leqq T)$ *which maximizes* $\int_0^T U[x(t), v(t), t]dt$ *subject to the conditions*

(a) $$\dot{x} = T[x(t), v(t), t],$$

*some constraints on the choices of the instruments, initial conditions on the state variables, and the terminal conditions,* $x_i(T) \geqq 0$ $(i = 1, \ldots, s)$. *Then there exist functions of time,* $p_i(t)$, *such that* (b) *and* (c) *of Proposition* 1 *hold, and for which*

(d) $$p_i(T) \geqq 0, \; p_i(T)x_i(T) = 0 \qquad (i = 1, 2, \ldots, s).$$

## 4. Continuous Time, Finite Horizon: Constraints Involving the State Variables

Up to this time, it has been implicitly assumed that the instruments at any moment of time can be chosen from a set of alternatives which do not depend on the state variables. Whether or not this condition is satisfied is partly a question of the form in which the problem is stated. Thus, if resource allocation is involved, the instruments may be stated either as the *proportions* or the *amounts* of given resources allocated to given purposes. In the first case, the instruments are nonnegative numbers adding up to one; the domain from which they are to be chosen is independent of the state of the system. In the second case, however, the amounts of resources devoted to particular purposes are constrained by the total amounts of resources available, which are in turn determined by the state variables. Since it is frequently more convenient to state the resource allocation problem in the second form, it is necessary to modify the previous results to include constraints on the instruments in which the contemporary values of the state variables enter. The following discussion is based on that of Pontryagin et al. (1962, chapter VI) and on the theory of nonlinear programming of Kuhn and Tucker (1951).

We assume that the choice of instruments at any moment $t$ with state $x$ must satisfy a set of inequality constraints,

$$F_j(x, v, t) \geqq 0 \qquad (j = 1, \ldots, m). \tag{1}$$

For example, if output is a function of the stock of capital, $F(K)$, and if output is to be divided between consumption, $C$, and investment, $I$, then the instruments $C$ and $I$ satisfy the condition,

$$F(K) - C - I \geq 0,$$

which involves the state variable $K$.

The previous propositions still remain valid. Indeed, the maximization in Proposition 1(b) is with respect to an admissible range of instruments, and it is in no way precluded by any of the preceding arguments that the admissible range at any moment of time might depend on the state variables and on time. However, a more explicit form can be given.

It is well known from the general theory of nonlinear programming that if $v^0$ maximizes $H$ subject to the constraints (1) and if these constraints satisfy a certain condition known as the constraint qualification (see Kuhn and Tucker 1951, pp. 483–84; Arrow, Hurwicz, and Uzawa 1961; Abadie 1967), then, at any moment of time, there exist multipliers $q_j^0$ $(j = 1, \ldots, m)$ such that

$$q_j^0 \geqq 0, \; q_j^0 F_j(x, v^0\, t) = 0 \qquad (j = 1, \ldots, m), \tag{2}$$

and

$$\partial L/\partial v_k = 0 \qquad (k = 1, \ldots, m) \text{ at } v = v^0, q = q^0, \tag{3}$$

where the *Lagrangian* $L$ is defined by

$$L = H + \sum_{j=1}^{m} q_j F_j, \tag{4}$$

and $q$ is an abbreviation for $q_1, \ldots, q_m$.

The constraint qualification is certainly satisfied in all cases discussed here.

Note that if $F_j(x, v^0, t) > 0$, then $q_j^0 = 0$; this will remain true for small variations in any state variable $x_i$, so that $\partial q_j^0/\partial x_i = 0$. Then, in any case,

$$F_j(x, v^0, t)(\partial q_j^0/\partial x_i) = 0, \text{ all } j. \tag{5}$$

Let

$$L^0(x, p, t) = L(x, v^0, p, q^0, t). \tag{6}$$

From (2), (4), and (6),

$$L^0(x, p, t) = H(x, v^0, p, t) = H^0(x, p, t), \tag{7}$$

from the definition 3.(8) of $H^0$. Since (7) is an identity in the state variables for any given values of the auxiliary variables and of time,

$$\partial L^0/\partial x_i = \partial H^0/\partial x_i. \tag{8}$$

But from (6), (4), (3), and (5), a modified form of the "envelope theorem" cited in section 3 holds here.

$$\begin{aligned}\partial L^0/\partial x_i &= (\partial L/\partial x_i) + \sum_{k=1}^{n} (\partial L/\partial v_k)(\partial v_k^0/\partial x_i) + \sum_{j=1}^{m} (\partial L/\partial q_j)(\partial q^0/\partial x_i) \\ &= (\partial L/\partial x_i) + \sum_{j=1}^{m} F_j(x, v^0, t)(\partial q_j^0/\partial x_i) = \partial L/\partial x_i. \end{aligned}\tag{9}$$

Since, by 3.(12),

$$\partial H^0/\partial x_i = \partial H/\partial x_i,$$

it follows from (8) and (9) that Proposition 1(c) can be restated:

$$\dot{p}_i = -\partial L/\partial x_i = -\partial H^0/\partial x_i. \tag{10}$$

Proposition 3 can now be restated as:

PROPOSITION 4. *Let* $v^*(t)$ *be a choice of instruments* ($0 \leqq t \leqq T$) *which maximizes* $\int_0^T U[x(t), v(t), t]dt$ *subject to the conditions*

(a) $$\dot{x} = T[x(t), v(t), t],$$

*a set of constraints,*

(b) $$F_j[x(t), v(t), t] \geqq 0 \qquad (j = 1, \ldots, m),$$

*on the instruments possibly involving the state variables, initial conditions on the state variables, and the terminal conditions,* $x_i(T) \geqq 0$. *If the constraint qualification holds, then there exist functions of time,* $p_i(t)$ *such that, for each t,*

(c) $v^*(t)$ *maximizes* $H[x(t), v, p(t), t]$ *subject to the constraints*

$$\text{(b), where } H(x, v, p, t) = U(x, v, t) + \sum_{i=1}^{s} p_i T_i(x, v, t);$$

(d) $\dot{p}_i = -\partial L/\partial x_i$, *evaluated at* $x = x(t)$, $v = v^*(t)$, $p = p(t)$,

*where*

(e) $$L(x, v, p, q, t) = H(x, v, p, t) + \sum_{j=1}^{m} q_j F_j(x, v, t),$$

*and the Lagrange multipliers* $q_j$ *are such that*

(f) $\partial L/\partial v_k = 0$, *all k, for* $x = x(t)$, $v = v^*(t)$, $p = p(t)$,

$q_j(t) \geqq 0$, $q_j(t)F_j[x(t), v^*(t), t] = 0$, *all j;*

*and*

(g) $$p_i(T) \geqq 0, \; p_i(T)x_i(T) = 0 \qquad (i = 1, 2, \ldots, s).$$

Note that the constraint functions $F_j$ depend upon the instruments, since we considered them as defining the range of admissible values of the instruments. Some of the constraints $F_j$ might, however, not involve the state variables; for example, nonnegativity constraints on the instruments would have to be included among the constraints $F_j$.

In many circumstances, however, it is reasonable to consider restrictions on the state variables that do not involve instruments. In particular, if the state variables are stocks of capital, negative values have no meaning; we require that

$$x_i(t) \geqq 0 \qquad (0 \leqq t \leqq T, \; i = 1, \ldots, s). \tag{11}$$

At any point where $x_i(t) > 0$, the corresponding constraint (11) is ineffective and can be disregarded. Suppose that $x_i(t) = 0$ over some interval. Then the instruments must be so constrained that $\dot{x}_i(t) \geqq 0$ over that interval. Since actually $x_i(t)$ is constant over the interval, this new constraint is effective. But $\dot{x}_i = T_i$, so the constraint $T_i \geqq 0$ is an effective constraint over the interval.

Suppose, for example, that $x_1(t) = 0$ over the interval, and $x_i(t) > 0$ $(i > 1)$. Then the constraint

$$T_1[x(t), v(t), t] \geqq 0 \tag{12}$$

is effective over the interval. Proposition 4 can be applied, and the constraint (12) can be regarded as being added to the original set of constraints (b). Let the $q_j$'s be the Lagrange multipliers associated with the original constraints $F_j \geqq 0$, and let $r_1$ be the Lagrange multiplier associated with the constraint (12). As before, $r_1 \geqq 0$. The Lagrangian becomes

$$L = H + \sum_{j=1}^{m} q_j F_j + r_1 T_1 .$$

Now define $r_i = 0$ $(i > 1)$. Note that we now have $r_i \geqq 0$, $r_i T_i = 0$ $(i = 1, \ldots, s)$, and also $r_i x_i = 0$ $(i = 1, \ldots, s)$.

PROPOSITION 5. *Let $v^*(t)$ be a choice of instruments $(0 \leqq t \leqq T)$ which maximizes $\int_0^T U[x(t), v(t), t]dt$ subject to the conditions*

(a) $$\dot{x} = T[x(t), v(t), t],$$

(b) $$F_j[x(t), v(t), t] \geqq 0 \qquad (j = 1, \ldots, m),$$

*involving the instruments and possibly the state variables, initial conditions on the state variables, and the nonnegativity conditions,*

(c) $$x_i(t) \geqq 0 \qquad (0 \leqq t \leqq T),$$

*on the state variables. If the constraint qualification holds, there exist functions of time, $p_i(t)$, such that for each $t$,*

(d) *$v^*(t)$ maximizes $H[x(t), v, p(t), t]$ subject to the constraints (b) and the additional constraints $T_i[x(t)v, t] \geqq 0$ for all $i$ for which $x_i(t) = 0$, where $H(x, v, p, t) = U(x, v, t) + \sum_{i=1}^{s} p_i T_i(x, v, t)$;*

(e) *$\dot{p}_i = -\partial L/\partial x_i$, evaluated at $x = x(t)$, $v = v^*(t)$, $p = p(t)$, $q = q(t)$, $r = r(t)$,*

*where*

(f) $$L(x, v, p, q, r, t) = H(x, v, p, t) + \sum_{j=1}^{m} q_j F_j(x, v, t) + \sum_{i=1}^{s} r_i T_i(x, v, t),$$

*and the Lagrange multipliers $q_j$ and $r_i$ are such that*

(g) $\partial L/\partial v_k = 0$, *all* $k$, *for* $x = x(t)$, $v = v^*(t)$, $p = p(t)$, $q_j(t) \geqq 0$, $q_j(t)F_j[x(t), v^*(t), t] = 0$, *all* $j$, $r_i(t) \geqq 0$, $r_i(t)x_i(t) = 0$, $r_i(t)T_i[x(t), v^*(t), t] = 0$, *all* $i$;

(h) $p_i(T) \geqq 0$, $p_i(T)x_i(T) = 0$, *all* $i$.

## 5. Continuous Time, Finite Horizon: The Sufficiency Theorem

The propositions proved in the last two sections are *necessary* conditions that a policy be optimum. The situation is precisely analogous to the usual problem in calculus; the condition that a derivative is zero is necessary for a maximum but certainly not sufficient in general. However, the condition is sufficient if the function being maximized is *concave*; i.e., if the values of the function on a straight line-segment joining two points are at least equal to the values of the linear interpolation to function between those points. A basic property of concave functions is the following:

If $f(x_1, \ldots, x_n)$ is a concave function, then for any given point $(x_1^*, \ldots, x_n^*)$ and any arbitrary point $(x_1, \ldots, x_n)$,

$$f(x_1, \ldots, x_n) \leqq f(x_1^*, \ldots, x_n^*) + \sum_{i=1}^{n} f_{x_i}^*(x_i - x_i^*), \tag{1}$$

where $f_{x_i}^* = \partial f/\partial x_i$, evaluated at $x_i = x_i^*$.

Geometrically, this says that the tangent hyperplane to the function always lies above the function. Concavity, of course, corresponds to the economic notions of diminishing marginal utility or productivity in any direction.

The following discussion is a minor variation of that of Mangasarian (1966). We make the assumption that

$$H^0(x, p, t) \text{ is a concave function of } x \text{ for given } p \text{ and } t, \tag{2}$$

where

$$H^0 = \max_v H(x, v, p, t). \tag{3}$$

This will certainly be true if $U(x, v, t)$ and $T(x, v, t)$ are concave in the variables $x$, $v$, taken together, but (2) may hold more generally. The definition of an instrument is somewhat arbitrary (thus, the ratio of two instruments can itself be considered an instrument), and it may sometimes be more convenient to state the instruments in such a form that the functions $U$ and $T$ are not concave in $x$ and $v$ jointly; however, transformations of the instruments have no effect on the concavity of $H^0$ with respect to $x$.

Let $v^*(t)$ be a policy satisfying the conditions of Proposition 5 (or 4, or, for that matter, 3, or 1 and 2), and let $x^*(t)$ be the corresponding evolution of the state variables, that is, the solution of the differential equations

$$\dot{x} = T[x, v^*(t), t], \tag{4}$$

with the initial conditions $x^*(0) = x$. Let $v(t)$ be any other policy satisfying all the constraints, and $x(t)$ the corresponding evolution of the state variables, with the same initial conditions. Let $p(t)$ be the paths of the auxiliary variables satisfying all the conditions of Proposition 5. By definition (3),

$$H[x(t), v(t), p(t), t] \leqq H^0[x(t), p(t), t]. \tag{5}$$

For given $p(t)$ and $t$, apply (1) to $H^0$, as is permitted by (2), with $x$ replaced by $x(t)$ and $x^*$ by $x^*(t)$.

$$H^0[x(t), p(t), t] \leqq H^0[x^*(t), p(t), t] + \sum_{i=1}^{s} H^0_{xi}[x^*(t), p(t), t][x_i(t) - x_i^*(t)],$$

and, in combination with (5),

$$\begin{aligned} H[x(t), v(t), p(t), t] \leqq\ & H[x^*(t), v^*(t), p(t), t] \\ & + \sum_{i=1}^{s} H^0_{xi}[x^*(t), p(t), t][x_i(t) - x_i^*(t)], \end{aligned} \tag{6}$$

where use has been made of Proposition 5(d). By definition of $H$ and the equations (a) of Proposition 5,

$$\begin{aligned} H[x(t), v(t), p(t), t] &= U[x(t), v(t), t] + \sum_{i=1}^{s} p_i(t) T_i[x(t), v(t), t] \\ &= U[x(t), v(t), t] + \sum_{i=1}^{s} p_i(t)\dot{x}_i(t), \end{aligned}$$

and in particular

$$H[x^*(t), v^*(t), p(t), t] = U[x^*(t), v^*(t), t] + \sum_{i=1}^{s} p_i(t)\dot{x}_i^*(t).$$

By 4.(10),

$$H^0_{xi}[x^*(t), p(t), t] = -\dot{p}_i(t).$$

Substitution into (6) yields

$$\begin{aligned} U[x(t), v(t), t] + \sum_{i=1}^{s} p_i(t)\dot{x}_i(t) \leqq\ & U[x^*(t), v^*(t), t] \\ & + \sum_{i=1}^{s} p_i(t)\dot{x}_i^*(t) - \sum_{i=1}^{s} \dot{p}_i(t)[x_i(t) - x_i^*(t)]. \end{aligned}$$

By transposition and grouping terms, it is found that

$$U[x^*(t), v^*(t), t] - U[x(t), v(t), t]$$
$$\geqq \sum_{i=1}^{s} \{p_i(t)[\dot{x}_i(t) - \dot{x}_i^*(t)] + \dot{p}_i(t)[x_i(t) - x_i^*(t)]\}$$
$$= (d/dt)\sum_{i=1}^{s} p_i(t)[x_i(t) - x_i^*(t)].$$

Now integrate both sides with respect to $t$ from 0 to $T$.

$$\int_0^T U[x^*(t), v^*(t), t]dt - \int_0^T U[x(t), v(t), t]dt$$
$$\geqq \sum_{i=1}^{s} p_i(t)[x_i(t) - x_i^*(t)]\Big|_0^T$$
$$= \sum_{i=1}^{s} p_i(T)[x_i(T) - x_i^*(T)] - \sum_{i=1}^{s} p_i(0)[x_i(0) - x_i^*(0)].$$

Since both $x(t)$ and $x^*(t)$ have the same initial conditions, it must be that

$$x_i(0) = x_i^*(0),$$

and the last term on the right-hand side vanishes. The first term can be written

$$\sum_{i=1}^{s} p_i(T)x_i(T) - \sum_{i=1}^{s} p_i(T)x_i^*(T).$$

But $x^*(t)$ satisfies the conditions of Proposition 5 and by (h) the second term vanishes. Since $p_i(T) \geqq 0$ and $x_i(T)$ is constrained to be nonnegative, the left-hand side is nonnegative; the utility attached to the path satisfying Proposition 5 must at least equal that of any other feasible path.

PROPOSITION 6. *In the notation of Proposition 5, if*

$$H^0(x, p, t) = \max_v H(x, v, p, t),$$

*where the maximization is over the range defined by the constraints* $F_j(x, v, t) \geqq 0$ *and* $T_i(x, v, t) \geqq 0$ *when* $x_i = 0$ *is a concave function of* $x$ *for given* $p$ *and* $t$, *then any policy satisfying all the hypotheses of Proposition 5 is optimal.*

## 6. Continuous Time, Infinite Horizon

The extension from the finite to the infinite horizon in continuous time optimization parallels very closely that in discrete time problems (see section 2). The utility function to be maximized is

$$\int_0^{+\infty} U[x(t), v(t), t]dt. \tag{1}$$

As in the discrete time case, there is no guarantee that this integral converges nor that an optimal policy exists even if it does [for discussion of a specific case of nonexistence, see section III.2 (remarks following Proposition 1), or, for a more extensive discussion of essentially the same case, Koopmans (1965, pp. 251–53)].

Suppose an optimal policy exists. The arguments for the necessity conditions, such as Proposition 5, remain valid, except possibly for the transversality conditions. Condition (h) in Proposition 5 would have as its infinite-horizon analogue,

$$\lim_{t \to +\infty} p_i(t) \geqq 0, \qquad \lim_{t \to +\infty} p_i(t)x_i(t) = 0. \tag{2}$$

It will be seen that in our problems this condition is indeed satisfied for the optimal policy, but a special argument seems to be needed in each case. Conditions (a)–(g) of Proposition 5 define a system of differential equations that have many solutions, since the number of initial conditions is too few. It turns out in many practical situations that, with a few exceptions, these solutions can be shown by some simple, direct argument to be clearly nonoptimal in the infinite-horizon case. However, it is certainly not true that conditions (2) are always necessary for an optimum, and we have no general theorem giving conditions under which they are necessary.[1] The argument for the finite horizon case fails to extend here because we do not have a meaningful analogue to the scrap value function. However, it is true that the sufficiency theorem remains intact, and its proof is exactly the same. Thus, we can use the transversality conditions (2) to establish sufficiency.

As in the discrete-time infinite-horizon model, it is customary and reasonable to assume that future felicities are discounted; i.e., the felicity obtained at time $t$ is multiplied by a *discount factor*, $\alpha(t)$, which is

[1] The following example, given by H. Halkin (personal communication) shows that (2) need not hold for an optimal policy in the infinite-horizon case. We suppose one state variable and one instrument. Let $U(x, v, t) = (1 - x)v$, and suppose that $\dot{x} = (1 - x)v$, with $x(0) = 0$. Let $v$ be constrained to the range $-1 \leqq v \leqq 1$. Then $\int_0^{+\infty} U(x, v, t)dt = \int_0^{+\infty} \dot{x}dt = \lim_{t \to +\infty} x(t)$. By direct integration, $x(t) = 1 - e^{-V(t)}$, where $V(t) = \int_0^t v(u)du$. Thus, $x(t) < 1$ for all $t$, and any choice of instruments for which $V(t)$ approaches infinity is optimal. In particular, the policy $v(t) = v_0$, where $0 < v_0 < 1$, is optimal.

In this problem, $H = (1 + p)(1 - x)v$. For $v = v_0$ to maximize $H$, it is necessary that $(1 + p)(1 - x) = 0$. Since $x < 1$, this means $p(t) = -1$, all $t$. This solution indeed satisfies the auxiliary equation, $\dot{p} = -\partial H/\partial x = (1 + p)v$, but then, since $x(t)$ approaches 1, $p(t)x(t)$ approaches $-1$ and not 0, violating the transversality conditions.

ordinarily taken to be a decreasing function of $t$. The utility function (1) is rewritten,

$$\int_0^{+\infty} \alpha(t)U[x(t), v(t), t]dt. \tag{3}$$

Ordinarily it is assumed that if the chosen policy leads to a constant felicity, the utility integral (3) will converge. This is equivalent to

$$\int_0^{+\infty} \alpha(t)dt \quad \text{converges}. \tag{4}$$

Now proceed parallel to the discrete-time infinite-horizon model. The (discounted) return function analogous to 2.(3) is

$$V(x, t_0) = \max \int_{t_0}^{+\infty} \alpha(t)U[x(t), v(t), t]dt, \quad \text{where} \quad x(t_0) = x, \tag{5}$$

and, as in 2.(4), this formula suggests that the *current-value return function*,

$$W(x, t_0) = V(x, t_0)/\alpha(t_0), \tag{6}$$

and the current-value marginal returns, $\partial W/\partial x_i$, will be of interest. We therefore change notation so that

$$p_i = \partial W/\partial x_i = (\partial V/\partial x_i)/\alpha. \tag{7}$$

In applying Proposition 5, then, $U(x, v, t)$ is replaced by $\alpha(t)U(x, v, t)$ and $p_i(t)$ by $\alpha(t)p_i(t)$. The Hamiltonian becomes

$$\alpha(t)U(x, v, t) + \sum_{i=1}^{s} \alpha(t)p_iT_i(x, v, t)$$
$$= \alpha(t)[U(x, v, t) + \sum_{i=1}^{s} p_iT_i(x, v, t)] = \alpha(t)H(x, v, p, t), \tag{8}$$

where we now define the *current-value Hamiltonian*:

$$H(x, v, p, t) = U(x, v, t) + \sum_{i=1}^{s} p_iT_i(x, v, t). \tag{9}$$

Thus, $\alpha(t)H$ must replace $H$ throughout the statements of Proposition 5.

Since $\alpha(t)$ is positive, the instruments chosen to maximize $\alpha(t)H$ are the same as those chosen to maximize $H$, so that Proposition 5(d) remains unchanged. If we interpret the Lagrange multipliers $q_j$ and $r_i$ as referring to the maximization of $H$ (as now defined) subject to the constraints, then $L$ must be replaced by $\alpha(t)L$. Then Proposition 5(e) becomes

$$\frac{d[\alpha(t)p_i]}{dt} = -\frac{\partial[\alpha(t)L]}{\partial x_i},$$

or

$$\dot{\alpha} p_i + \alpha \dot{p}_i = -\alpha(\partial L / x_i).$$

Divide through by $\alpha$, and define

$$\rho(t) = -\dot{\alpha}(t)/\alpha(t). \tag{10}$$

$$\dot{p}_i = \rho(t) p_i - (\partial L / \partial x_i). \tag{11}$$

Note that $\rho(t)$ is essentially a short-term interest rate, corresponding to the system of discount factors, $\alpha(t)$. The definition (10) can be integrated back to yield the familiar form

$$\alpha(t) = e^{-\int_0^t \rho(u) du},$$

for discounting derived from a short-term interest rate varying in time. If (11) is written

$$\dot{p}_i + (\partial L / \partial x_i) = \rho(t) p_i,$$

it is the familiar equilibrium relation for investment in capital goods; the sum of capital gains and marginal productivity should equal the interest on the investment.

The infinite-horizon analogue of Proposition 5 (without the transversality conditions) becomes

Proposition 7. *Let $v^*(t)$ be a choice of instruments ($t \geqq 0$) which maximizes $\int_0^{+\infty} \alpha(t) U[x(t), v(t), t] dt$ subject to the conditions*

(a) $$\dot{x} = T[x(t), v(t), t],$$

*a set of constraints*

(b) $$F_j[x(t), v(t), t] \geqq 0 \qquad (j = 1, \ldots, m),$$

*involving the instruments and possibly the state variables, initial conditions on the state variables, and the non-negativity conditions*

(c) $$x_i(t) \geqq 0 \qquad (t \geqq 0,\ i = 1, 2, \ldots, s),$$

*on the state variables. If the constraint qualification holds, then there exist functions of time, $p_i(t)$, such that for each $t$,*

(d) *$v^*(t)$ maximizes $H[x(t), v, p(t), t]$ subject to the constraints (b) and the additional constraints $T_i[x(t), v, t] \geqq 0$ for all $i$ for which $x_i(t) = 0$, where $H(x, v, p, t) = U(x, v, t) + \sum_{i=1}^{s} p_i T_i(x, v, t)$;*

(e) *$\dot{p}_i = \rho(t) p_i - (\partial L / \partial x_i)$, evaluated at $x = x(t)$, $v = v^*(t)$, $p = p(t)$, where $\rho(t) = -\dot{\alpha}(t)/\alpha(t)$ and*

(f) $$L(x, v, p, q, r, t) = H(x, v, p, t) + \sum_{j=1}^{m} q_j F_j(x, v, t) + \sum_{i=1}^{s} r_i T_i(x, v, t),$$

*and the Lagrange multipliers* $q_j$ *and* $r_i$ *are such that*

(g) $\partial L/\partial v_k = 0$, *all* $k$, for $x = x(t)$, $v = v^*(t)$, $p = p(t)$,
$q_j(t) \geqq 0$, $q_j(t)F_j[x(t), v^*(t), t] = 0$, *all* $j$, $r_i(t) \geqq 0$,
$r_i(t)x_i(t) = 0$, $r_i(t)T_i[x(t), v^*(t), t] = 0$, *all* $i$.

The sufficiency theorem, Proposition 6, requires the transversality condition as part of its hypotheses. A slight restatement is:

Proposition 8. *In the notation of Proposition* 7, *if*

$$H^0(x, p, t) = \max_v H(x, v, p, t),$$

*is a concave function of* $x$ *for given* $p$ *and* $t$ [*where the maximization is over the range specified in Proposition* 7(d)], *then any policy is optimal that satisfies the conditions of Proposition* 7 *and the transversality conditions*

$$\lim_{t\to+\infty} \alpha(t)p_i(t) \geqq 0, \qquad \lim_{t\to+\infty} \alpha(t)p_i(t)x_i(t) = 0.$$

As in the discrete-time case, it is frequently appropriate to make an assumption of stationarity analogous to 2.(8):

$$\begin{aligned} U(x, v, t) &= U(x, v), \\ T(x, v, t) &= T(x, v), \\ F_j(x, v, t) &= F_j(x, v) \\ \rho(t) &= \rho, \end{aligned}$$

where the right-hand sides are independent of $t$. With $\rho$ constant, it follows from its definition (10), and the convention that $\alpha(0) = 1$, that

$$\alpha(t) = e^{-\rho t},$$

and then the convergence condition (4) becomes simply

$$\rho > 0. \tag{12}$$

Exactly as in 2.(12), it then follows simply that $W(x, t)$, as defined by (5) and (6), is independent of $t$; this can be seen by writing

$$\begin{aligned} W(x, t_0) &= (1/e^{-\rho t_0}) \max \int_{t_0}^{+\infty} e^{-\rho t} U[x(t), v(t)]dt \\ &= \max \int_{t_0}^{+\infty} e^{-\rho(t-t_0)} U[x(t), v(t)]dt, \end{aligned}$$

so that replacing $t_0$ by 0, say, leaves the form of the optimum policy completely unaffected. But if $W(x, t) = W(x)$, independent of $t$, then, from (7), $p_i$ is completely determined by $x$ in the following sense: Suppose we have two optimization problems of the type dealt with in Proposition 7 (but satisfying the stationarity conditions) that are identical in all respects except for initial conditions. Let $x^1(t)$ and $x^2(t)$ be the paths of the state variables along the optimal solutions for the two problems, respectively, and let $p^1(t)$ and $p^2(t)$ be the corresponding paths of the auxiliary variables. Then, if $x^1(t) = x^2(t')$, $p^1(t) = p^2(t')$.

Note that since $p$ is determined by $x$, and $U$ and $T$ do not depend on $t$, $H(x, v, p, t)$ is a function of $x$ and $v$ alone, and therefore the value of $v$ which maximizes $H$ depends only on $x$. The optimum policy can, in the language of section 2, be represented as a strategy completely determined by the state of the system.

Also note that, for given $x$, $v$, and $p$, $H$ is independent of $t$, and therefore Proposition 7(d) by itself implies that $v^*$ is determined by $x$ and $p$, independent of $t$. The stationarity assumptions then imply that $t$ does not enter explicitly into the system of differential equations defined by (a) and (e). Such a system is termed *autonomous.*

PROPOSITION 9. *Under the assumptions and in the notation of Proposition* 7, *suppose in addition that*

(a) $$U(x, v, t) = U(x, v), \qquad T(x, v, t) = T(x, v),$$
$$F_j(x, v, t) = F_j(x, v), \qquad \text{and } \rho(t) = \rho, \text{ all independent of } t.$$

*Then,*

(b) *the optimal policy,* $v^* = v^*(x)$, *and the values of the auxiliary variables along the optimal path, are functions of* $x$ *alone, independent of* $t$ *for given* $x$;

(c) *the system of differential equations defined by* (a), (d), *and* (e) *is autonomous.*

In the case of an autonomous system, considerable interest is usually focused on its stationary point or *equilibrium*, where all motion ceases; i.e., the values of $x$ and $p$ for which $\dot{x} = 0$ and $\dot{p} = 0$. This notion in economics is that of long-run stationary equilibrium (as opposed to temporary or short-run equilibrium in which the capital stocks are given). In the present system an equilibrium is defined by $x^*$, $p^*$, $v^*$, satisfying the conditions

$$T(x^*, v^*) = 0,$$
$$\rho p_i^* = L_{x_i}^*,$$
$$v^* \text{ maximizes } H(x^*, v, p^*) \text{ under the constraints } F_j(x^*, v) \geqq 0,$$
$$T_i(x^*, v) \geqq 0 \quad \text{if} \quad x_i^* = 0.$$

If the initial state of the system is $x^*$, then all the conditions of Proposition 7 can be satisfied by simply setting $x(t) = x^*$, $v(t) = v^*$, $p(t) = p^*$ for all $t$. The question may be asked: Under what conditions is this solution optimal? More generally, suppose we can find a path satisfying the conditions of Proposition 7 that converges to the stationary values: When is this optimal?

For simplicity of reference, we define a *Pontryagin path* as a system, $x(t)$, $p(t)$, $v^*(t)$, satisfying the conditions of Proposition 7.

PROPOSITION 10. *Let $x(t)$, $p(t)$, $v^*(t)$ be a Pontryagin path for the problem of Proposition 7. Suppose further that the concavity hypothesis of Proposition 8 and the stationarity hypothesis (a) of Proposition 9, with $\rho > 0$, are satisfied. Then, if $x(t)$ and $p(t)$ converge to an equilibrium $x^*$, $p^*$ where $p_i^* \geqq 0$, they constitute an optimal path.*

*Proof*: From Proposition 8 it suffices to note that the transversality condition, $\alpha(t)p_i(t)x_i(t)$ approaches zero, is satisfied. But $p_i(t)$ and $x_i(t)$ converge to finite limits, and $\alpha(t) = e^{-\rho t}$ approaches zero since $\rho > 0$.

It should be remarked, however, that (a) there may be more than one equilibrium, and (b) optimal paths may exist which do not converge to any finite equilibrium; for example, see Kurz (1968*a* and 1968*b*, section B) and section IV.4, especially Figure 9.

## 7. Jumps in the State Variables

Under certain circumstances, it is possible that among the policy choices available to an individual is that of arranging for a discontinuous change in one or more state variables. For example, a firm may change its capital stock by a sudden purchase of a large block of capital goods as well as by a gradual change through investment. Such a jump may be accompanied by a reward, which will typically be negative (i.e., a cost). We confine ourselves here to the case where the reward or cost of a jump is proportional to its magnitude. The determination of optimal policies for this extension has been studied by Rishel (1965), Warga (1966) and Vind (1967), using similar methods; we follow here the exposition of Vind.

The transition equations without jumps discussed thus far, e.g., 3.(1), can be written in integrated form as

$$x(t') - x(0) = \int_0^{t'} T[x(t), v(t), t]dt. \tag{1}$$

Now suppose that upward jumps are permitted in some but not necessarily all the state variables, for definiteness in the state variables

$x_i(i = 1, \ldots, \bar{s})$. Let the successive times at which jumps occur in one or more of these state variables be designated by $t_1, t_2, \ldots, t_j, \ldots$. For a state variable $x_i$, let $x_i^-(t_j)$ and $x_i^+(t_j)$ be the values before and after the jump; they might of course be the same for some state variable if there is another that has a jump at $t_j$. Then the transition equation for $x_i(i = 1, \ldots, \bar{s})$ can be written in integrated form as

$$x_i(t') - x_i(0) = \int_0^{t'} T_i[x(t), v(t), t]dt + \sum_{t_j<t'} [x_i^+(t_j) - x_i^-(t_j)]. \tag{2}$$

If $t'$ were itself a jump point, then (2) defines $x_i^-(t')$. Equation (1) holds for $i = \bar{s} + 1, \ldots, s$.

Then let $U_i(i = 1, \ldots, \bar{s})$ be the utility associated with a unit jump in state variable $i$. In general, we may suppose $U_i$ to be a function of time. Then the utility associated with a jump in state variable $x_i$ at jump time $t_j$ is $U_i(t_j)[x_i^+(t_j) - x^-(t_j)]$. Note that this magnitude is a *utility*, not a *felicity*, i.e., a stock magnitude, not a flow. The total utility derived from all jumps is the sum of these magnitudes over all $i = 1, \ldots, \bar{s}$ and all jump points $t_j$. Thus, the utility associated with a given policy, including jumps, is,

$$\int_0^T U[x(t), v(t), t]dt + \sum_j \sum_{i=1}^{\bar{s}} \bar{U}_i(t_j)[x_i^+(t_j) - x_i^-(t_j)], \tag{3}$$

plus a possible scrap value which we ignore here.

It is then sought to maximize (3) subject to (1), (2), and any constraints on the instruments $v(t)$, where the location and magnitudes of the jumps are also under the control of the maximizer.

Vind's idea is to introduce an artificial time, say $\bar{t}$, which coincides with natural time, $t$, between jumps. A jump is considered to be an interval in artificial time during which each state variable capable of jumps varies at a constant rate. Such an interval will be termed a *jump interval.* Then if a jump at $t_j$ is identified with a jump interval $\langle \bar{t}_j, \bar{t}_j^+ \rangle$, we introduce a new instrument, $\bar{v}_i$, for each such state variable so that the jump in that variable,

$$x_i^+(t_j) - x_i^-(t_j) = (\bar{t}_j^+ - \bar{t}_j^-)\bar{v}_i,$$

which can also be written

$$x_i^+(t_j) - x_i^-(t_j) = \int_{t_j^-}^{t_j^+} \bar{v}_i(\bar{t})d\bar{t}, \tag{4}$$

if $\bar{v}_i(\bar{t})$ is constant over the interval. Because we are only considering upward jumps, $\bar{v}_i \geqq 0$.

Let $v_0(\bar{t})$ be an instrument variable defined to be 0 on a jump interval and 1 elsewhere. Then we can write,

$$\int_0^{t'} T[x(t),\, v(t),\, t]dt = \int_0^{\bar{t}'} v_0(\bar{t})T[x(\bar{t}),\, v(\bar{t}),\, t]d\bar{t}, \tag{5}$$

where $\bar{t}'$ is the point in artificial time corresponding to $t'$ in natural time; it is defined by

$$\bar{t}' = t' + \sum_{t_j < t'} (\bar{t}_j^+ - \bar{t}_j^-). \tag{6}$$

From (4) and (5), (2) can be written,

$$x_i(\bar{t}') - x_i(0) = \int_0^{\bar{t}'} v_0(\bar{t})T_i[x(\bar{t}), v(\bar{t}), t]d\bar{t} + \int_0^{\bar{t}'} [1 - v_0(\bar{t})]\bar{v}_i(\bar{t})d\bar{t}$$

By differentiation with respect to $\bar{t}'$, we can write the transition equations in a form corresponding to that of the earlier sections,

$$dx_i/d\bar{t} = v_0(\bar{t})T_i[x(\bar{t}),\, v(\bar{t}),\, t] + [1 - v_0(\bar{t})]\bar{v}_i(\bar{t}). \tag{7}$$

It must be observed that natural time, $t$, still enters into (7), because $T$ may depend explicitly on $t$. It will therefore be necessary to introduce $t$ as a new state variable. It will of course satisfy the equation

$$dt/d\bar{t} = v_0(\bar{t}). \tag{8}$$

For the state variable $x_i$ with $i > \bar{s}$, it is clear that (7) also holds if it is understood that $v_i(\bar{t}) = 0$ for them; i.e., they are not permitted to jump.

With the notation just introduced, a completely parallel argument shows that (3) can be written,

$$\int_0^{\bar{T}} \left\{ v_0(\bar{t})U[x(\bar{t}),\, v(\bar{t}),\, t] + [1 - v_0(\bar{t})]\sum_{i=1}^{\bar{s}} \bar{U}_i(t)\bar{v}_i(\bar{t}) \right\} d\bar{t}. \tag{9}$$

So far it has been assumed that $\bar{v}_i(\bar{t})$ is constant throughout a jump interval, a restriction of a form not introduced in the earlier discussion of the Pontryagin principle. It is clear from (7) and (9) however that $\bar{v}_i(\bar{t})$ enters only through its integral over the jump intervals,

$$\int_{\bar{t}_j^-}^{\bar{t}_j^+} \bar{v}_i(\bar{t})d\bar{t}.$$

If we permit $\bar{v}_i(\bar{t})$ to be any (nonnegative) function over the jump interval, we can always find another which is constant over jump intervals and which satisfies (7) and yields the same utility (9), since the pattern in natural time is the same. On the one hand, then, we can consider the problem to be stated in completely standard Pontryagin form and apply Proposition 1. On the other hand, we can without loss of generality assume that the optimal policy is one for which $\bar{v}_i$ is constant over jump intervals. It is also clear that if $\bar{v}_i = 0$ for all $i$ over a jump interval, no jump has really occurred; we could therefore find another choice of instruments, specifically of $v_0$ as a function of $\bar{t}$, which would yield the same outcome in natural time and which would eliminate that jump interval.

At some optimal policy, $\bar{v}_i(\bar{t})$ constant over jump intervals, $\bar{v}_i(\bar{t}) \neq 0$ for some $i$ for $\bar{t}$ in a jump interval. (10)

We now apply Proposition 1 to the maximization of (9) subject to (7) and (8). As before, let $p_i$ be the auxiliary variable corresponding to the $i^{\text{th}}$ equation in (7), and let $p_0$ be that corresponding to (8). We will let $H$ be defined as before,

$$H = U(x, v, t) + \sum_i p_i T_i(x, v, t), \tag{11}$$

and let $\bar{H}$ be the Hamiltonian of the new problem.

$$\bar{H} = v_0 U(x, v, t) + (1 - v_0)\sum_{i=1}^{\bar{s}} \bar{U}_i(t)\bar{v}_i + \sum_i p_i v_0 T_i(x, v, t)$$

$$+ \sum_{i=1}^{\bar{s}} p_i(1 - v_0)\bar{v}_i + p_0 v_0 = v_0(H + p_0) + (1 - v_0)\tilde{H}, \tag{12}$$

where

$$\tilde{H} = \sum_{i=1}^{\bar{s}} [U_i(t) + p_i]\bar{v}_i. \tag{13}$$

The maximization of $\bar{H}$ with respect to all the instruments, $v$, $v_0$, and $\bar{v}_i$, entails, for fixed $v_0$, the maximization of $H$ with respect to $v$ and of $\tilde{H}$ with respect to the $\bar{v}_i$'s. If we let

$$H^0 = \max_v H, \qquad \tilde{H}^0 = \max_{\bar{v}} \tilde{H}, \qquad \bar{H}^0 = \max_{v, v_0, \bar{v}_i} \bar{H}, \tag{14}$$

then, since $v_0$ takes on only the values 0 and 1,

$$\bar{H}^0 = \max_{v_0} [v_0(H^0 + p_0) + (1 - v_0)\tilde{H}^0] = \max (H^0 + p_0, \tilde{H}^0), \tag{15}$$

$$H^0 + p_0 \leqq \tilde{H}^0 \text{ if } v_0 = 0, \qquad H^0 + p_0 \geqq \tilde{H}^0 \text{ if } v_0 = 1. \tag{16}$$

Since $\tilde{H}$ is linear in the $\bar{v}_i$'s, which are only constrained to be nonnegative, it follows by familiar arguments that $\bar{U}_i + p_i$ must be nonpositive for all $i = 1, \ldots, \bar{s}$. For if $\bar{U}_{i'}(t) + p_{i'}(\bar{t}) > 0$ for some $i'$ at some point on the optimal trajectory, then by choosing $\bar{v}_{i'}(\bar{t})$ arbitrarily large, we can make $\tilde{H}$ and therefore $\bar{H}$ arbitrarily large, by (13) and (15), and no maximum of $\bar{H}$ would exist.

$$\bar{U}_i(t) + p_i(\bar{t}) \leqq 0 \text{ for all } i = 1, \ldots, \bar{s}. \tag{17}$$

It follows immediately that $\tilde{H}$ can never be positive; on the other hand it can always be made equal to 0 by setting $\bar{v}_i = 0$, all $i$.

$$\tilde{H}^0 = 0 \text{ everywhere}, \tag{18}$$

and, from (16),

$$H^0 + p_0 \leqq 0 \text{ if } v_0 = 0, \qquad H^0 + p_0 \geqq 0 \text{ if } v_0 = 1. \tag{19}$$

If the strict inequality held everywhere in (17), then the unique optimizing choice of the $\bar{v}_i$'s is 0 for all; from (10), this cannot occur during a jump interval.

$$\text{In a jump interval, } \bar{U}_i(t) + p_i(\bar{t}) = 0 \text{ for some } i \leqq \bar{s}. \tag{20}$$

By Proposition 1(c), the motion of the auxiliary variables is governed by the differential equations,

$$dp_i/d\bar{t} = -\partial\bar{H}/\partial x_i, \; dp_0/d\bar{t} = -\partial\bar{H}/\partial t.$$

Since $x_i$ does not appear in $\tilde{H}$ by (13) it follows from (12) that,

$$dp_i/d\bar{t} = -v_0(\partial H/\partial x_i). \tag{21}$$

Also from (12),

$$dp_0/d\bar{t} = -v_0(\partial H/\partial t) - (1 - v_0)(\partial\tilde{H}/\partial t). \tag{22}$$

In a jump interval, where $v_0 = 0$, $dp_i/d\bar{t} = 0$, so that $p_i(\bar{t})$ is constant there. Hence, $p_i$ is a function of $t$ (natural time), and satisfies the usual equation,

$$dp_i/dt = -\partial H/\partial x_i\,; \tag{23}$$

it is to be noted, though, that the right-hand side depends on $x$, which varies discontinuously at a jump; thus the left- and right-hand natural time derivatives of $p_i$ may differ at a jump.

From (13), $\partial\tilde{H}/\partial t = \sum_{i=1}^{\bar{s}}(d\bar{U}_i/dt)\bar{v}_i(\bar{t})$. From (10), we can assume $\bar{v}_i(\bar{t})$ constant in a jump interval, and therefore the same is true of $\partial\tilde{H}/\partial t$. From (22), $dp_0/d\bar{t} = -(\partial\tilde{H}/\partial t)$, a constant, in the jump interval, so that,

$$p_0(\bar{t}) \text{ is linear in } \bar{t} \text{ over a jump interval}. \tag{24}$$

By integration, over a jump interval, it is immediately seen that, in natural time,

$$p_0^+(t_j) - p_0^-(t_j) = -\sum_{i=1}^{\bar{s}} \bar{U}_i'(t_j)[x_i^+(t_j) - x_i^-(t_j)]. \tag{25}$$

where $p_0^+(t)$ and $p_0^-(t)$ are the right- and left-hand time limits of $p_0(t)$, respectively.

From (7), since $\bar{v}_i$ is constant over a jump interval,

$$x(\bar{t}) \text{ is linear over a jump interval.} \tag{26}$$

At the upper end of the jump interval, $\bar{t}_j$, $v_0$ changes from 0 to 1. By (19) and continuity, $H^0[x(\bar{t}_j^+), p(\bar{t}_j^+), t_j] + p_0(\bar{t}_j^+) = 0$.

At the lower end of a jump interval the same holds, provided $\bar{t}_j^- > 0$; otherwise we cannot say that $v_0(\bar{t}) = 1$ for smaller values of $\bar{t}$. Of course, $\bar{t}_j^- = 0$ if and only if $t_j = 0$ [from (6)]. From (25), then, we can write, in natural time, that

$$H^0[x^+(t_j), p(t_j), t_j] - H^0[x^-(t_j), p(t_j), t_j] = \sum_{i=1}^{\bar{s}} \bar{U}_i'(t_j)[x_i^+(t_j) - x_i^-(t_j)] \tag{27}$$

provided $t_j > 0$.

Now suppose that $H^0(x, p, t)$ is strictly concave in $x$ for fixed $p$ and $t$. Then, since $x$ varies over a jump, $H^0[x(\bar{t}), p(t), t]$ is strictly concave in $\bar{t}$ over a jump interval in view of (26). From (24), it follows that $H^0[x(\bar{t}), p(t), t] + p_0(\bar{t})$ is strictly concave in $\bar{t}$ over a jump interval. If this function is 0 at both ends of the interval, it must be positive in the interior, in contradiction to (19). It has therefore been shown that if $H^0$ is strictly concave in $x$, it will never jump except possibly at $t = 0$.

This result is reasonable. Under concavity conditions, a firm might, to get started, acquire a block of capital; but afterwards, its optimal policy would never involve discontinuities.

Proposition 11. *Suppose all the assumptions of Proposition 1 are satisfied except that jumps are permitted in the state variables. Specificially, let $v^*(t)$ be a choice of instruments, $t_j^*$ a set of chosen jump points in time, and $x_i^+(t_j^*)$ the value to which state variable $x_i$ jumps at time $t_j^*$ which maximize*

$$\int_0^T U[x(t), v(t), t]dt + \sum_j \sum_{i=1}^{\bar{s}} \bar{U}_i(t_j)[x_i^+(t_j) - x_i^-(t_j)],$$

*subject to the conditions*

(a) $$x(t') - x(0) = \int_0^{t'} T[x(t), v(t), t]dt + \sum_{t_j < t'} [x^+(t_j) - x^-(t_j)],$$

*some constraints on the choices of the instruments, initial conditions on the state variables, and the restriction that* $x_i^+(t_j) \geqq x_i^-(t_j)$ *for* $i \leqq \bar{s}$, $x_i^+(t_j) = x^-(t_j)$ *for* $i > \bar{s}$, *where* $x^-(t_j)$ *is the left-hand limit of* $x(t)$ *as* $t$ *approaches* $t_j$. *Then there exist auxiliary variables,* $p_i(t)$, *such that, for each* $t$,

(b) $v^*(t)$ *maximizes* $H[x(t), v, p(t), t]$, *where* $H(x, v, p, t) = U(x, v, t) + \sum_{i=1}^{\bar{s}} p_i T_i(x, v, t)$,

*the functions* $p_i$ *satisfy the differential equations,*

(c) $\dot{p}_i = -\partial H/\partial x_i$ *evaluated at* $x = x(t)$, $p = p(t)$, *and the conditions,*

(d) $$\bar{U}_i(t) + p_i(t) \leqq 0 \text{ for all } t \text{ and all } i \leqq \bar{s},$$

(e) $$\bar{U}_i(t_j^*) + p_i(t_j^*) = 0 \text{ if } x_i^+(t_j^*) > x_i^-(t_j^*),$$

*and the jumps satisfy the condition,*

(f) $$H^0[x^+(t_j^*), p(t_j^*), t_j^*] - H^0[x^-(t_j^*), p(t_j^*), t_j^*] = \sum_{i=1}^{\bar{s}} \bar{U}_i'(t_j^*)[x_i^+(t_j^*) - x_i^-(t_j^*)] \quad \text{if } t_j > 0.$$

PROPOSITION 12.[2] *Suppose in addition to the assumptions of Proposition 11 that* $H^0(x, p, t)$ *is strictly concave in* $x$ *for given* $p$ *and* $t$. *Then a jump can never be optimal except possibly at the initial time point.*

[2] This proposition was conjectured by us and proved in some special applications: Arrow (1968, pp. 7–8), Arrow and Kurz (1969, section 5). We are greatly indebted to Karl Vind for observing that this proposition can be inferred from his treatment of the control problem with jumps in the state variables.

# III

# OPTIMAL INVESTMENT PLANNING IN A ONE-COMMODITY MODEL

## 0. Introduction

In this chapter we review in detail the simplest possible capital accumulation model. This was first studied by Ramsey (1928), though only in the context of an economy with stationary population and technology. Here, we assume that there is only one commodity, which can be either consumed or invested. We consider the situation in which a government is in a position to control the economy completely and to plan perfectly so as to optimize with respect to all possible control variables of the economic system—in this case only investment and consumption (only one of which can be chosen freely). The purpose of this chapter is to illustrate in the simplest case the modes of analysis applied to subsequent models involving both public and private investment. Our analysis owes much to the important work of Mirrlees (1967) and Koopmans (1965).

In section 1 we use relatively informal arguments; in section 2 we go over the same ground with the aid of a rigorous use of Pontryagin's maximum principle. In section 3 we give an interpretation of the investment and interest rate policy implied by the results of the preceding sections and show how the model can be used to derive computationally useful approximations. Section 4 is devoted to an alternative mode of presenting the constraints, which is applied to develop the optimal policy when investment is irreversible; i.e., when capital, once formed, cannot subsequently be consumed. Finally, in section 5 we briefly discuss a particular generalization to increasing returns to scale.

## 1. Optimization in the One-Sector Model: Informal Discussion

We assume here that there is a single commodity which, at any instant of time, may be either added to capital or consumed. In accordance with the discussion in section I.4 applied to an economy with no government sector (thus, public capital does not appear in the objective function), the aim of the economy is to maximize the utility functional:

$$V = \int_0^\infty e^{-\rho t} P(t) U[\tilde{c}(t)] dt, \tag{1}$$

where $\rho$ = felicity rate of discount; $P$ = population; $\tilde{c}$ = per capita consumption; $U(\tilde{c})$ = felicity of consumption (the contribution to utility made by the consumption at any instant); $t$ = time.

The production conditions are defined by the expression:

$$Y(t) = F[K(t), e^{\tau t} L(t)], \tag{2}$$

where $Y$ = total output; $L$ = labor force; $K$ = capital; $\tau$ = rate of labor-augmenting (Harrod-neutral) technological progress. For the present it is assumed that

$$F(K, L) \text{ is concave and homogeneous of degree 1 in } K \text{ and } L; \tag{3}$$

generalization with regard to increasing returns is discussed in section 5.

The labor force and population are assumed to grow at the same rate:

$$L(t)/P(t) = \text{constant rate of labor force participation.} \tag{4}$$

Aggregate consumption equals $P(t)\tilde{c}(t)$; hence, the conservation of product flow is written

$$\dot{K}(t) = Y(t) - P(t)\tilde{c}(t). \tag{5}$$

The aim of our policy is to choose the time function $\tilde{c}(t)$ so as to maximize expression (1), taking into account the initial conditions—in this case, the initial stock of capital, $K_0$. Before a rigorous analysis, some heuristic remarks will be useful.

Suppose we have adopted a particular policy and have therefore defined a stream of consumption for each individual. The consumption discount factor for time $t$ is simply the marginal rate of substitution between future and present consumption, and hence is the ratio of their marginal felicities, modified by the discount on future felicities.

$$\text{Consumption discount factor} = (\text{felicity discount factor}) \times \left(\frac{\text{marginal felicity of future consumption}}{\text{marginal felicity of present consumption}}\right).$$

Since the (proportional) rate of change of a product is the sum of the rates of change of the factors, it follows from this last remark that

$$\text{consumption rate of interest} = (\text{felicity rate of interest}) - (\text{rate of change of marginal felicity of consumption}).$$

Now,

rate of change of marginal felicity of consumption

$$= \frac{1}{U'(\tilde{c})}\frac{dU'(\tilde{c})}{dt} = \frac{U''(\tilde{c})}{U'(\tilde{c})}\frac{d\tilde{c}}{dt} = \frac{U''(\tilde{c})\tilde{c}}{U'(\tilde{c})}\frac{1}{\tilde{c}}\frac{d\tilde{c}}{dt}.$$

Since we ordinarily assume that felicity is a concave function of consumption (diminishing marginal felicity), $U''$ will be negative. It is convenient, then, to define elasticity of marginal felicity of consumption $= \sigma = -\frac{U''\tilde{c}}{U'}$. If we let $r_c$ = consumption rate of interest, the preceding discussion can be summarized in the simple formula:

$$r_c = \rho - d(\log U')/dt = \rho + \sigma(1/\tilde{c})(d\tilde{c}/dt). \tag{6}$$

This result is essentially that of Eckstein (1957) and is implicit in Ramsey (1928); by considering time to be continuous rather than discrete, the exposition and resulting formulas can be given a simpler form than Eckstein's.

As Frisch (1964) has noted with respect to a similar formula, the first term on the right-hand side of (6) is Böhm-Bawerk's second ground for the existence of interest (the systematic undervaluation of future felicities), while the second term is his first ground (the decrease in the marginal felicity of consumption owing to its growth).

From the definition of the consumption rate of interest, it follows that an individual would be indifferent between lending and borrowing an infinitesimal amount of consumption goods for an infinitesimal time period at that rate of interest. Now consider an act of real investment. In our one-commodity world, the marginal rate of transformation between investment and consumption is 1, as expressed in equation (5). If capital can always be decumulated and turned into consumption goods without loss, then investment can be regarded as a loan of arbitrarily short duration, and hence at the margin the marginal productivity of capital (which is its return) should equal the consumption rate of interest:

$$F_K = r_c. \tag{7}$$

Even if investment is not reversible, we may expect (7) to be valid in a growing economy. If the amount of capital per capita is increasing, then the representative individual will not disinvest even if permitted to. Hence, the same conclusions hold. Investment is thus being made on what may be termed "myopic" grounds; the marginal productivity of capital at any instant should be equated to an appropriately chosen short-term rate of interest (see Marglin 1963, pp. 20–27; Arrow 1964*b*).[1]

[1] The short-term rate needed here is that appropriate to a nonmonetary full-employment economy; the rate actually observed is probably overly influenced by monetary and cyclical factors.

This does not mean that the current investment decision is independent of the future since the "correct" short-term rate of interest must in full equilibrium reflect future movements of profitability throughout the economy.

It should be emphasized that the assumption of a single type of capital which is *malleable* (to use Meade's term) is crucial to the argument [this assumption is contained in the aggregate production function (5) since output depends merely on the total supply of capital, not on its distribution to different uses]. Under this assumption it would not pay, for example, to make an investment that would earn less than the consumption rate of interest in the immediate future; if it would earn higher returns at some time in the future, it would be even better to postpone the investment.[2]

Since capital in the real world is not in fact malleable but has been created by physical processes that cannot be reversed without loss, are

[2] The determination of investment by equating the current marginal productivity with an interest rate at least apparently sharply contrasts with more familiar formulations, such as Keynes's "marginal efficiency of capital" calculation (1936, chapter 11). The latter asserts that an investment is justified if and only if the sum of discounted returns at least equals the cost. There are, however, two ambiguities in this statement; if they are resolved in what appears to be economically the most natural way, the rule is myopic. (1) What is meant by the return to a particular investment? In fact, it varies with the total volume of capital in the system. The only consistent interpretation, at least if capital is malleable, is to take the given investment as being the marginal investment in every future period. Then the return in any period is simply the marginal productivity of capital. (2) By what rate are future returns discounted to the present? If the rate used in discounting a return $t$ years hence is taken to be the marginal rate of substitution between consumption then and now, the short-term interest rate at any time is $r_c$, and the long-term interest rates are the simple averages of the short-term rates in the intervening period. If the short-term rates are not constant, then neither will the long-term rates be constant.

If it is assumed that an optimal policy will be followed in the future, so that $F_K = r_c(t)$ at all future $t$, it follows easily enough that a current investment will be justified only so long as $F_K \geqq r_c$ today, since future returns to the marginal investment will barely justify it. In this sense the Keynes formulation is accurate, but it is not a very useful sense because the optimal policy is determined first. Further, the Keynes formulation can easily be misunderstood to mean that, in evaluating future returns, the new investment today is to be regarded as marginal not to the future optimal stock of capital but to the present stock of capital. With a growing labor force and technological progress, the marginal productivity of any fixed amount of capital will rise over time. Thus, with constant interest rates, for example, the marginal product of capital will exceed the interest rate for all $t > 0$ if the initial stock of capital is optimal in the sense of satisfying (7). Thus, the marginal efficiency of capital will exceed cost, and the rule would appear to justify a stock of capital in excess of the optimal. The Keynes rule is thus either useless for calculation or wrong.

Fisher's "rate of return over cost" appears to have the same defects as Keynes's "marginal efficiency of capital," but in fact Fisher hedged by considering the returns and costs to be alternative returns and costs measured relative to the next best alternative (see Fisher 1930, pp. 155–58). Since the alternatives could clearly include postponement, Fisher's results are formally correct, though no simple way of implementing them is presented.

these models of any use? At several points in this study we note the possibility of a more general analysis that takes explicit account of the irreversibility of specific capital investments (see section 4). But it can be maintained that in an economy where all forms of investment are growing, the embodiment of some capital in specific form does not limit the direction of future investments. Hence, the economy will grow as if capital were malleable, for it would never pay to take advantage of the possibility of shifting capital among different forms. Further, it is not even necessary that the desired rate of investment in all activities be positive; it suffices that the desired rate of disinvestment not exceed the rate of depreciation.[3] (In our formal models we do not consider depreciation, but this can be included by reinterpretation as shown in section 4.)

Let us return to the equations so far derived. The basic relations are (5), (6), and (7). Suppose we start with a given stock of capital and a given level of consumption. Then the marginal productivity of capital is determined and, from (7), the consumption rate of interest, $r_c$. From (6), this determines $d\tilde{c}/dt$, since $\tilde{c}$ is given. But from the production relations (3) and (4), and the capital accumulation equation (5), $\dot{K}$ is determined by the present values of $K$ and $\tilde{c}$. Hence, the rates of change of both capital and consumption are determined. After a short period of time, then, new levels of capital and consumption are determined, and the calculations can be started again.

Thus, the whole time path of the optimal accumulation policy is determined by these relations plus the initial values of capital and consumption. The initial stock of capital must be regarded as given by historical circumstances; but consumption is a flow, not a stock, and can be changed at will by the planner. The initial value should therefore be chosen optimally. It will be seen that in fact it can only be chosen in one particular way to ensure that the resulting time path of consumption and capital is not either infeasible or wildly unstable.

The long-run properties of the optimal path are worth some attention. Assume that population is growing at a constant rate, $\pi$. It is plausible to suppose (and will be rigorously validated below under appropriate assumptions) that the evolving system will settle down into a state of steady growth, in which the savings ratio tends to a constant. Then, as we know from the standard theory of growth (see section I.5), both the capital stock and consumption will grow at the *natural rate*, $\gamma = \pi + \tau$. Hence, we will define

$$k = Ke^{-\gamma t}, \tag{8}$$

[3] Cf. Solow (1963, p. 2): "There is a case for saying that these one-period rates of return are the fundamental ones because in a highly developed and complex growing economy, saving-investment decisions come up for consideration every period and can easily be changed or even undone."

the ratio of capital to effective labor force (labor force adjusted for improvements in technological efficiency). The assumptions of constant returns to scale and labor-augmenting technological progress imply

$$F[K(t), e^{\tau t}L(t)] = F[K(t), L_0 e^{\gamma t}] = e^{\gamma t}F[K(t)e^{-\gamma t}, L_0] = e^{\gamma t}f[k(t)], \quad (9)$$

where we define $f(k) = F(k, L_0)$; i.e., output per effective worker as a function of capital per effective worker. If we differentiate with respect to $K$, we find

$$F_K = e^{\gamma t}f'[k(t)](\partial k/\partial K) = e^{\gamma t}f'[k(t)]e^{-\gamma t} = f'[k(t)]. \quad (10)$$

Now let us make the additional simplifying assumption that the total and marginal felicity functions have constant elasticities with respect to per capita consumption, so that $\sigma$ is constant. In a state of steady growth, total consumption must be rising at the rate $\gamma$ and, therefore, per capita consumption at the rate $\tau = \gamma - \pi$. If we use the superscript $^\infty$ to denote values in the state of steady growth, it then follows from (6) that

$$r_c^\infty = \rho + \sigma\tau = \omega, \quad (11)$$

say. But then (10) and (7) tell us that

$$f'(k^\infty) = \omega, \quad (12)$$

so that the ratio of capital to effective labor is determined along the balanced growth path. Total capital is, from (8), determined by $K(t) = k^\infty e^{\gamma t}$, so that $\dot{K}(t) = \gamma k^\infty e^{\gamma t}$; total output is, from (9), $Y(t) = e^{\gamma t}f(k^\infty)$, and hence, from (5), per capita consumption is given by

$$\tilde{c}(t) = \frac{1}{P(0)} e^{-\pi t}[e^{\gamma t}f(k^\infty) - e^{\gamma t}\gamma k^\infty] = \frac{1}{P(0)} e^{\tau t}[f(k^\infty) - \gamma k^\infty]. \quad (13)$$

The savings ratio, $\dot{K}/Y$, can be calculated from the above results to be

$$\gamma k^\infty/f(k^\infty) = \gamma/[f(k^\infty)/k^\infty] = \gamma/[F(K, e^{\tau t}L)/K],$$

a constant equal to the ratio between the natural rate of growth and the average productivity of capital along the balanced growth path (a familiar Harrod-Domar conclusion).

Hence, in the simple Ramsey model, we expect the ratio of capital to effective labor to move from its initial given value to the asymptotic level, $k^\infty$. At each moment of time the ratio of capital to effective labor and the rate of increase of per capita consumption are related by the equation:

$$f'(k) = \omega = \rho + \sigma(1/\tilde{c})(d\tilde{c}/dt), \quad (14)$$

and we also observe that $(1/\tilde{c})(d\tilde{c}/dt)$ tends to the limit, $\tau$, the actual level of $\tilde{c}$ being determined by (12).

## 2. Optimization in the One-Sector Model: Application of the Pontryagin Maximum Principle

Under the hypotheses of the previous section, including the constancy of $\sigma$—the elasticity of the marginal felicity of consumption—the Pontryagin principle developed in chapter II provides an expeditious means of setting forth an explicit solution.

To repeat 1.(1), the maximand is

$$\int_0^{\infty} e^{-\rho t} P(t) U[\tilde{c}(t)] dt, \tag{1}$$

and from 1.(2) and 1.(5), the constraint is

$$\dot{K} = F[K(t), e^{\tau t} L(t)] - P(t)\tilde{c}(t), \tag{2}$$

and finally $\tilde{c}(t)$ is the single control variable. Then (see Proposition II.7), the current-value Hamiltonian is

$$H = P(t) U[\tilde{c}(t)] + q\{F[K(t), e^{\tau t} L(t)] - P(t)\tilde{c}_t\}, \tag{3}$$

where $q$ is the auxiliary variable associated with the constraint (2). The maximum principle instructs us to maximize (3) with respect to $\tilde{c}(t)$. If we assume $U'(0) = +\infty$, as is natural, the maximum must be interior, and we have

$$P(t) U'[\tilde{c}(t)] - qP(t) = 0,$$

or

$$U'[\tilde{c}(t)] = q. \tag{4}$$

Thus, $q$, the price of capital, is also the marginal felicity of consumption, a natural result in a world where the one commodity can be used indifferently for investment or consumption. We can also compute

$$\partial H / \partial K = qF_K = qf'(k),$$

where use is made of 1.(10). Then the auxiliary variable $q$ satisfies the differential equation [see Proposition II.7(e)]:

$$\dot{q} = \rho q - qf'(k),$$

or

$$\dot{q}/q = \rho - f'(k). \tag{5}$$

The equations (2), (4), and (5), together with the definition 1.(8) of $k$ in terms of $K$ and time, constitute a complete system of differential equations. However, further clarity can be achieved by some changes of variables, which exploit the assumptions of exponential trends in technology and population and of a constant elasticity of felicity with respect to consumption.

First, we will eliminate $K$ from (2) by using the definition of $k$. From the definition, it follows immediately that

$$\dot{k} = e^{-\gamma t}\dot{K} - \gamma k .$$

Substitute from 1.(9) into (2) and then substitute the resulting expression in the formula for $\dot{k}$:

$$\dot{k} = f(k) - \gamma k - P(t)e^{-\gamma t}\tilde{c}(t) . \tag{6}$$

Introduce the abbreviation:

$$c(t) = P(t)e^{-\gamma t}\tilde{c}(t) ; \tag{7}$$

$c(t)$ is proportional to consumption per effective worker. If the marginal felicity of consumption has constant elasticity $\sigma$, then

$$U'(\tilde{c}) = U'(ce^{\gamma t}/P) = (e^{\gamma t}/P)^{-\sigma}U'(c) . \tag{8}$$

Let us introduce a new "price" for consumption per effective worker, say $p$. We wish to define $p$ so that

$$U'(c) = p . \tag{9}$$

The necessary definition, then, from (8) and (4) is

$$p = (e^{\gamma t}/P)^{\sigma}q . \tag{10}$$

We now need a differential equation for $p$ to replace (5) for $q$. Take natural logarithms in (10):

$$\log p = \sigma(\gamma t - \log P) + \log q .$$

Differentiate with respect to time:

$$\dot{p}/p = \sigma[\gamma - (\dot{P}/P)] + (\dot{q}/q) .$$

We now use the assumption that population is growing at a steady rate, $\pi$. Then $\dot{P}/P = \pi$, and $\gamma - \pi = \tau$, the rate of technological progress. If, finally, we substitute for $\dot{q}/q$ from (5), we have

$$\dot{p}/p = \rho + \sigma\tau - f'(k) = \omega - f'(k) , \tag{11}$$

from 1.(11).

It is convenient to rewrite (6) with the aid of (7):

$$\dot{k} = f(k) - \gamma k - c . \tag{12}$$

Equations (11), (12), and (9) constitute a complete system, which is now autonomous, in the sense that time does not enter explicitly. This will permit a simple two-dimensional analysis of the path of the system.

Figure 2 shows a phase diagram for the path of solutions to the two equations, (11) and (12); it will be understood that $c$ is a function of $p$, defined by (9), the essential property of which is that $c$ is a decreasing function of $p$. From (11), $p$ is stationary ($\dot{p} = 0$) whenever $k = k^{\infty}$, defined by $f'(k^{\infty}) = \omega$.

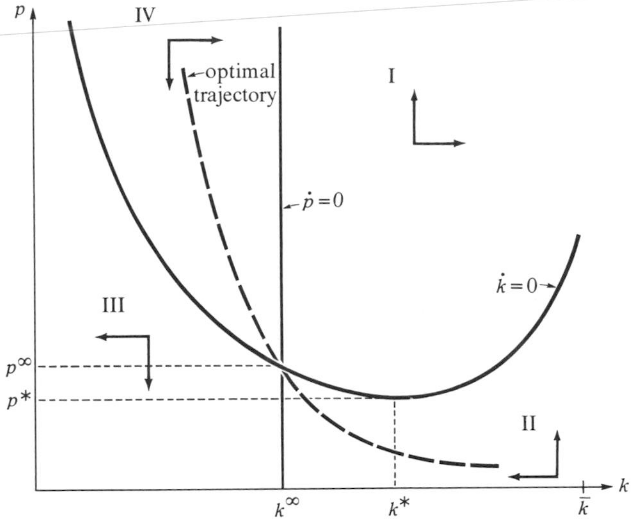


**Figure 2**

In the $(k, p)$-plane, $\dot{p} = 0$ is then a vertical line. Under the assumption of concavity of the production function (diminishing marginal productivity of capital), $f'(k)$ is decreasing; hence, $\omega - f'(k) > \omega - f'(k^{\infty}) = 0$ for $k > k^{\infty}$, and from (11) $p$ is increasing for $k > k^{\infty}$ and decreasing for $k < k^{\infty}$. The movements of $p$ in different quadrants of the diagram are represented by small vertical arrows.

Similarly, $\dot{k} = 0$, from (12), whenever $c(p) = f(k) - \gamma k$. The function $f(k) - \gamma k$ is a concave function since its second derivative is negative. It has its maximum at $k = k^*$, defined by $f'(k^*) = \gamma$; this is the so-called golden rule point.[4] In drawing figure 2 we have assumed $k^* > k^{\infty}$; we return to this assumption later. Since $c(p)$ is a decreasing function of $p$, it follows that, along the curve for which $\dot{k} = 0$, $p$ has its minimum

[4] Among all possible ratios of capital to effective labor for which balanced growth is possible, this yields the highest consumption stream. This property was discovered independently by Phelps (1961), Swan (1964, p. 7), Desrousseaux (1961), von Weizsäcker (1962, p. 79), Joan Robinson (1962), and doubtless several others. As the above analysis shows, transformation of the variables reduces the general case of balanced growth to that of the maximization of steady consumption in stationary states, which had been analyzed thoroughly by Allais (1947, pp. 179–228).

at $k = k^*$. Since $U'(c)$ has constant elasticity, $U'(0)$ must be infinite, so that $c(p) = 0$ only when $p = +\infty$. Since $f(0) = 0$, $f(k) - \gamma k = 0$ when $k = 0$, and again for some $\bar{k} > k^\infty$, so that the curve, $\dot{k} = 0$, is asymptotic to the $p$-axis and to the parallel line, $k = \bar{k}$.

Consider any point above the curve $\dot{k} = 0$; there is a point on the curve with the same $k$ and smaller $p$. Since $c$ decreases as $p$ increases, it follows that $\dot{k}$ increases as $p$ increases, $k$ being held constant, from (12). Hence, $\dot{k} > 0$ for $k$ above the curve $\dot{k} = 0$, $\dot{k} < 0$ below the curve. The movements of $k$ are denoted by small horizontal arrows.

The two curves, $\dot{p} = 0$ and $\dot{k} = 0$, divide the plane into four quadrants, labeled with roman numerals on the diagram. In each, the direction of movement of a solution of the pair of differential equations (11)–(12) is the resultant of the two vectors denoted by small arrows.

The equilibrium of the system is represented by the intersection of the two curves. Its $k$-coordinate is $k^\infty$, already defined; call its $p$ coordinate $p^\infty$. It is easy to see that if we start from some arbitrary point in the $(p, k)$-plane, we do not in general approach the equilibrium. Consider first a starting point in quadrant I. Here, both $p$ and $k$ are increasing. Hence, the only boundary of quadrant I that can be crossed is the curve $\dot{k} = 0$. But if the path reaches this boundary, then $\dot{p} > 0$ while $\dot{k} = 0$, and the moving point goes right back into quadrant I. Hence, a path starting in quadrant I never leaves it, and $p$ and $k$ increase steadily. In particular, $k(t) \geqq k(0) > k^\infty$; since $f'(k)$ is decreasing,

$$f'[k(t)] \leqq f'[k(0)] < f'(k^\infty) = \omega$$

and, from (11),

$$\dot{p}/p = \omega - f'[k(t)] \geqq \omega - f'[k(0)].$$

Since the right-hand side is a positive constant, $p(t)$ must approach infinity. For some $t_0$, then, $p(t) > p^\infty$ for $t \geqq t_0$. Since $c(p)$ is a decreasing function of $p$, $c(t) = c[p(t)] < c(p^\infty)$ for $t \geqq t_0$. Clearly, such a path would not be optimal since it would be dominated by another path that coincided with the given one until time $t_0$, then had a brief period of very high consumption until $k$ was reduced from $k(t_0)$ to $k^\infty$ and coincided with the equilibrium point (which has a higher consumption) thereafter.

Now consider a path starting in quadrant III; $p$ and $k$ are both decreasing in that quadrant. We will consider not only the case shown in figure 2 but also the alternative possibility that $k^* < k^\infty$. By differentiation of (12),

$$\ddot{k} = (f' - \gamma)\dot{k} - c'\dot{p},$$

where the double dot denotes the second derivative with respect to time, and primes denote differentiation. We first show that a path starting in quadrant III must remain in that quadrant. Since $k$ is decreasing in that quadrant, $f'(k)$ is increasing and consequently, from (11), $\dot{p}/p$ is decreasing and therefore negative. Hence, if the path leaves quadrant III, with $p$ and $k$ positive, it cannot cross the line $\dot{p} = 0$ but rather must cross the curve $\dot{k} = 0$. But at such a point,

$$\ddot{k} = -c'\dot{p}.$$

Since $c' < 0$, and $\dot{p} < 0$, $\ddot{k} < 0$ at the point of crossing. But since $\dot{k} < 0$ for smaller values of $t$, $\dot{k} = 0$ at the crossing, we must have $\ddot{k} \geqq 0$, a contradiction.

From the fact that a path starting in quadrant III remains in quadrant III, we can infer that the path becomes infeasible in finite time; specifically, that $k(t) = 0$ for some finite $t$. Since $\dot{k} < 0$, all $t$, and $\dot{p}/p$ is decreasing and therefore negative and bounded away from 0, it follows that $p(t)$ approaches 0 so that $c(t)$ approaches $+\infty$. Since $0 \leqq k < k^{\infty}$ in quadrant III, $f(k) - \gamma k$ is bounded there; hence,

$$\dot{k} = f(k) - \gamma k - c(p)$$

is negative and bounded away from 0 for sufficiently large $t$; i.e.,

$$\dot{k}(t) \leqq M < 0 \qquad \text{for} \qquad t \geqq t_0,$$

and therefore $k(t) \leqq k(t_0) + M(t - t_0) \to -\infty$, which implies that $k(t) = 0$ for some finite $t$.

[To be rigorous, we also have to consider the possibility that $p(t)$ reaches 0 in finite time, for then the equation system ceases to have any meaning. But it is easy to see that if this occurs, then $k(t)$ also approaches 0 in finite time. For suppose that $p(t_0) = 0$, with $p(t) > 0$ for $t < t_0$. If $k(t_0) > 0$, then

$$\dot{p}/p \geqq \omega - f'[k(t_0)] \qquad \text{for} \qquad t < t_0,$$

and therefore, by integration,

$$p(t_0) \geqq p(0)e^{\{\omega - f'[k(t_0)]\}t_0} > 0,$$

which contradicts the assumption that $p(t_0) = 0$.]

The discussion of the remaining two quadrants can be reduced to the previous cases. In quadrant IV, $k$ is increasing, $p$ decreasing. If the path remains in the quadrant, then both must approach limits which can only be the equilibrium values. Otherwise, the path must leave the quadrant; it may either cross the line $\dot{p} = 0$, in which case it enters quadrant I, diverges from equilibrium, and is nonoptimal; or it crosses the curve $\dot{k} = 0$, in which case it enters quadrant III and becomes nonoptimal, as already shown. Then it is intuitively clear from the diagram that for each $k_0 < k^\infty$, there is exactly one value of $p = p_0$ such that a path starting from the point $(k_0, p_0)$ will converge to the equilibrium $(k^\infty, p^\infty)$. To see this rigorously, let us introduce the following argument which has considerable further interest of its own.

Along a path in quadrant IV, $k$ is increasing with $t$. Hence, we can change our independent variable from $t$ to $k$. Then, from (11) and (12), we have

$$(1/p)(dp/dk) = (\dot{p}/p)/\dot{k} = [\omega - f'(k)]/[f(k) - \gamma k - c]. \qquad (13)$$

Since $c$ decreases as $p$ increases, and the numerator is negative, $(1/p)(dp/dk)$ is an increasing function of $p$ for fixed $k$. If $p^1(k)$ and $p^0(k)$ are two solutions to (13) with starting points $(p_1, k_0)$ and $(p_0, k_0)$, respectively, then $d \log [(p^1(k)/p^0(k)]/dk > 0$ whenever $p^1(k) > p^0(k)$. But since $p^1(k_0) = p_1 > p_0 = p^0(k_0)$, there can be no larger value of $k$ (within quadrant IV) for which $p^1(k) \leqq p^0(k)$, since $\log [p^1(k)/p^0(k)]$ would have to be decreasing at some smaller value of $k$, and this is impossible for the smallest such value. Therefore, $\log [p^1(k)/p^0(k)]$ is increasing with $k$. In particular, as $k$ approaches $k^\infty$ it is impossible that $p^1(k)$ and $p^0(k)$ both approach the same limit, $p^\infty$. Thus, for any given $k_0$ there can be at most one $p_0$ for which the path approaches the equilibrium; by continuity there must be at least one. This point is the start of the only possible optimal path with initial capital $k_0$.

An exactly parallel argument applies to quadrant II. A path starting there will pass into quadrant I and then diverge, or pass into quadrant III where it will become infeasible in finite time, or approach equilibrium. Again the last can occur for points along that solution of the differential equation (13) which passes through the equilibrium point. By simple continuity considerations it is clear that for $k$ slightly larger than $k^\infty$, there will be a value of $p$ such that the path beginning there converges to $(k^\infty, p^\infty)$. But then the solution to (13) can be continued for all values of $k$. For it is certainly downward-sloping, and hence can have difficulty only by crossing the $k$-axis. Suppose then that the solution to (13) in question (the broken curve in figure 2) tends to a point with $p = 0$ and $k = k_1$. Write (13) as

$$d \log p/dk = [\omega - f'(k)]/[f(k) - \gamma k - c]. \qquad (14)$$

Since $p$ tends to 0 as $k$ approaches $k_1$, $\log p$ tends to $-\infty$ and therefore $d \log p/dk$ must take on indefinitely large negative values. But the numerator is bounded; and, since $c(p)$ approaches $+\infty$ as $p$ approaches 0, the denominator approaches $-\infty$ so that $d \log p/dk$ approaches 0, a contradiction. Hence, the solution to (13) can be extended to all values of $k$. Thus, we can conclude:

Proposition 1. *For any given initial capital,* $K(0) = k(0)$, *there is determined* $p(0)$ *such that the solution of the differential equation system* (9), (11), and (12) *with those initial values converges to the long-run equilibrium values* $k^\infty$, $p^\infty$. *If any other initial value* $p(0)$ *were chosen, the resulting solution would either diverge to* $+\infty$ *in both variables and be clearly nonoptimal or it would become nonfeasible, with capital stock becoming zero in finite time. From the definitions,* $K(t) = e^{\gamma t}k(t)$ *and* $\tilde{c}(t) = [e^{\gamma t}/P(t)]c(t)$, *the consumption and investment policies which satisfy the Pontryagin maximum principle can be numerically determined.*

We have not said yet that this solution is indeed optimal. As already seen in chapter II, the Pontryagin solution is indeed optimal if there is any optimal solution; but with an infinite horizon, existence is not guaranteed. The problem is not just a question of mathematical delicacy, to be avoided by sufficiently strong regularity conditions. It is in fact the same as what has sometimes been referred to as the *paradox of growth stocks* (Durand 1957); if the expected rate of capital appreciation of a common stock exceeds the rate of interest, then the buyer ought rationally to be willing to pay any price for it.

Paradoxes of this kind relate to the far distant future or, more precisely, to the way magnitudes behave as time approaches infinity. Hence, the relevant comparison is between the asymptotic rate of interest and the asymptotic rate of growth or, in the notation of section 1, between $\omega$ and $\gamma$ [see especially the discussion of 1.(8)–1.(12)]. To see the problem in more detail, suppose that the rate of interest in the appropriate sense is less than the natural rate of growth of the economy; i.e., that $\omega < \gamma$. From the definitions of $k^\infty$ and $k^*$—i.e., $f'(k^\infty) = \omega, f'(k^*) = \gamma$—and from the fact that $f'(k)$ is decreasing as $k$ increases (diminishing marginal productivity of capital), it follows that

$$k^\infty > k^*. \tag{15}$$

It will now be demonstrated that under these circumstances the Pontryagin path is not optimal (and therefore that there is no optimal path). Since $f(k) - \gamma k$ has its maximum at $k = k^*$, we have [see figure 2, but understand that (15) holds],

$$c(p^\infty) = f(k^\infty) - \gamma k^\infty < f(k^*) - \gamma k^* = c(p^*).$$

Since $c(p)$ is a decreasing function of $p$,

$$p^\infty > p^*. \tag{16}$$

Consider now the Pontryagin path, $k(t)$, $p(t)$, which converges to $k^\infty$, $p^\infty$. From (15) and (16), it must be that eventually

$$k(t) > k^*, \; p(t) > p^* \qquad \text{for} \qquad t \geqq t_0, \tag{17}$$

for some $t_0$ and, therefore, since $c(p)$ is a decreasing function of $p$,

$$c(t) < c^* \quad \text{for} \quad t \geqq t_0, \tag{18}$$

where $c(t) = c[p(t)]$ is the consumption along the Pontryagin path, and $c^* = c(p^*)$ is the attainable steady-state consumption at the golden-rule point $(k^*, p^*)$. We now construct a path superior to the Pontryagin path, namely, follow that path up to time $t_0$, and then change consumption per effective worker to the constant level, $c^*$, for all subsequent $t$. Since by (18) consumption is always higher along the alternative path than along the Pontryagin path beginning with $t_0$ and the two paths coincide before $t_0$, the alternative path is certainly superior, provided it is feasible. But beginning at time $t_0$, the capital stock satisfies the differential equation:

$$\dot{k} = f(k) - \gamma k - c^* = f(k) - \gamma k - [f(k^*) - \gamma k^*], \tag{19}$$

with $k(t_0) \geqq k^*$. Since $f(k) - \gamma k$ attains its maximum at $k^*$, it is clear that $\dot{k} < 0$ whenever $k \neq k^*$. However, since $k(t_0) > k^*$, $k(t)$ satisfying (19) cannot fall below $k^*$ since that is an equilibrium point of (19). Therefore, $k(t)$ never falls to zero, and the alternative path is feasible and therefore superior to the Pontryagin path.[5]

It may appear puzzling to assert that there is no optimal path, and interpretation of this phenomenon appears to be rather difficult. We will add only this. It might appear that the whole difficulty arises because of our assumption of an infinite horizon which is, after all, an artifice introduced for analytic and conceptual convenience; astronomers assure us that the world as we know it will end in some few billions of years. With a finite horizon, existence of an optimal path is guaranteed with little difficulty (Yaari 1964*b*). For a finite horizon it is intuitively obvious that an optimal path will call for zero capital at the terminal time. Suppose that the horizon is very far off and that the initial value of $k$ (ratio of capital to effective workers) is well below the long-run stationary value $k^\infty$. Then the optimal path will involve first an increase in $k$ to some level close to $k^\infty$ (the more extended the horizon, the closer the maximum value of $k$ achieved is to $k^\infty$), and then a decrease in $k$ to zero at the horizon. Let us call the period of increasing $k$ the *accumulation period*, and that of decreasing $k$ the *potlatch*. If $\omega > \gamma$, the present value of the felicity of consumption during the potlatch becomes relatively unimportant compared with that during the accumulation period, but if $\omega < \gamma$, the economy, because of its high rate of growth as compared with the discounting of the future, receives a major part of its total utility from the potlatch, and a low initial rate of consumption which

[5] It may be helpful to note that if $k(t_0)$ were less than $k^*$, $k(t)$ satisfying (19) would decrease and in fact become zero in finite time.

aims to accumulate capital in order to increase the potlatch is justified. But as the time horizon becomes infinite, the potlatch recedes to infinity and, so to speak, disappears. When $\omega > \gamma$, the potlatch is of vanishing importance anyway, but in the opposite case the disappearance of the potlatch phase represents a major discontinuity at infinity; the Pontryagin path calls for an accumulation of capital, which has no ultimate use in further consumption, to the end of time.

Probably all this means that the case $\omega < \gamma$ is somehow not a model which properly reflects reality. The assumption of constant exponential trends in population and technology is clearly too strong; certainly population must have a limit for physical reasons if nothing else.

We will now show that the assumption $\omega > \gamma$ is sufficient for the Pontryagin principle to yield an optimum. We rely here on the sufficiency theorem, Proposition II.8. Since all the concavity assumptions made there hold for the optimization studied in this chapter, it is sufficient to show that the present value of the state variables tends to 0 for any feasible path, where the state variables are evaluated by the auxiliary variables in the Pontryagin solution. In the one-sector world, there is only one state variable: the stock of capital, $K$. The corresponding auxiliary variable has $q(t)$ as its current value, and therefore $e^{-\rho t}q(t)$ as value discounted to time 0. The sufficient condition for the Pontryagin path to be optimal is that $\lim_{t\to\infty} e^{-\rho t}q(t)K(t) = 0$. But from 1.(8) and (10) we can rewrite this condition in terms of $p$ and $k$:

$$e^{-\rho t}q(t)K(t) = e^{-\rho t}(e^{\gamma t}/P)^{-\sigma}e^{\gamma t}p(t)k(t).$$

Since $P(t) = P(0)e^{\pi t}$ and $\gamma - \pi = \tau$,

$$\begin{aligned} e^{-\rho t}q(t)K(t) &= e^{-(\rho+\sigma\tau-\gamma)t}[P(0)]^{\sigma}p(t)k(t) \\ &= e^{-(\omega-\gamma)t}[P(0)]^{\sigma}p(t)k(t). \end{aligned}$$

With $\omega > \gamma$, this will approach zero since $p(t)$ and $k(t)$ converge to the finite limits $p^{\infty}$, $k^{\infty}$, respectively.

To sum up the conclusions on optimal growth in the one-sector world:

PROPOSITION 2. *The aim of the economy is to maximize* $\int_0^{\infty} e^{-\rho t}P(t)U(\tilde{c})dt$, *where* $\rho$ *is the subjective rate of discount,* $P(t)$ *is population assumed to be growing exponentially at rate* $\pi$, $\tilde{c}$ *is per capita consumption, and* $U(\tilde{c})$ *is the utility of an average individual for consumption* $\tilde{c}$, *where it is assumed that* $U'(\tilde{c})$ *has a constant elasticity* $\sigma$. *The growth of the economy is subject to the constraint* $\dot{K} + P(t)\tilde{c} = F[K(t), e^{\tau t}L(t)]$ *with* $K(0)$ *given, where* $K$ *is the stock of capital,* $L(t)$ *is the labor force assumed proportional to population, and* $\tau$ *is the rate of labor-augmenting technological progress.*

*F is assumed to be concave and homogeneous of degree 1. Define* $\gamma = \pi + \tau$ *(the natural rate of growth);* $\omega = \rho + \sigma\tau$ *(the asymptotic rate of interest);* $k(t) = e^{-\gamma t}K(t)$ *(capital per effective worker);* $f(k) = F(k, L_0)$*; and* $c(t) = P(t)e^{-\gamma t}\bar{c}(t)$ *(consumption per effective worker). If* $\omega < \gamma$*, there is no optimal policy. If* $\omega > \gamma$*, there is an optimal policy which may be characterized as follows: Introduce a new variable, p, and consider the system of two differential equations:*

$$\text{(a)} \qquad \dot{k} = f(k) - \gamma k - c,$$

$$\text{(b)} \qquad \dot{p}/p = \omega - f'(k),$$

*and the ordinary equation*

$$\text{(c)} \qquad U'(c) = p.$$

*Then for any given initial value,* $k(0) = K(0)$*, there is one and only one value,* $p(0)$*, for which the solution of the above system with initial values* $k(0)$*,* $p(0)$ *converges to a limit and has positive capital stock everywhere. This solution defines the optimal path for* $k(t)$ *and* $c(t)$*. The limits of the quantities* $k(t)$*,* $p(t)$*,* $c(t)$ *along this solution are defined by the equations*

$$\text{(d)} \qquad f'(k^\infty) = \omega, \qquad c^\infty = f(k^\infty) - \gamma k^\infty, \qquad p^\infty = U'(c^\infty).$$

*Since k and c approach positive finite limits, the capital stock K is asymptotically growing exponentially at the natural rate of growth, and per capita consumption is asymptotically growing exponentially at the rate of labor-augmenting technological progress.*

## 3. Interpretations and Approximations

The starting point of this entire inquiry was the determination of the rate of interest appropriate for making investment decisions. At first blush, the conclusion is banal; the rate of interest is the marginal productivity of capital. In fact, however, we must look at the entire system to fully appreciate its implications. First suppose the system is in long-run steady growth. Then, from Proposition 2(d), we see that the rate of interest or the marginal productivity of capital must equal $\omega$, which is determined by the basic parameters of the system: specifically, the subjective rate of discount, $\rho$; the elasticity of the marginal utility of consumption, $\sigma$; and the rate of labor-augmenting technological progress, $\tau$. Now consider the case where the system is not in a state of balanced growth. Then the marginal productivity of capital differs from the asymptotic rate of interest. The marginal productivity of capital is, at the moment, whatever has been determined by history, but the discrepancy determines the investment and consumption patterns, which in turn alter $k$ (the ratio of capital to effective workers) and thereby move the rate of interest toward its asymptotic level. We will discuss this interaction in more detail below, but one simple relation can be seen by comparing 1.(6) with 1.(11); the consumption rate of interest is $r_c = \rho + \sigma(1/\bar{c})(d\bar{c}/dt)$ and this must equal $f'(k)$, while the asymptotic rate of interest is $\omega = \rho + \sigma\tau$; hence,

$$(1/\bar{c})(d\bar{c}/dt) = \tau + [f'(k) - \omega]/\sigma = [f'(k) - \rho]/\sigma.$$

Thus, the rate of growth of per capita consumption will differ from its long-term value so long as the rate of interest differs from its asymptote. However, we will need more information to determine the actual level of consumption and therefore of investment, which is output less consumption. This additional information is contained in the requirement that the initial value be so chosen that the solution to the system of differential equations should converge to a stationary value.

It follows that knowledge of the rate of interest does not suffice to determine the rate of investment, a point which deserves some emphasis. The rate of interest determines the stock of capital, or, more precisely, the stock of capital adjusted for growth. Investment is the rate of change of the capital stock: therefore investment, or at least its capital-deepening component, depends on the rate of change of the interest rate, not merely the interest rate itself. The point can be made most sharply by considering the case of an economy that is not growing; i.e., for which $\gamma = 0$, and therefore the rates of both technological progress, $\tau$, and population growth, $\pi$, are zero. Then $\omega = \rho$, and the stability condition $\omega > \gamma$ reduces to $\rho > 0$; i.e., a positive rate of subjective time discount. In this case, $k = K$, and at the long-run steady state both are constant so that there is no capital accumulation. Now suppose the economy has a capital stock, $K$, which is not the steady-state value, $k^\infty$; i.e., $f'(K) \neq \rho$. Then an optimal policy calls for capital accumulation (or decumulation if $K > k^\infty$). Thus, the interest rate by itself does not determine the direction of capital change; rather it is the discrepancy between the interest rate at the moment and the subjective interest rate. Since the subjective discount rate is the long-term steady state interest rate, we may say that it requires the future to determine the present resource allocation.

It follows that the concept of a schedule relating investment to the rate of interest, common in post-Keynesian models, is incorrect and indeed meaningless, a point which has been made most ably by Haavelmo (1960, chapters 25, 28, and 29).

The usual language of benefit-cost analysis might also suggest a functional relation between the volume of investment and the rate of interest; i.e., given the rate of interest (and the benefits and costs of all possible projects), the volume of investment is governed by the rule of accepting every project for which the discounted benefits exceed or equal the costs. But if in fact society chooses to invest more than this, all that happens is that the rate of interest moves down so that the equality of the rate of interest and the rate of return remains true at the margin.

It follows, then, that an analysis of the rate of interest in an optimal growth policy is insufficiently revealing without a simultaneous estimation of the rate of investment, and we shall use the results of section 2 to derive approximations to it. (Of course, since at any given moment total output is determined by capital stock and exogenous factors, population, and technology, the determination of the rate of investment is equivalent to that of the rate of consumption.) Before turning to the approximation procedure, we shall examine the connection between the instantaneous rates of interest thus far studied and the long-term rates used in the usual formulation for discounting future benefits.

Assuming that there is completely malleable capital is essentially equivalent to assuming that all investment projects can be treated as if they were of infinitesimal duration. One cannot, in strict logic, speak within this model of capital locked up in a project and yielding its fruits gradually. However, one can imagine that in a world of generally malleable capital there is an isolated project in the usual sense of benefit-cost analysis; i.e., a prescribed time sequence of inputs and outputs. In the present one-commodity world it can be described by a function, $r(t)$, where $r$ is the amount of output from the project at time $t$, taken negative during an input (construction) phase. At what rate should the return at time $t$ be discounted? Since the instantaneous rate of interest at any time $t$ is $f'[k(t)]$ (the marginal productivity of capital at time $t$), the usual rules of financial mathematics suggest that the rate at which a return at time $t$ should be discounted is $e^{-\int_0^t f'[k(u)]du}$, so that the criterion for accepting the project is

$$\int_0^\infty e^{-\int_0^t f'[k(u)]du} r(t)dt \geqq 0. \tag{1}$$

This can also be seen by an argument closer to the Pontryagin principle and its interpretation. Recall that $e^{-\rho t}q(t)$ is the variation in total discounted utility due to an increase of one unit in capital at time $t$ [interpreted as infinitesimal movements, of course; see chapter II.3.(6)]. Hence, adoption of a small project with return function $r(t)$ will increase total discounted utility by $\int_0^\infty e^{-\rho t}q(t)r(t)dt$. But now we recall the basic equation for $q(t)$, 2.(5):

$$\dot{q}/q = \rho - f'(k),$$

which, on integration, yields

$$q(t) = q(0)e^{\int_0^t \{\rho - f'[k(u)]\}du} = q(0)e^{\rho t}e^{-\int_0^t f'[k(u)]du},$$

so that the project will increase total discounted utility (or not decrease it) if and only if

$$q(0)\int_0^{\infty} e^{-\int_0^t f'[k(u)]du} r(t)dt \geqq 0,$$

which is equivalent to (1).

The criterion (1) shows an additional aspect of the relation between the rate of investment and the rate of interest; in order to know the long-term rates of interest for discounting future benefits from a project, one must know future short-term interest rates which, in turn, are determined by the course of capital accumulation through its effect on marginal productivity of capital. It is also important to note that unless the economy is already at its steady state, the discounting of future benefits does *not* occur at a constant rate. If initially the capital stock is below its long-run relation to effective labor force, then the short-term interest rate is expected to fall over time from its current value $f'(k)$ to $\omega$, and the rate at which far distant benefits are to be discounted is lower than that for those in the near future. Only in the steady state are all benefits, near and far, discounted at the same rate, $\omega$.

We now proceed to develop approximations to the time movements of $k$ and of the related interest rates. Our starting point is the characterization of the optimal policy given in Proposition 2 at the end of section 2, but we will first bring out more clearly the stationary nature of our optimization problem, which is not clear in its original form. To see this, we first need a more explicit form for $U(\tilde{c})$ in the maximand $\int_0^{\infty} e^{-\rho t}P(t)U(\tilde{c})dt$. Since $U'(\tilde{c})$ has a constant elasticity, $\sigma$, $U'(\tilde{c})$ must be proportional to $\tilde{c}^{-\sigma}$. But clearly $U(\tilde{c})$, and therefore $U'(\tilde{c})$, can be altered by multiplication by a positive constant without any essential change; the maximand is multiplied by that constant and the maximum is therefore attained for the same policy. Hence, we can assume $U'(\tilde{c}) = \tilde{c}^{-\sigma}$ without loss of generality. By integration, for $\sigma \neq 1$,

$$U(\tilde{c}) = \tilde{c}^{1-\sigma}/(1-\sigma) + A,$$

where $A$ is an arbitrary constant which can be taken to be 0. Then $U(\tilde{c})$ is homogeneous of degree $1 - \sigma$, and

$$U(\tilde{c}) = U(e^{\gamma t}c/P) = U[e^{\tau t}c/P(0)] = e^{\tau(1-\sigma)t}U(c)/[P(0)]^{1-\sigma}.$$

Thus, the maximand becomes, with the substitution $P(t) = P(0)e^{\pi t}$,

$$[P(0)]^{\sigma} \int_0^{\infty} e^{-[\rho-\pi-(1-\sigma)\tau]t} U(c)dt = [P(0)]^{\sigma} \int_0^{\infty} e^{-(\omega-\gamma)t} U(c)dt.$$

Define

$$\lambda = \omega - \gamma. \tag{2}$$

Then, since $P(0) > 0$, the original problem is equivalent to maximizing

$$\int_0^{\infty} e^{-\lambda t} U[c(t)]dt. \tag{3}$$

The constraint can be written as before [see 2.(12) or Proposition 2(a)]:

$$\dot{k} = f(k) - \gamma k - c. \tag{4}$$

The maximization of (3) subject to (4) is now completely stationary in the sense used in section II.6, and we may apply Proposition II.9 to observe that the choice of instrument, $c$, and the auxiliary variable, $p$, are both functions of the one state variable, $k$.

The case $\sigma = 1$ has not been covered in the above argument. When we integrate $U'(\tilde{c}) = \tilde{c}^{-1}$, we have $U(\tilde{c}) = \log \tilde{c}$ plus an arbitrary constant which can be taken to be 0. Then $U(\tilde{c}) = U[e^{\tau t}c/P(0)] = \tau t - \log P(0) + U(c)$. In this case, $\omega = \rho + \tau, \gamma = \pi + \tau$, so that $\lambda = \omega - \gamma = \rho - \pi$. The maximand becomes

$$P(0) \int_0^{\infty} e^{-(\rho-\pi)t}[\tau t - \log P(0)]dt + P(0) \int_0^{\infty} e^{-(\omega-\gamma)t} U(c)dt.$$

The first integral is convergent and constant, independent of the control variables. Optimization then means maximization of the second integral only, and the rest of the argument is as before.

We now examine in detail the determination of $p$, and therefore $c$, by $k$.

Since the optimal path lies entirely in quadrants II and IV, we have either $\dot{p} < 0$ and $\dot{k} > 0$, or vice versa, so that $dp/dk < 0$ except possibly at the stationary point, $k^{\infty}$, $p^{\infty}$. Now $\dot{k}$ and $\dot{p}$ are functions of $k$ and $p$, as defined by Proposition 2, equations (a) and (b), respectively, where $c$ is taken to be a function of $p$ defined by equation (c). Since, however, $p$ is a function of $k$, we can consider $\dot{k}$ and $\dot{p}$ to be functions of $k$ alone.

$$\dot{p} = \phi(k), \qquad \dot{k} = \psi(k). \tag{5}$$

Then, as already argued in connection with 2.(13), $p(k)$ satisfies the differential equation

$$p'(k) = \phi(k)/\psi(k). \tag{6}$$

Further, we know one point on the function $p(k)$; namely,

$$p(k^\infty) = p^\infty, \tag{7}$$

where $k^\infty$ and $p^\infty$ are defined by Proposition 2(d). Thus, $p(k)$ is a solution of (6) with initial conditions (7). We now study the behavior of this solution for values of $k$ near $k^\infty$ to arrive at approximations to the optimal policy.

We first note that there are in fact two solutions of (6) with initial conditions (7), though it is easy to select the correct solution. The first step is the evaluation of $p'(k)$ for $k = k^\infty$. Since $k^\infty$ is a stationary point, both $\dot{k}$ and $\dot{p}$ must be 0 or, by (5), $\phi(k^\infty) = \psi(k^\infty) = 0$, so that, from (6), $p'(k)$ is indeterminate. By L'Hospital's rule, then,

$$p'(k^\infty) = \phi'(k^\infty)/\psi'(k^\infty). \tag{8}$$

From (5) and Proposition 2(a,b),

$$\phi(k) = [\omega - f'(k)]p(k), \qquad \psi(k) = f(k) - \gamma k - c[p(k)],$$

and differentiation yields

$$\phi'(k) = [\omega - f'(k)]p'(k) - f''(k)p(k),$$
$$\psi'(k) = f'(k) - \gamma - c'(p)p'(k).$$

Let $k = k^\infty$; recall that $f'(k^\infty) = \omega$ and that $p(k^\infty) = p^\infty$. Then

$$\phi'(k^\infty) = -f''(k^\infty)p^\infty, \tag{9}$$

$$\psi'(k^\infty) = \omega - \gamma - c'(p^\infty)p'(k^\infty) = \lambda - c'(p^\infty)p'(k^\infty), \tag{10}$$

with the notation of (2). If we substitute (9) and (10) into (8), we find that $p'(k^\infty)$ appears on the left-hand side and in the denominator of the right-hand side. After clearing of fractions, it can be seen that $p'(k^\infty)$ satisfies a quadratic equation, and thus has two possible values that correspond to the two possible solutions of (6) with initial condition (7). However, as will be seen, one of the roots is positive and the other negative, and only the latter corresponds to the desired optimal policy, as is obvious from figure 2 and the supporting analysis.

The results take a simpler form when expressed in terms of elasticities. For any function $F(x)$, we shall use the notation

$$EF/Ex = (x/F)dF/dx.$$

The elasticities of the functions $p(k)$ and $f'(k)$, evaluated at $k = k^\infty$, will be denoted:

$$Ep/Ek = E_p^\infty \text{ at } k = k^\infty, \qquad Ef'/Ek = E_{f'}^\infty \text{ at } k = k^\infty. \tag{11}$$

Then (8) can be rewritten:

$$E_p^\infty = (k^\infty/p^\infty)\phi'(k^\infty)/\psi'(k^\infty). \tag{12}$$

From (9),

$$(k^\infty/p^\infty)\phi'(k^\infty) = -k^\infty f''(k^\infty) = -f'(k^\infty)E_{f'}^\infty = -\omega E_{f'}^\infty. \tag{13}$$

To restate (10) in elasticity form, we first take elasticities of the formula $U'(c) = p$:

$$(EU'/Ec)(Ec/Ep) = 1.$$

But since, by assumption, $U'(c)$ has a constant elasticity $\sigma$, then $Ec/Ep = -1/\sigma$ for all $p$. Then

$$c'(p)p'(k) = \frac{c}{p}\frac{Ec}{Ep}\frac{p}{k}\frac{Ep}{Ek} = \frac{c}{k}\frac{Ec}{Ep}\frac{Ep}{Ek} = -\frac{1}{\sigma}\frac{c}{k}\frac{Ep}{Ek},$$

and in particular for $k = k^\infty$,

$$c'(p^\infty)p'(k^\infty) = -(1/\sigma)(c^\infty/k^\infty)E_p^\infty.$$

Substitution into (10) yields

$$\psi'(k^\infty) = \lambda + (1/\sigma)(c^\infty/k^\infty)E_p^\infty. \tag{14}$$

It may be recalled at this point that $c^\infty$ is defined by Proposition 2(d):

$$c^\infty = f(k^\infty) - \gamma k^\infty. \tag{15}$$

We can now substitute (13) and (14) into (12):

$$E_p^\infty = -\omega E_{f'}^\infty/[\lambda + (1/\sigma)(c^\infty/k^\infty)E_p^\infty],$$

or, by multiplying through by the denominator of the right-hand side, we see that $E_p^\infty$ satisfies the quadratic equation:

$$(1/\sigma)(c^\infty/k^\infty)(E_p^\infty)^2 + \lambda E_p^\infty + \omega E_{f'}^\infty = 0. \tag{16}$$

The coefficient of the quadratic term is positive, while the constant term is negative, since $f'' < 0$ and therefore $E_{f'}^\infty < 0$. Since the product of the roots of (16) equals the ratio of the constant term to the coefficient of the quadratic term (by a well-known algebraic theorem), the product of the roots is negative, one being positive and one negative. The analysis of section 2 shows that $p(k)$ is decreasing, at least for $k \neq k^\infty$; by continuity $p(k)$ cannot be increasing at $k = k^\infty$. Therefore, the negative root of (16) is the one relevant to the optimal policy. Given this value of $Ep/Ek$ at $k = k^\infty$, and consequently the value of $p'(k^\infty) = (p^\infty/k^\infty)E_p^\infty$, there is a unique solution of the differential equation (6), and the optimal policy can be stated in the following alternative way to Proposition 2:

PROPOSITION 3. *If $\omega > \gamma$, an optimal policy, defined by a function $p(k)$, exists in the sense that at any time $t$, per capita consumption, $c(t)$, is defined by the following equations:*

(a) $\bar{c}(t) = e^{rt}c(t)/P(0)$, $U'(c) = p[k(t)]$, $k(t) = e^{-\gamma t}K(t)$.

*The function* $p(k)$ *is defined as that solution of the differential equation,*

(b) $p'(k) = [\omega - f'(k)]p(k)/[f(k) - \gamma k - c(p)]$,

*with the initial condition* $p(k^\infty) = p^\infty$ *and the additional condition that* $Ep/Ek$ *at* $k = k^\infty$ *is the negative root of the equation:*

(c) $(1/\sigma)(c^\infty/k^\infty)(E_p^\infty)^2 + \lambda E_p^\infty + \omega E_{f'}^\infty = 0$.

In principle, be it noted, all the coefficients of (c) are easily computable from the data.

Now, by assuming that $k$ is sufficiently close to $k^\infty$ so that linear approximations are valid, we can approximate expressions for the rate of investment, and from that for the rates of interest, discount, and consumption. We first solve for $\psi'(k^\infty)$ in (12) and substitute from (13):

$$\psi'(k^\infty) = -\omega E_{f'}^\infty / E_p^\infty, \tag{17}$$

all the components of which are calculable. Since $\psi(k^\infty) = 0$ and $\dot{k} = \psi(k)$, we have approximately

$$\dot{k} \approx -(\omega E_{f'}^\infty / E_p^\infty)(k - k^\infty). \tag{18}$$

The rate of investment, properly speaking, is not $\dot{k}$ but $\dot{K}$; since $K = e^{\gamma t}k$,

$$\begin{aligned} \dot{K} &= \gamma K + e^{\gamma t}\dot{k} \approx \gamma K - (\omega E_{f'}^\infty / E_p^\infty)(e^{\gamma t}k - e^{\gamma t}k^\infty) \\ &= \gamma K - (\omega E_{f'}^\infty / E_p^\infty)(K - e^{\gamma t}k^\infty) \\ &= [\gamma - (\omega E_{f'}^\infty / E_p^\infty)]K + (\omega E_{f'}^\infty / E_p^\infty)e^{\gamma t}k^\infty. \end{aligned} \tag{19}$$

This is an approximate rule giving the volume of investment as a function of the capital stock and time.

We can derive similarly an approximation for the rate of interest as a function of $k$ (capital per effective worker). By linear approximation,

$$f'(k) \approx f'(k^\infty) + f''(k^\infty)(k - k^\infty) = \omega + \omega E_{f'}^\infty[(k/k^\infty) - 1]. \tag{20}$$

This is not too useful for calculation of the short-term interest rate at any moment, since presumably $f'(k)$ itself could be computed with no more information than is needed to compute the approximation. This formula can, however, be used to predict future short-term interest rates and therefore compute rates for discounting future returns; but for this purpose the interest rate has to be expressed as a function of time. By integration of (18) it can be seen that

$$k(t) - k^\infty \approx e^{-(\omega E_{f'}^\infty / E_p^\infty)t}[k(0) - k^\infty].$$

Then the short-term rate of interest at time $t$ can be approximated by substitution into (20):

$$f'[k(t)] \approx \omega + \omega E_{f'}^\infty e^{-(\omega E_{f'}^\infty / E_p^\infty)t}[(k(0)/k^\infty) - 1]. \tag{21}$$

The rate at which a benefit at time $t$ is discounted back to time 0 is

$$\int_0^t f'(k)dt \approx \omega t - E_p^\infty[e^{-(\omega E_{f'}^\infty/E_p^\infty)t} - 1][(k(0)/k^\infty) - 1]. \tag{22}$$

In both (21) and (22) the second term becomes vanishingly small compared with the first for large $t$, as is to be expected.

The two basic results are the rate of investment, given by (19); and the rate at which future returns are discounted, given by (22). Take the present time as 0, so that $t = 0$ and $k(0) = K$, where $K$ is the present stock of capital. Recall that the units in which $k$, and therefore $k^\infty$, are measured depend on the choice of origin, so that $k^\infty$ is directly comparable dimensionally to the initial $K$.

PROPOSITION 4. *If the stock of capital $K$ is not too different from $k^\infty$, as defined by Proposition 2(d), then for an optimal path the current rate of investment is approximately*

(a) $$\dot{K} \approx [\gamma - (\omega E_{f'}^\infty/E_p^\infty)]K + (\omega E_{f'}^\infty/E_p^\infty)k^\infty,$$

*and the rate at which benefits or costs accruing at time $t$ are discounted is approximately*

(b) $$\omega t - E_p^\infty[e^{-(\omega E_{f'}^\infty/E_p^\infty)t} - 1][(K/k^\infty) - 1].$$

Higher order approximations can be obtained; for details the reader is referred to the work of Mirrlees (1967, pp. 104).

## 4. Alternative Formulations of the Controls and Irreversibility of Investment

In the development in sections 1 and 2 we have taken consumption as the variable to be controlled; investment appears as a residual. Obviously, we could equally well have taken investment as the control variable and consumption as the residual. When we analyze more complex models with several different kinds of investment, a more symmetrical formulation simplifies the notation and algebra; all uses of output are treated as control variables but subject to a constraint that total use should not exceed total output. As in static problems in economics, this leads to the use of Lagrange multipliers; the applicable form of Pontryagin's principle has been cited in chapter II, section 4.

To illustrate with the one-sector model of this chapter, we take both $\bar{c}$, per capita consumption, and $I$, total investment, as control variables. The maximand remains

$$\int_0^\infty e^{-\rho t}P(t)U(\bar{c})dt, \tag{1}$$

the capital accumulation equation takes the simple form

$$\dot{K} = I, \tag{2}$$

and the control variables $I$ and $\tilde{c}$ are subject to the joint constraint

$$P(t)\tilde{c} + I = F(K, e^{\tau t}L). \tag{3}$$

It will be most straightforward to transform the variables so that the problem is in stationary form, as in section 3. Then the instruments are best written:

$$c = P(t)\tilde{c}e^{-\gamma t}, \qquad i = Ie^{-\gamma t}. \tag{4}$$

From 3.(3), the maximand is

$$\int_0^\infty e^{-\lambda t}U[c(t)]dt, \tag{5}$$

while the constraints (2) and (3) can be rewritten, by substitution of (4) and simplification along lines that are by now familiar:

$$\dot{k} = i - \gamma k, \tag{6}$$

$$c + i = f(k). \tag{7}$$

We now apply Proposition II.7. The current-value Lagrangian is

$$L = U(c) + p(i - \gamma k) + q[f(k) - i - c], \tag{8}$$

where $q$ is the Lagrange multiplier corresponding to (7).

The maximum principle in this case requires the choice of $c$ and $i$ to maximize (8), where $q$ is so chosen that the maximizing solution satisfies (7). Differentiating with respect to $c$ yields

$$U'(c) = q. \tag{9}$$

In maximizing with respect to $i$ we note that $L$ is linear in $i$, with coefficient $p - q$. For the present assume, as we have done to this point, that $i$ can take on any value, positive or negative; in particular, it is possible to disinvest and use existing capital for consumption. Then if $p \neq q$, there is no finite optimum value of $i$; if $p > q$, then the larger the $i$ the better, and if $p < q$, then $i$ should have as large a negative value as possible. Thus, for the optimum to exist it is necessary that

$$p = q. \tag{10}$$

Finally, the differential equation governing the auxiliary variable is, as before,

$$\dot{p} = \lambda p - (\partial L/\partial k)$$

which, from (8), becomes

$$\dot{p} = \lambda p + \gamma p - qf'(k). \tag{11}$$

Then if we substitute (10) into (9) and (11), and also substitute 3.(2) into (11), we derive precisely equations (b) and (c), respectively, of Proposition 2, and the analysis proceeds as before.

The Lagrangian presentation not only permits greater symmetry but also allows us to treat the case where investment is irreversible. Suppose that decumulation of capital is not possible; then $I \geqq 0$ necessarily. We will parallel the previous discussion. From (4), the constraint $I \geqq 0$ is equivalent to

$$i \geqq 0. \tag{12}$$

The current-value Lagrangian is still given by (8), to be maximized with respect to $i$ and $c$, subject to the constraint (12). The maximum with respect to $c$ is interior, so that (9) still holds. The control variable $i$ enters into (8) linearly with coefficient $p - q$. Clearly, if $p > q$, as before no maximum is possible since it pays to increase $i$ indefinitely. Thus

$$p \leqq q. \tag{13}$$

But the same argument cannot be raised against the possibility that $p < q$, since $i$ cannot be lowered below 0, which is then the optimum value. This is, of course, a most elementary linear programming argument.

$$\text{If } p < q, \text{ then } i = 0. \tag{14}$$

Finally, the auxiliary variable, $p$, is governed by the equation (11):

$$\dot{p} = \omega p - qf'(k). \tag{15}$$

If at any point on the optimal path $i > 0$, then, from (13) and (14), $p = q$ and the equations reduce to the same set as those governing the reversible case, as might be expected. On the other hand, if $i = 0$, we must have $p \leqq q$. Then any optimal path will consist in general of alternating segments: in one type of time interval, $i = 0$ and therefore, from (7), $c = f(k)$ (i.e., no investment and all output consumed); in the other type, $p = q$, and $c$ is determined by (9), while $p$ evolves according to the differential equation applicable to the reversible case.

The stationary character of the optimization problem is equally valid for the irreversible case; the argument is exactly as before since the only additional constraint, (12), does not involve time explicitly. Then $c$ and $i$ are functions of $k$, independent of time. In more detail, $c$, $i$, and $q$ can be determined as functions of $p$ and $k$ by (7), (9), (13), and (14); i.e., either

$$U'(c) = p, \qquad i = f(k) - c, \qquad q = p, \tag{16}$$

or

$$c = f(k), \qquad i = 0, \qquad q = U'[f(k)], \tag{17}$$

where (16) holds if $p \geqq U'[f(k)]$ (since $i \geqq 0$, $c \leqq f(k)$, and $p = U'(c) \geqq U'[f(k)]$), and (17) holds in the contrary case. Then there is a function $p(k)$, which is the solution of a differential equation obtained by dividing (15) by (6):

$$p' = [\omega p - qf'(k)]/(i - \gamma k). \tag{18}$$

We can thus divide the $k$-axis into intervals in which (16) and (17) hold alternately. An interval in which (16) holds will be called a *free* interval; one in which (17) holds will be called a *blocked* interval. It is conceivable, of course, that the solution for the reversible case, in which (16) is assumed to hold for all $k$, will satisfy the condition $p \geqq U'[f(k)]$ for all $k$ or, equivalently, $i \geqq 0$; in that case, the solution of section 2 is also valid for the case of irreversible investment. However, in any case the solution for the reversible case calls for $\dot{k} \geqq 0$ when $k \leqq k^{\infty}$ and, since $i = \dot{k} + \gamma k$ from (6), that $i > 0$ for $k \leqq k^{\infty}$; by continuity we see that $i \geqq 0$ in an interval $0 \leqq k \leqq \bar{k}$, where $\bar{k} > k^{\infty}$. Hence, this is a free interval.

Also, $\dot{k} = -\gamma k < 0$ in a blocked interval. Hence, any $k$ for which $\dot{k} = 0$ must lie in a free interval, with $p = q$. If $\dot{k} = 0$, then, from (6), $i = \gamma k$; from (18) this is only possible if the numerator vanishes, which, with $p = q$, implies that $k = k^{\infty}$. Since the reversible solution is valid for the irreversible case for some $k > k^{\infty}$ and $\dot{k} < 0$ there, it must be that $\dot{k} < 0$ for all $k > k^{\infty}$; otherwise there would be a value of $k > k^{\infty}$ for which $\dot{k} = 0$.

A description of the solution for the irreversible case can now be given. First we find the solution for the reversible case for the interval from 0 to $k^{\infty}$ and continue for larger values of $k$ until we reach $\bar{k}$, defined by

$$p(\bar{k}) = U'[f(\bar{k})].$$

At this point we switch to a blocked regime; substituting (17) into (18) yields

$$p' = \{U'[f(k)]f'(k) - \omega p\}/\gamma k. \tag{19}$$

This is to be solved beginning at $\bar{k}$ with the initial condition $p = p(\bar{k})$, and continued as long as $p \leqq U'[f(k)]$. When this condition ceases to hold, we switch back to a free interval, with the initial $p$-value being that found at the end of the previous blocked interval. This process can then be repeated.

However, while in principle and indeed in practice the optimal policy for the irreversible case can be effectively computed, not much can be said as to its general characteristics; in particular, the number of alternations from free to blocked intervals can be arbitrarily large or infinite. For a more detailed study, see Arrow and Kurz (1970).

Until now we have not introduced depreciation into this model; for the exponential case this requires only reinterpretation of symbols. The amount of capital that disappears is proportional to $K$; thus, the equation for capital accumulation becomes

$$\dot{K} = I - \delta K.$$

The model is otherwise unaltered. In intensive units, the capital accumulation relation becomes

$$\dot{k} = i - (\gamma + \delta)k. \tag{20}$$

Following the lines of previous arguments, we see that the optimization problem can be stated as the maximization of (5) subject to (20) [instead of (6)]; (7); and, in the irreversible case, (12). We see that the problem has exactly the same form as before, with $\lambda$ unchanged and $\gamma$ increased by $\delta$ [and therefore, from 3.(2), $\omega$ increased by $\delta$]. In terms of the original parameters—$\rho$, $\pi$, $\tau$, and $\sigma$—we can say that $\rho$ and $\pi$ have both been increased by $\delta$, and $\tau$ and $\sigma$ remain unaltered.

## 5. Increasing Returns

In section I.5, it was seen that the theory of growth models with fixed savings ratios could easily be extended from the case of constant returns to certain cases of increasing returns. By using the transformations introduced there, we shall show that the same generalization can be made for the optimization models of the present chapter, where the savings ratio is not fixed but is chosen optimally.

We assume that the production function is given by I.5.(30), modified to incorporate labor-augmenting technological progress:

$$Y = F(K, L, t) = G\{K, H[K, (e^{\tau' t}L)^{\delta}]\}, \tag{1}$$

where $G$ and $H$ are both concave and homogeneous of degree 1 and strictly increasing in both variables. Then [see I.5.(31)], the natural rate of growth must be

$$\gamma = (\pi + \tau')\delta. \tag{2}$$

Let

$$\tau = \gamma - \pi. \tag{3}$$

Make the transformations:

$$k = Ke^{-\gamma t}, \qquad c = P\tilde{c}e^{-\gamma t}. \tag{4}$$

Then, as indicated in I.5.(32),

$$F(K, L, t) = e^{\gamma t} f(k),$$

where

$$f(k) = G[k, H(k, L_0^\delta)]$$

is a strictly concave function. The equation of motion of the system, $\dot{K} = F(K, L, t) - P\tilde{c}$, can be written

$$\dot{k} = f(k) - \gamma k - c, \tag{5}$$

which is also 3.(4). The argument leading to writing the maximand as 3.(3), $\int_0^\infty e^{-\lambda t} U[c(t)]dt$, remains valid. Hence, with the foregoing reinterpretation of symbols, the whole of the preceding analysis remains valid for this case of increasing returns.

From the viewpoint of a planning model, there is nothing further to discuss. But since there are increasing returns, the possibility of implementing the optimal policy through decentralized methods is altered. Specifically, it is impossible to pay both capital and labor their marginal products.

Since, in this model, the supply of labor is inelastic, it follows that labor can be paid less than its marginal product without loss of efficiency. What institutional arrangements should be made in any given case depends on the way the production functions for individual firms aggregate into the social production function shown here.

# IV

# OPTIMAL INVESTMENT IN A TWO-SECTOR MODEL

## 0. Introduction

While in chapter III we dealt with the aggregate program of economic growth, no distinction was made between private and public capital. This allocation problem has many dimensions which have already been discussed in chapter I. More specifically, the introduction of public capital raises the whole problem of increasing returns to scale and external economies. In this chapter we shall attempt to provide a comprehensive study of the optimal programs of investments under a variety of conditions regarding increasing returns and externalities.

In the major part of the chapter we shall discuss the optimal program under constant returns to scale, but with external economies allowed; the last section will deal with the case of increasing returns to scale. As discussed in chapter I, external effects of public investments appear in the economy either as an effect of public goods on private productivity or as the direct public services which appear as aggregate "consumption benefits." These ideas will be stated explicitly below.

Although our aim is to treat public and private capital as distinct goods, the treatment in this chapter essentially retains the physical similarity of the two goods while distinguishing between the different decisions involved in the optimization procedure. Thus, in the following model there is only one good that can be either consumed or accumulated as a stock of public or private capital. A stronger "physical" distinction could be made by insisting that investment decisions would be irreversible so that before the act of investment there would be only one homogeneous commodity, while after the investment has been undertaken the commodity would fix its shape either as a private or public capital good.

Although we shall work mostly with the assumption of reversible investment decisions in this chapter, we shall make explicit comments regarding the nature of the results which could be obtained under the irreversibility assumption.

## 1. General Formulation

As in sections III.1 and III.2, we shall first set up the problem in its general form; later we shall specialize the assumptions. The following notation will be used:

$$
\begin{aligned}
K_p(t) &= \text{total capital employed in the private sector at } t,\\
K_g(t) &= \text{total capital employed in the public sector at } t,\\
\tilde{k}_g(t) &= \text{per capita capital employed in the public sector at } t,\\
K(t) &= K_p(t) + K_g(t),\\
\tilde{c}(t) &= \text{per capita consumption at } t,\\
L(t) &= \text{labor supply at } t \text{ proportional to population, } P(t), \text{ at } t,\\
P(t) &= \text{total population at } t,\\
I_p(t) &= \text{investment in the private sector at } t,\\
I_g(t) &= \text{investment in the public sector at } t,\\
Y(t) &= \text{output at time } t.
\end{aligned}
$$

Thus, we assume that output is determined by

$$Y(t) = F[K_p(t), K_g(t), e^{\tau t}L(t)], \tag{1}$$

where $F$ is a concave production function and $\tau$ is the percentage rate of technological progress (labor-augmenting).

On the other hand, in the absence of depreciation,

$$\dot{K}_p(t) = I_p, \tag{2a}$$

$$\dot{K}_g(t) = I_g. \tag{2b}$$

Thus, our natural constraint is

$$I_p(t) + I_g(t) + P(t)\tilde{c}(t) \leqq F[K_p(t), K_g(t), e^{\tau t}L(t)]. \tag{3}$$

The mathematical expression of irreversible investment decisions in the absence of depreciation is the pair of additional constraints $I_p \geqq 0$, $I_g \geqq 0$. However, this assumption will be discussed only briefly, in section 7. The addition of depreciation to the models studied could be carried out straightforwardly along the lines sketched at the end of section III.4.

Finally, the maximand is

$$\int_0^\infty e^{-\rho t}P(t)U[\tilde{c}(t), \tilde{k}_g(t)]dt, \tag{4}$$

where $U$ is a concave felicity function. Note that the utility function evaluates the per capita consumption and services of public goods. The reader is referred to I.4 for a discussion of this point. The introduction of $K_g/P$ into the utility function was anticipated earlier by our discussion of the dual function of public capital. It could conceivably be argued that public capital should be broken into two parts: $K_g^1$, the fraction of total public capital that provides direct production benefits, and $K_g^2$, the fraction that provides direct consumption benefits ($K_g = K_g^1 + K_g^2$). If $K_g^1$ and $K_g^2$ are proportional to each other, then our formulation above is adequate. If this proportionality assumption does not hold, then the allocation between $K_g^1$ and $K_g^2$ could be considered to be part of the optimization problem. This procedure is certainly possible but lacks realism: public goods seem to produce "joint" products. For instance, education yields both increased productivity and direct consumption benefits; a highway can be used both by business firms in their productive activities and by the individual traveler in his trips to the countryside. This joint production is reflected in the appearance of the same $K_g(t)$ in the production and utility functions.

Under the shiftability assumption (reversible investment decisions) our problem can be formulated as follows:

$$\text{Maximize} \int_0^\infty e^{-\rho t} P(t) U[\tilde{c}(t), \tilde{k}_g(t)]dt, \tag{5a}$$

subject to

$$\dot{K}(t) = F[K_p(t), K_g(t), e^{\tau t}L(t)] - P(t)\tilde{c}(t), \tag{5b}$$

$$K(t) \geqq K_p(t) + K_g(t). \tag{5c}$$

Because of the assumption of free transferability of capital between sectors, we do not consider the two stocks, $K_p(t)$ and $K_g(t)$, as state variables but rather as control variables. This gives rise to an optimization problem with only one state variable; namely, the total capital stock $K(t)$.

The following assumptions will be made in this chapter—A.1 will be replaced by an alternative assumption in section 8, but A.2 and A.3 will be retained throughout:

A.1. *$F(K_p, K_g, L)$ is a concave function, homogeneous of degree 1, and twice differentiable.*

A.2. *$L(t) = L(0)e^{\pi t}$, where $\pi > 0$ is the growth rate of population.*

A.3. *$U(\tilde{c}, \tilde{k}_g)$ is concave, homogeneous of degree $1 - \sigma$, $\sigma > 0$, and twice differentiable.*

## 2. Optimal Growth under Constant Returns to Scale: General Analysis

The assumption that $F(K_p, K_g, e^{\tau t}L)$ is homogeneous of degree 1 in all three variables means that there are diminishing returns to scale in the production function of the private sector (using private inputs). Thus, the lack of production externalities will allow us to think of the private sector as operating in perfect competition. The assumption of constant returns to scale simplifies matters considerably, just as it did in sections III.1–4. To see this, note that output can now be written as

$$F(K_p, K_g, e^{\tau t}L) = e^{\gamma t}f(k_p, k_g)\,, \tag{1}$$

where

$$k_p = K_p e^{-\gamma t}, \qquad k_g = K_g e^{-\gamma t} = P(t)\bar{k}_g e^{-\gamma t} = P(0)\bar{k}_g e^{-\tau t}\,; \tag{2}$$

$$f(k_p, k_g) = F(k_p, k_g, L_0)\,; \tag{3}$$

$$\gamma = \pi + \tau. \tag{4}$$

Then $f(k_p, k_g)$ is a strictly concave function of its two arguments.

Now define

$$c = P\tilde{c}e^{-\gamma t} = P(0)\tilde{c}e^{-\tau t}, \tag{5}$$

$$k = Ke^{-\gamma t}\,; \tag{6}$$

then the constraints 1.(5b)–(5c) can be reformulated as follows:

$$k(t) \geqq k_p(t) + k_g(t)\,,$$

and, since $\dot{k} = \dot{K}e^{-\gamma t} - \gamma k$,

$$\dot{k} = f[k_p(t), k_g(t)] - \gamma k(t) - c(t)\,.$$

Finally, by Assumption A.3 and (2) and (5),

$$\begin{aligned} e^{-\rho t}P(t)U(\tilde{c}, \bar{k}_g) &= e^{-\rho t}P(0)e^{\pi t}U[ce^{\tau t}/P(0), k_g e^{\tau t}/P(0)] \\ &= [P(0)]^{\sigma}e^{-\rho t}e^{\pi t}e^{\tau(1-\sigma)t}U(c, k_g) \\ &= [P(0)]^{\sigma}e^{-\lambda t}U(c, k_g)\,, \end{aligned}$$

where we define, as in III.1.(11) and III.3.(2),

$$\omega = \rho + \sigma\tau, \qquad \lambda = \omega - \gamma. \tag{7}$$

We can subsume $[P(0)]^{\sigma}$ into the utility function and reformulate our problem as

$$\text{Maximize} \int_0^{\infty} e^{-\lambda t}U[c(t), k_g(t)]dt, \tag{8}$$

subject to

$$k(t) \geqq k_g(t) + k_p(t), \tag{9}$$

$$\dot{k}(t) = f[k_p(t), k_g(t)] - \gamma k(t) - c(t). \tag{10}$$

Since $U$ and $f$ are strictly increasing in their arguments, the equality sign holds in (9), and the Pontryagin maximum principle can readily be used. Write the current-value Lagrangian:

$$L = U(c, k_g) + p[f(k_p, k_g) - \gamma k - c] + q(k - k_p - k_g), \tag{11}$$

and maximize with respect to the instruments, $k_p$, $k_g$, and $c$ (see Proposition II.7).

$$pf_p = q, \tag{12}$$

$$U_g + pf_g = q, \tag{13}$$

$$U_c = p, \tag{14a}$$

where

$$U_c = \partial U/\partial c, \qquad U_g = \partial U/\partial k_g, \qquad f_p = \partial f/\partial k_p, \qquad f_g = \partial f/\partial k_g.$$

Eliminate $q$ from (12) and (13):

$$U_g + p(f_g - f_p) = 0, \tag{14b}$$

which expresses the equality of value of capital in its two uses. Recall equation (9):

$$k = k_p + k_g. \tag{14c}$$

Equations (14a)–(14c) represent the short-term equilibrium of the system: For any given time $t$, $k$ and $p$ are given; then (14a)–(14c) yield essentially the "derived demand equations" for each moment of time as functions of $k$ and $p$. We can visualize the system solved, so we can write

$$c = c(k, p), \qquad k_p = k_p(k, p), \qquad k_g = k_g(k, p). \tag{15}$$

These three yield the optimal allocation of current output between consumption and savings, and the optimal allocation of the existing capital stock between the private and public sectors. From the strict concavity of $U$ and $f$, it follows that these maximizing values are unique.

It is important to note that, because of the assumption of free transferability of capital between the sectors, the control variables $k_p(t)$ and $k_g(t)$ do not have to be continuous functions; indeed, the optimal policy calls in general for a discontinuous transfer of capital (i.e., a jump) at time 0 to correct the initial allocation of capital between the two sectors. Although further transfers of capital at later dates are feasible, we shall show that such transfers are not optimal.

From the Pontryagin principle we also obtain the differential equation which governs the behavior of $p$:

$$\dot{p} = \lambda p - (\partial L/\partial k).$$

Computation of this derivative yields

$$\dot{p} = \lambda p + \gamma p - q$$

and, from (12) and (7),

$$\dot{p}/p = \omega - f_p. \qquad (16)$$

These results are summarized in Proposition 1.

PROPOSITION 1. *Assume that the aim of the economy is to maximize* $\int_0^\infty e^{-\rho t}P(t)U(\tilde{c}, \tilde{k}_g)dt$, *where* $\rho$ *is the subjective rate of discount,* $P(t)$ *is population assumed to be growing exponentially at rate* $\pi$, $\tilde{c}$ *is per capita consumption,* $\tilde{k}_g$ *is per capita government capital, and* $U(\tilde{c}, \tilde{k}_g)$ *is the felicity of consumption* $\tilde{c}$ *and per capita government capital* $\tilde{k}_g$; $U(\tilde{c}, \tilde{k}_g)$ *is assumed concave, twice differentiable, and homogeneous of degree* $1 - \sigma$, $\sigma > 0$. *The growth of the different magnitudes is subject to the constraints* $\dot{K}_p + \dot{K}_g + P(t)\tilde{c} = F[K_p(t), K_g(t), e^{\tau t}L(t)]$, *with* $K_p(0)$ *and* $K_g(0)$ *given, where* $K_p$ *and* $K_g$ *are the total stocks of private and government capital, respectively,* $L(t)$ *is the labor force assumed proportional to population, and* $\tau$ *is the rate of labor-augmenting technological progress.* $F$ *is assumed concave, twice differentiable, and homogeneous of degree 1. Define* $\gamma = \pi + \tau$; $\omega = \rho + \sigma\tau$; $k_p(t) = e^{-\gamma t}K_p(t)$; $k_g(t) = e^{-\gamma t}K_g(t)$; $k = k_p + k_g$; $f(k_p, k_g) = F(k_p, k_g, L_0)$, *and* $c(t) = P(0)\tilde{c}(t)e^{-\tau t}$. *Then the optimal policy satisfies the following necessary conditions: Let* $c(k, p)$, $k_p(k, p)$, $k_g(k, p)$ *be the solution of the following equations:*

(a) $$U_c = p,$$

(b) $$U_g + p(f_g - f_p) = 0,$$

(c) $$k_p + k_g = k.$$

*Then* $k(t)$ *and* $p(t)$ *satisfy the differential equations:*

(d) $$\dot{k} = f[k_p(k, p), k_g(k, p)] - \gamma k - c(k, p),$$

(e) $$\dot{p}/p = \omega - f_p[k_p(k, p), k_g(k, p)].$$

*If* $\omega > \gamma$, *then any solution of equations* (d) *and* (e) *that converges to a bounded limit is an optimal solution.*

*Remark.* The allocation of a given capital, $k$, between the two sectors is governed by conditions (a)–(c). Since $p$ and $k$ are continuous functions of time, $k_p$ and $k_g$ will also be continuous for $t > 0$; but the historically given $k_p(0)$ and $k_g(0)$ need not satisfy (a)–(c), so that, as indicated earlier, a jump may take place then.

We shall turn now to the analysis of these conditions. First, we shall investigate the nature of the short-term "derived demand functions," and then the dynamic character of the optimal path.

## 3. Analysis of the Short-Run Equilibrium

We have noticed earlier that it follows from the concavity of $U$ and $f$ that the short-term equilibrium is unique. The analysis of comparative statics carried out in this section will clarify some important points pertaining to the dynamic analysis following in section 4.

To start with, let us differentiate totally the system, Proposition 1.(a)–(c).

$$\left.\begin{aligned} U_{cc}dc \quad\quad + U_{cg}dk_g \quad\quad\quad\quad &= dp \\ U_{gc}dc + [U_{gg} + p(f_{gg} - f_{pg})]dk_g + p(f_{gp} - f_{pp})dk_p &= -(f_g - f_p)dp \\ dk_g \quad + \quad dk_p &= dk \end{aligned}\right\} \quad (1)$$

The matrix of coefficients on the left-hand side of the above system has the following principal minors:

$$\Delta_1 = U_{cc} \, ;$$
$$\Delta_2 = (U_{cc}U_{gg} - U_{cg}^2) + p(f_{gg} - f_{pg})U_{cc} \, ;$$

and the determinant $\Delta$ is

$$\Delta = (U_{cc}U_{gg} - U_{cg}^2) + pU_{cc}(f_{gg} + f_{pp} - 2f_{gp}) \, .$$

By assumption, $U(c, k_g)$ is strictly concave and homogeneous of degree $1 - \sigma$ $(\sigma > 0)$; thus, $U_{cc} < 0$, $U_{gg} < 0$, and $U_{cc}U_{gg} - U_{cg}^2 > 0$. We now make Assumption

A.4. $\quad f_{pp} - f_{pg} < 0$ *and* $f_{gg} - f_{gp} < 0$.

This "dominant diagonal" assumption is reasonable in two senses. First, we would expect private and public capital to interact in the productive sector so as to complement each other, thus, $f_{pg} \geq 0$ would be the case, and A.4 would hold. Even if $f_{pg} < 0$, we would hardly expect the marginal product of private capital to fall more if a unit of government capital were added than it would if a unit of private capital were added, and similarly if we interchange the two kinds of capital.

Now, instead of considering the matrix of the system (1), consider the following matrix:

$$\begin{bmatrix} U_{cc} & U_{cg} & 0 \\ U_{gc} & U_{gg} + p(f_{gg} - f_{pg}) & p(f_{gp} - f_{pp}) \\ 0 & -1 & -1 \end{bmatrix}$$

This matrix is obtained simply by reversing the sign of the last row.

(a) All principal minors of the first order are negative:

$$U_{cc} < 0, \qquad U_{gg} + p(f_{gg} - f_{pg}) < 0, \qquad -1 < 0.$$

(b) All principal minors of the second order are positive:

$$(U_{cc}U_{gg} - U_{cg}^2) + pU_{cc}(f_{gg} - f_{pg}) > 0$$
$$-U_{cc} > 0$$
$$-U_{gg} - p(f_{gg} - f_{pg}) + p(f_{gp} - f_{pp}) > 0.$$

(c) The determinant is:

$$-(U_{cc}U_{gg} - U_{cg}^2) - pU_{cc}(f_{gg} + f_{pp} - 2f_{gp}) < 0.$$

Thus, by Theorem 4 of Gale and Nikaidô (1965), the solution is unique. This is an alternative way of showing the uniqueness of the solution of the derived demand equations, Proposition 1.(a)–(c).

From the system (1) we can solve for all the partial derivatives of the derived demand equations. These are:

$$\frac{\partial c}{\partial p} = \frac{U_{gg} + p(f_{pp} + f_{gg} - 2f_{gp}) + (f_g - f_p)U_{cg}}{\Delta} < 0, \tag{2a}$$

$$\frac{\partial c}{\partial k} = \frac{pU_{cg}(f_{gp} - f_{pp})}{\Delta}, \tag{2b}$$

$$\frac{\partial k_g}{\partial p} = -\frac{U_{cc}(f_g - f_p) + U_{gc}}{\Delta} < 0, \tag{2c}$$

$$\frac{\partial k_g}{\partial k} = -\frac{U_{cc}p(f_{gp} - f_{pp})}{\Delta} > 0, \tag{2d}$$

$$\frac{\partial k_p}{\partial p} = -\frac{\partial k_g}{\partial p} = \frac{U_{cc}(f_g - f_p) + U_{gc}}{\Delta} > 0, \tag{2e}$$

$$\frac{\partial k_p}{\partial k} = 1 - \frac{\partial k_g}{\partial k} = \frac{(U_{cc}U_{gg} - U_{cg}^2) + pU_{cc}(f_{gg} - f_{pg})}{\Delta} > 0. \tag{2f}$$

To justify the signs in (2a)–(2f), note first that since $f_{gp} - f_{pp} > 0$, $f_{gg} - f_{pg} < 0$ and $\Delta > 0$, the concavity of $U(c, k_g)$ explains the signs of (2d) and (2f). The justification of (2a), (2c), and (2e) follows from the following argument: Since $U(c, k_g)$ was assumed homogeneous of degree $1 - \sigma$, $U_g$ and $U_c$ are homogeneous of degree $-\sigma$; thus,

$$U_{gg}k_g + U_{gc}c = -\sigma U_g$$
$$U_{cg}k_g + U_{cc}c = -\sigma U_c$$

and we have the relationships (since $c$ and $k_g$ are positive):

$$c = \frac{\begin{vmatrix} U_{gg} & -\sigma U_g \\ U_{cg} & -\sigma U_c \end{vmatrix}}{\begin{vmatrix} U_{gg} & U_{gc} \\ U_{cg} & U_{cc} \end{vmatrix}} > 0, \tag{3a}$$

$$k_g = \frac{\begin{vmatrix} -\sigma U_g & U_{gc} \\ -\sigma U_c & U_{cc} \end{vmatrix}}{\begin{vmatrix} U_{gg} & U_{gc} \\ U_{cg} & U_{cc} \end{vmatrix}} > 0, \tag{3b}$$

and by concavity of $U(c, k_g)$ and $\sigma > 0$, we must have

$$U_{gg}U_c - U_gU_{cg} < 0, \tag{4a}$$
$$U_{cc}U_g - U_cU_{gc} < 0. \tag{4b}$$

Note, however, that the equality $f_g - f_p = -U_g/U_c$ holds; thus, by inserting this expression into (2a), (2c), and (2e) one shows, with the aid of (4a)–(4b), the sign relationships stated.

As for (2b), the sign of $\partial c/\partial k$ depends on $U_{cg}$; if $U_{cg} > 0$, then $\partial c/\partial k > 0$, and if $U_{cg} < 0$, then $\partial c/\partial k < 0$.

## 4. Analysis of the Optimal Path

In order to analyze the dynamic nature of the optimal path, we return to the differential equations, Proposition 1.(d)–(e); i.e.,

$$\dot{p}/p = \omega - f_p, \tag{1}$$
$$\dot{k} = f(k_p, k_g) - \gamma k - c, \tag{2}$$

where $c$, $k_p$, and $k_g$ are understood to be the solutions of the short-term equilibrium conditions, Proposition 1.(a)–(c).

We shall start by investigating the stationary solutions of (1) and (2), subject to the first-order conditions.

Let

$$\phi(p, k) = \omega - f_p, \tag{3}$$

$$\psi(p, k) = f(k_p, k_g) - \gamma k - c. \tag{4}$$

We start by determining the general shape of the curve $\phi(p, k) = 0$. From (3),

$$\frac{\partial \phi}{\partial p} = -f_{pp}\left(\frac{\partial k_p}{dp}\right) - f_{pg}\left(\frac{\partial k_g}{\partial p}\right),$$

and since $\dfrac{\partial k_p}{\partial p} = -\dfrac{\partial k_g}{\partial p}$ and $\dfrac{\partial k_g}{\partial p} < 0$ [see 3.(2c)], we have

$$\begin{aligned}\frac{\partial \phi}{\partial p} &= f_{pp}\frac{\partial k_g}{\partial p} - f_{pg}\frac{\partial k_g}{\partial p} \\ &= (f_{pp} - f_{pg})\frac{\partial k_g}{\partial p} > 0.\end{aligned} \tag{5}$$

On the other hand,

$$\begin{aligned}\frac{\partial \phi}{\partial k} &= -f_{pp}\frac{\partial k_p}{\partial k} - f_{pg}\frac{\partial k_g}{\partial k} \\ &= -f_{pp} + (f_{pp} - f_{pg})\frac{\partial k_g}{\partial k} \\ &= -f_{pp} - \frac{U_{cc}p}{\Delta}(f_{gp} - f_{pp})(f_{pp} - f_{gp}) \\ &= -\frac{f_{pp}(U_{cc}U_{gg} - U_{gc}^2) + f_{pp}pU_{cc}(f_{gg} + f_{pp} - 2f_{gp}) - pU_{cc}(f_{pg} - f_{pp})^2}{\Delta} \\ &= -\frac{f_{pp}(U_{cc}U_{gg} - U_{gc}^2)}{\Delta} \\ &\qquad - \frac{pU_{cc}}{\Delta}\{f_{pp}f_{gg} + f_{pp}^2 - 2f_{gp}f_{pp} - f_{gp}^2 + 2f_{gp}f_{pp} - f_{pp}^2\} \\ &= -\frac{f_{pp}(U_{cc}U_{gg} - U_{gc}^2)}{\Delta} - \frac{pU_{cc}}{\Delta}\{f_{pp}f_{gg} - f_{pg}^2\} > 0.\end{aligned} \tag{6}$$

Thus, we have demonstrated that $\dfrac{\partial \phi}{\partial p} > 0$ and $\dfrac{\partial \phi}{\partial k} > 0$. This means that

$$\left.\frac{dp}{dk}\right|_{\phi(p,\,k)\,=\,0} = -\frac{\partial\phi}{\partial k}\bigg/\frac{\partial\phi}{\partial p} < 0. \tag{7}$$

This analysis shows that from the relation $\phi(p, k) = 0$ we can obtain $k = \eta(p)$ with $\eta'(p) < 0$. Now define $\underline{k} = \inf \eta(p)$; the curve $\phi(p, k) = 0$ can be described in figure 3:

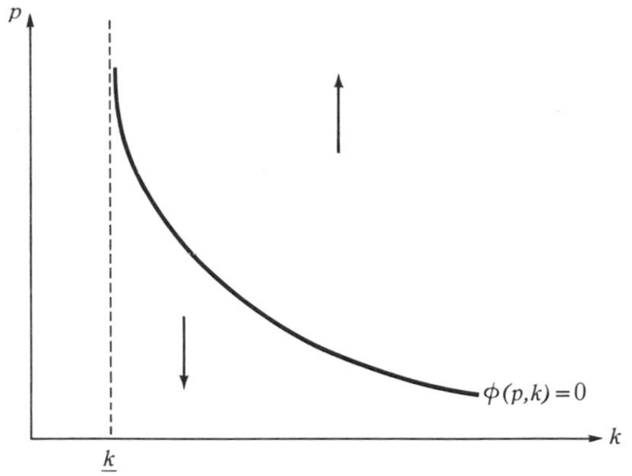


**Figure 3**

Let $\underline{p}$ be such that $\lim_{p \to \underline{p}} \eta(p) = \underline{k}$. Clearly, $\underline{p} = +\infty$, for otherwise, if $\underline{k} > 0$, then $\eta(p)$ would have a finite derivative at $p = \underline{p}$ and would be defined for larger $p$ and therefore take on smaller values of $k$ than $\underline{k}$, a contradiction. If $\underline{k} = 0$, then $c = 0$, and if $U_c(0, k_g) = +\infty$, then $p = +\infty$. The arrows in figure 3 indicate the direction of movement of $p$ in positions above or below the curve $\phi(p, k) = 0$.

We shall see below that $\underline{k} > 0$ is a sufficient condition for the existence of a stationary solution. Thus, we shall now investigate the conditions which will ensure $\underline{k} > 0$. We introduce two assumptions:

A.5 (*substitution between consumption and public goods*). *For any fixed* $k_g > 0$, *the utility function satisfies the following conditions:*

(a) $$U_c(0, k_g) = +\infty,$$

(b) $$U_g(0, k_g) \text{ finite}.$$

Assumption A.5 means that the marginal utility of consumption is $+\infty$ at the point $(c = 0, k_g)$, while the marginal utility of public goods is finite for $k_g > 0$. This means that substitution possibilities between consumption and public goods are limited. However, this does not preclude $U_g(c, 0) = +\infty$. Note that if $U_{gc}(c, k_g) > 0$ for small $c$, then A.5.(b) is satisfied.

A.6. $$f_p(0, k_g) = +\infty, f_p(\infty, k_g) = 0 \text{ for all } k_g;$$
$$f_g(k_p, 0) = +\infty, f_g(k_p, \infty) = 0 \text{ for all } k_p.$$

The above set of "derivative conditions" is not new in the economic literature; it is well known that in most cases they are excessive in the sense that at the origin they are only required to be larger than some parameters. In fact, this is the way that A.6 should be understood.

Now for any $k$, the following maximization problem has a solution [by the concavity of $f(k_p, k_g)$]:

$$g(k) = \max_{k_p+k_g=k} f(k_p, k_g), \tag{8}$$

and we shall write the solution for this problem in the form:

$$k_p = k_p^*(k)$$
$$k_g = k_g^*(k).$$

Since these solutions are obtained from the system

$$\left.\begin{aligned} f_p(k_p, k_g) - f_g(k_p, k_g) &= 0 \\ k_p + k_g &= k \end{aligned}\right\}, \tag{9}$$

it follows from Assumption A.6 that $k_p^*(k)$ and $k_g^*(k)$ are *positive finite for any positive finite* $k$.

Now choose an arbitrary $k_0$. We shall show that the pair $(k_0, \infty)$, with $k_{g0} = k_g^*(k_0)$, $k_{p0} = k_p^*(k_0)$, constitutes a short-term equilibrium. To see this, note first that short-term equilibrium is defined by

$$U_c(c, k_g) = p$$
$$f_p(k_p, k_g) - f_g(k_p, k_g) = \frac{U_g(c, k_g)}{U_c(c, k_g)}$$
$$k_g + k_p = k$$

Insert into this system the fixed values $k_0$, $k_p^*(k_0)$, $k_g^*(k_0)$, and let $p \to +\infty$. From A.5 we see that for $U_c[c, k_g^*(k_0)]$ to tend to $+\infty$, $c$ must tend to 0. From A.5, $U_g[c, k_g^*(k_0)]$ is bounded. Thus, $\dfrac{U_g[c, k_g^*(k_0)]}{U_c[c, k_g^*(k_0)]} \to 0$ as $p \to +\infty$. As we let $p \to +\infty$ and set $k_p = k_p^*(k_0)$, $k_g = k_g^*(k_0)$, we have

$$f_p[k_p^*(k_0), k_g^*(k_0)] - f_g[k_p^*(k_0), k_g^*(k_0)] = 0,$$
$$k_p^*(k_0) + k_g^*(k_0) = k_0,$$

which is consistent with (9). Finally, since $k_p(k, p)$, $k_g(k, p)$ and $c(k, p)$ are continuous functions, it follows that

$$\lim_{p\to\infty} k_p(k, p) = k_p^*(k) \text{ for } k > 0,$$

$$\lim_{p\to\infty} k_g(k, p) = k_g^*(k) \text{ for } k > 0,$$

$$\lim_{p\to\infty} c(k, p) = 0 \qquad \text{for } k > 0.$$

To obtain a solution for $\underline{k}$ we note that $(\underline{k}, \infty)$ must be a short-term equilibrium while satisfying the condition $f_p(k_p, k_g) = \omega$ as well. In other words, $\underline{k}$ is defined by the system

$$\begin{aligned} f_p[k_p^*(\underline{k}), k_g^*(\underline{k})] &= \omega, \\ f_g[k_p^*(\underline{k}), k_g^*(\underline{k})] &= \omega, \\ k_p^*(\underline{k}) + k_g^*(\underline{k}) &= \underline{k}. \end{aligned} \tag{10}$$

From A.6 it follows that $0 < k_p^*(\underline{k}) < \infty$ and $0 < k_g^*(\underline{k}) < \infty$; thus, $0 < \underline{k} < \infty$.

It is interesting to note the interpretation of $\underline{k}$. Suppose we consider the case in which $k_g$ does not appear in the objective function so that $U(c)$ is free of $k_g$. Then the curve $\phi(p, k) = 0$ will *not* depend on $p$ and thus will be a vertical line in the $(p, k)$ space. The solution of $\phi(k) = 0$ is precisely $\underline{k}$.

We now consider the curve $\psi(p, k) = 0$. Since $\psi(p, k) = f(k_p, k_g) - c - \gamma k$, where $k_p(k, p)$, $k_g(k, p)$ and $c(k, p)$ satisfy Proposition 1.(a)–(c), we have

$$\frac{\partial\psi}{\partial p} = f_p \frac{\partial k_p}{\partial p} + f_g \frac{\partial k_g}{\partial p} - \frac{\partial c}{\partial p}.$$

Since $\partial k_p/\partial p = -\partial k_g/\partial p > 0$, we have

$$\begin{aligned} \frac{\partial\psi}{\partial p} &= f_p \frac{\partial k_p}{\partial p} - f_g \frac{\partial k_p}{\partial p} - \frac{\partial c}{\partial p} \\ &= (f_p - f_g) \frac{\partial k_p}{\partial p} - \frac{\partial c}{\partial p}. \end{aligned}$$

By Proposition 1.(b), $f_p - f_g > 0$ and by 3.(2a) and 3.(2e), we have $\partial k_p/\partial p > 0$, $\partial c/\partial p < 0$, thus proving that

$$\frac{\partial\psi}{\partial p} > 0. \tag{11}$$

The last derivative we need, namely $\frac{\partial\psi}{\partial k}$, is the problematic one.

Computing it, we have

$$\frac{\partial \psi}{\partial k} = f_p \frac{\partial k_p}{\partial k} + f_g \frac{\partial k_g}{\partial k} - \frac{\partial c}{\partial k} - \gamma$$

$$= f_p + (f_g - f_p) \frac{\partial k_g}{\partial k} - \frac{\partial c}{\partial k} - \gamma. \tag{12}$$

Since the sign of $\partial c/\partial k$ is ambiguous, the sign of $\partial \psi/\partial k$ is also ambiguous.

Before examining the various possibilities of the optimal path, we wish to establish the existence of at least one stationary state. We have already seen the behavior of the curve $\phi(p, k) = 0$.

As already seen, $c(k, \infty) = 0$; $k_p(k, \infty) = k_p^*(k)$; $k_g(k, \infty) = k_g^*(k)$ for all $k > 0$ and, in particular, for $k = \underline{k}$. For $g(k)$ defined in (8), it follows from (9)–(10) that $g'(\underline{k}) = \omega > \gamma$. Since $g(k) - \gamma k$ is a concave function vanishing at the origin and, as just shown, increasing at $k = \underline{k}$, clearly

$$g(\underline{k}) - \gamma \underline{k} > 0.$$

Hence,

$$\psi(\infty, \underline{k}) = f[k_p(\underline{k}, \infty), k_g(\underline{k}, \infty)] - \gamma \underline{k} - c(\underline{k}, \infty)$$
$$= g(\underline{k}) - \gamma \underline{k} > 0.$$

On the other hand, $U_c(c, k_g)$ is positive if $c$ and $k_g$ are both finite. Hence, Proposition 1(a) with $p = 0$,

$$U_c[c(k, 0), k_g(k, 0)] = 0,$$

implies that $c(k, 0) = +\infty$ since $k_g(k, 0) \leqq k$ and is therefore finite.

$$\psi(0, k) = f[k_p(k, 0), k_g(k, 0)] - \gamma k - c(k, 0) = -\infty, \tag{13}$$

since $f(k_p, k_g)$ is certainly bounded when $k_p + k_g = k$ and $k$ is finite. In particular, (13) holds for $k = \underline{k}$; in conjunction with the statement that $\psi(\infty, \underline{k}) > 0$, the existence of a finite $p$ for which $\psi(p, \underline{k}) = 0$ is demonstrated. This solution is unique by (11). Since $\phi(\infty, \underline{k}) = 0$, it follows that the locus $\psi(p, k) = 0$ lies below the locus $\phi(p, k) = 0$ for $k$ in a right-hand neighborhood of $\underline{k}$.

To show the existence of at least one stationary equilibrium, it is now sufficient to show that the locus $\psi(p, k) = 0$ lies above the locus $\phi(p, k) = 0$ for large $k$; more precisely, we will show that, along the locus $\psi(p, k) = 0$, $p$ approaches infinity as $k$ approaches a suitable chosen finite value. From (13) we know that $\psi(0, k) < 0$, all $k$; hence, it suffices to show that $\psi(p, k) < 0$, all $p$, for $k$ sufficiently large. We assume the following, which is equivalent to assuming the existence of a golden rule path for any natural rate of growth:

A.7 *For any* $\epsilon$ *there exists* $M$ *such that* $k_p + k_g > M$ *implies* $f(k_p, k_g)/(k_g + k_g) < \epsilon$.

That is, output per unit capital approaches zero (for fixed labor force) no matter how the capital is allocated between the two sectors.

Then,

$$\psi(p, k) = f[k_p(k, p), k_g(k, p)] - \gamma k - c(k, p)$$
$$\leqq k\left\{\frac{f[k_p(k, p), k_g(k, p)]}{k_p(k, p) + k_g(k, p)} - \gamma\right\} < 0$$

if $k = k_p(k, p) + k_g(k, p)$ is sufficiently large.

Combining these results with the analysis of the curve $\phi(p, k) = 0$, we have proved that at least one stationary point, $(p^\infty, k^\infty)$, exists at which $\phi(p^\infty, k^\infty) = \psi(p^\infty, k^\infty) = 0$.

Turning now to the other properties of the curve $\psi(p, k) = 0$, note that if we assume $U_{cg} > 0$, then $\partial c/\partial k > 0$ and the sign of $\partial\psi/\partial k$ depends only on the difference $f_p - \gamma$. Suppose that for some allocation of $k_g$ and $k_p$ we had $f_p = \gamma$, then for that allocation $U_{cg} > 0$ implies $\partial\psi/\partial k < 0$ and thus $\left.\frac{dp}{dk}\right|_{\psi(p, k) = 0} > 0$. This will also be true for a small open set of values of $k$ that will generate a small difference $f_p - \gamma$. These considerations are important for the evaluation of the stationary points.

Suppose $(p^\infty, k^\infty)$ is a stationary point for which $\phi(p^\infty, k^\infty) = \psi(p^\infty, k^\infty) = 0$. Since $f_p(k_p^\infty, k_g^\infty) = \omega$ and $\omega > \gamma$, it follows that $f_p - \gamma > 0$ at that stationary point, and thus the sign of $\partial\psi/\partial k$ is ambiguous. Figures 4 and 5 depict two possible patterns for the curve $\psi(p, k) = 0$. The

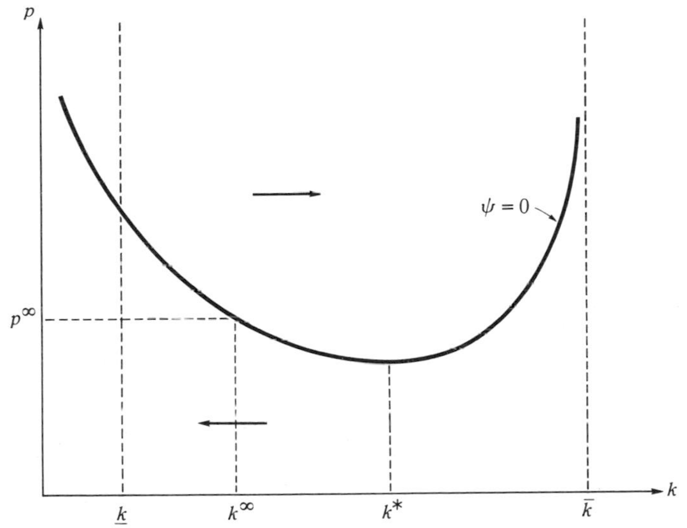


**Figure 4**

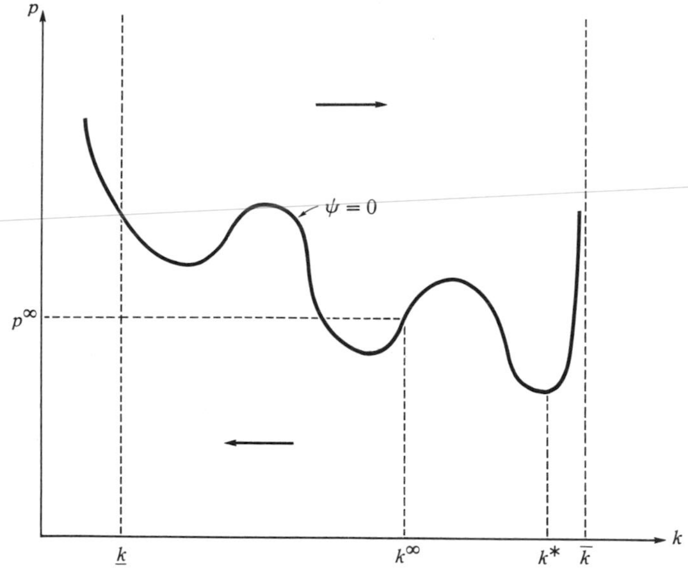


Figure 5

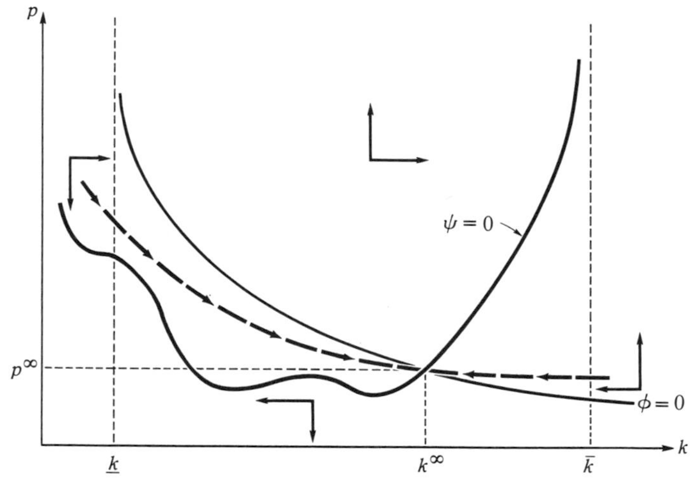


Figure 6

stationary point $(p^{\infty}, k^{\infty})$ may be on a positively or negatively sloped segment of the $\psi = 0$ curve. However, the discussion above suggests that when $\omega - \gamma$ is sufficiently small, then the assumption $U_{cg} > 0$ will ensure that at the stationary point $\partial\psi/\partial k < 0$, and thus $\left.\frac{dp}{dk}\right|_{p^{\infty}, k^{\infty}} > 0$; thus, we can discuss two cases: (a) $\omega - \gamma$ is sufficiently small to ensure $\left.\frac{dp}{dk}\right|_{(p^{\infty}, k^{\infty})} > 0$; (b) $\omega > \gamma$ with a significant difference between these two constants.

*Case a:* $\omega$ is sufficiently close to $\gamma$. In this case, $\left.\frac{dp}{dk}\right|_{(p^{\infty}, k^{\infty})} > 0$ (see figure 6). Although the curve $\psi = 0$ is not monotonic, it cuts $\phi = 0$ from below, and thus the stationary point $(p^{\infty}, k^{\infty})$ is unique. Note that this stationary point is indeed a saddle point, as indicated by the arrows pointing the direction of movement. The proximity of $\omega$ and $\gamma$ ensures that the stationary point lies on a positively sloping segment of the $\psi = 0$ curve. If there had been more than one stationary point, then at least one of these points must have been on a negatively sloped segment of the curve $\psi = 0$; this was precluded by the assumptions $U_{cg} \geqq 0$ and $|\omega - \gamma|$ sufficiently small.

In figure 6 we drew the broken bold line through the stationary point; this is the optimal path for a problem such as this; it is a function $p = p(k)$ which specifies the initial value $p(0)$ which must be chosen for each initial $k(0)$ (see Proposition II.9).

*Case b:* If $\omega$ is sufficiently greater than $\gamma$, an arbitrary number of stationary solutions may exist. At any such stationary point $f_p = \omega > \gamma$, the relation $f_p - \gamma > 0$ does not ensure the condition $\left.\frac{dp}{dk}\right|_{\psi = 0} > 0$ at that point. The stationary point $(p^{\infty}, k^{\infty})$ may lie either on a declining or on a rising segment of the curve $\psi(p, k) = 0$. Many situations could arise; three of these are described in figures 7, 8, and 9:

In figure 7 the stationary point is on the rising part of the $\psi = 0$ curve, and this yields a unique stationary point. In figure 8, the stationary point is on the downward sloping segment of the $\psi = 0$ curve, but still we have a unique stationary point. In figure 9 the situation is different. Three different points—$(p_1^{\infty}, k_1^{\infty})$, $(p_2^{\infty}, k_2^{\infty})$, and $(p_3^{\infty}, k_3^{\infty})$—exist at which the curves $\phi = 0$ and $\psi = 0$ intersect. All three are stationary solutions, and the optimal path is the broken line that goes through all three points. The interesting fact, explained by the arrows in figure 9, is that the two

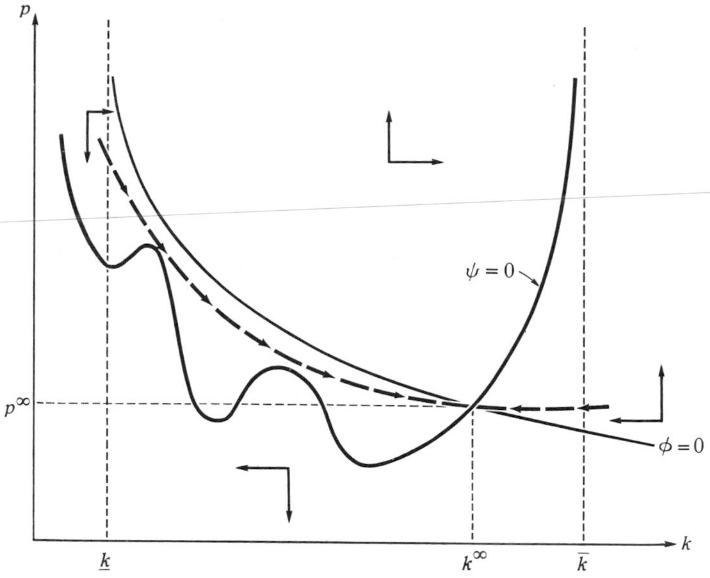


Figure 7

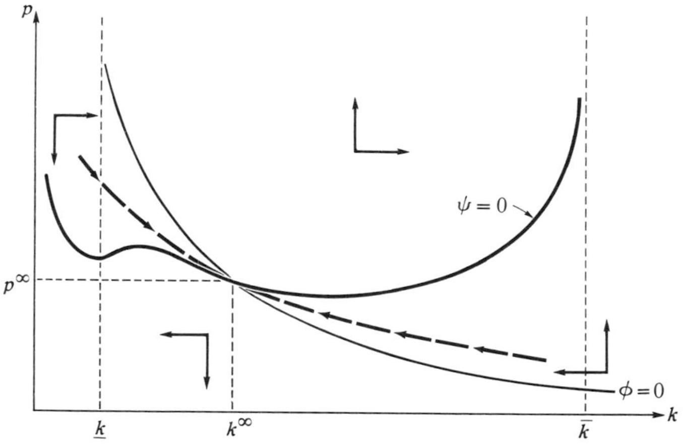


Figure 8

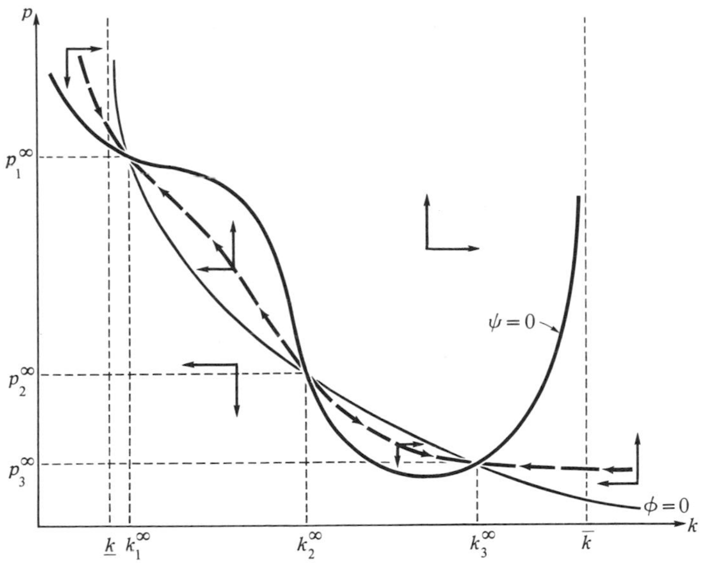


**Figure 9**

stationary points, $(p_1^\infty, k_1^\infty)$ and $(p_3^\infty, k_3^\infty)$, are saddle points, while $(p_2^\infty, k_2^\infty)$ is a totally unstable point. Thus, if the initial capital stock, $k(0)$, is $k(0) > k_2^\infty$, then the optimal policy calls for convergence to $k_3^\infty$ either from below or above. If, however, $k(0) < k_2^\infty$, then the optimal policy calls for convergence to $k_1^\infty$. If the initial capital stock is $k(0) = k_2^\infty$, then the total amount of savings should be just enough to maintain $k(t) = k_2^\infty$. Thus, the point $(p_2^\infty, k_2^\infty)$ acts as a threshold: initial conditions above it lead to an optimal program which converges to one stationary point, while initial conditions below it lead to an optimal program which converges to the second stationary point.

It is clear that in general it is possible to construct curves $\phi = 0$ and $\psi = 0$ for which there will exist an arbitrarily large odd number of stationary points and the optimal policy will have a character similar to the program analyzed in figure 9.

PROPOSITION 2. *In addition to the assumptions of Proposition 1, assume the following:*

(a) $U_c(0, k_g) = +\infty$, $U_g(0, k_g)$ *finite for any* $k_g > 0$;

(b) $f_p(0, k_g) = +\infty$, $f_p(\infty, k_g) = 0$ *for all* $k_g$,
$f_g(k_p, 0) = +\infty$, $f_g(k_p, \infty) = 0$ *for all* $k_p$;

(c) $f(k_p, k_g)/(k_p + k_g)$ *can be made arbitrarily small for* $k_p + k_g$ *large.*

*Then there is at least one stationary equilibrium for the differential equation system, Proposition 1*(d)–(e). *There is a function,* $p(k)$, *satisfying the differential equation:*

$$\text{(d)} \qquad \frac{dp}{dk} = \frac{p\{\omega - f_p[k_p(k, p), k_g(k, p)]\}}{f[k_p(k, p), k_g(k, p)] - \gamma k - c(k, p)}$$

*and passing through all the equilibria. The optimal policy is defined by this function in the sense that, for any* $k$, *the optimal consumption (normalized for growth) is* $c(k) = c[k, p(k)]$; *the optimal accumulation of capital is output less consumption; and the allocation of capital between private and government capital is determined by the functions* $k_p[k, p(k)]$ *and* $k_g[k, p(k)]$, *respectively.*

*There will be a unique equilibrium, which will be a saddle point, if* $\omega - \gamma$ *is sufficiently small and* $U_{cg} \geqq 0$. *In general there will be an odd number of equilibria; every other one, beginning with the one with the smallest value of* $k$, *will be a saddle point, while those remaining are totally unstable. If the initial capital (normalized for growth) stock corresponds to one of the totally unstable equilibria, then the optimal policy calls for keeping it constant; otherwise the growth-normalized capital stock converges to the value corresponding to one of the saddle points.*

## 5. Balanced Growth

The short-term equilibrium, Proposition 1.(a)–(c), defines the derived demand equations $c(k, p)$, $k_p(k, p)$, $k_g(k, p)$. In a state of balanced growth, $\dot{k} = 0$, $\dot{p} = 0$, thus making available two other equations from Proposition 1.(d)–(e):

$$f_p(k_p^\infty, k_g^\infty) = \omega, \tag{1}$$

$$f(k_p^\infty, k_g^\infty) = c(k^\infty, p^\infty) + \gamma k^\infty. \tag{2}$$

The interpretation of these conditions is partly familiar: Proposition 1.(a) says that the shadow price, $p$, must be equal to the marginal utility, $U_c$, and equation (2) says that at a stationary point, output is divided between consumption and a level of gross investments which is just needed to keep $k(t)$ at its stationary level $k^\infty$ (constant capital-labor ratio). The conditions, Proposition 1.(b) and equation (1), deserve more attention.

In the short-term condition, Proposition 1.(b), the benefits from investments are examined. If a unit of capital is invested in the public sector, it yields direct marginal consumption benefits equal to $U_g$ in addition to the production values $pf_g$. Thus, the total benefits are $U_g + pf_g$. The benefits from a unit of capital invested in the private sector are valued at $pf_k$, and thus the equilibrium condition, Proposition 1.(b), requires the equality of these streams; i.e., $U_g + pf_g = pf_p$.

Since $f_p$ is the rate of return on capital, the stationarity condition $f_p = \omega$ means that the rate of return on capital should be constant and equal to $\omega$. But $\omega = \rho + \sigma\tau$, which is the familiar asymptotic consumption rate of interest. Thus, the stationarity condition, $f_p = \omega$, means the equality of the rate of return on capital with the consumption interest rate.

If we combine equation (1) with Proposition 1.(b), we find the rate of interest on government investment under conditions of balanced growth:

$$f_g(k_p^\infty, k_g^\infty) = \omega - [U_g(k_p^\infty, k_g^\infty)/p^\infty]. \tag{3}$$

Finally, since at the stationary point $k^\infty$, $k_g^\infty$, $k_p^\infty$, and $c^\infty$ are all constants, it follows from the transformations 2.(2) that, in original units, consumption and both forms of capital grow at the natural rate, $\gamma$. This result has already been encountered in chapter III (see end of section 1 and Proposition III.1).

## 6. The Special Case $U_g \equiv 0$

The special case $U_g \equiv 0$ amounts to assuming that the utility function is of the form $U(c)$. Thus, it ignores the potential direct consumption benefits of public investments.

In this case, the first-order conditions, Proposition 1.(a)–(c), of the optimization simplify to

$$U_c = p, \tag{1a}$$

$$f_g = f_p, \tag{1b}$$

$$k = k_g + k_p. \tag{1c}$$

Thus, the equality of the shadow price $p$ to the marginal utility $U_c$ still holds, but $f_g = f_p$ says that the stock of capital is to be allocated between private and public use in such a way that the rates of return on these two uses are equalized. Note that this allocation does not depend any more on the price $p$ of capital goods; thus, the derived demand equations in this case are simpler than those in 2.(15):

$$c = c(p), \tag{2a}$$

$$k_g = k_g(k), \tag{2b}$$

$$k_p = k_p(k). \tag{2c}$$

The system 3.(1) is now replaced by

$$\begin{aligned} U_{cc}dc \qquad\qquad\qquad\qquad\qquad\qquad &= dp \\ p(f_{gg} - f_{pg})dk_g + p(f_{gp} - f_{pp})dk_p &= 0 \\ dk_g + \qquad\qquad\qquad dk_p &= dk\,, \end{aligned}$$

and the principal minors are simply

$$\Delta_1 = U_{cc} < 0\,, \tag{3a}$$

$$\Delta_2 = pU_{cc}(f_{gg} - f_{pg}) > 0\,, \tag{3b}$$

$$\Delta = pU_{cc}(f_{gg} + f_{pp} - 2f_{gp}) > 0\,. \tag{3c}$$

If we multiply the last equation by $-1$, the matrix becomes

$$\begin{bmatrix} U_{cc} & 0 & 0 \\ 0 & p(f_{gg} - f_{pg}) & p(f_{gp} - f_{pp}) \\ 0 & -1 & -1 \end{bmatrix}$$

This is a $P$-matrix; thus it follows from Gale and Nikaidô (1965, Theorem 4) that the short-term equilibrium solution is unique.

Turning now to the dynamics of the system, we have from 4.(3)–(4):

$$\phi(k) = \omega - f_p[k_p(k), k_g(k)]\,, \tag{4}$$

$$\psi(p, k) = f[k_p(k), k_g(k)] - \gamma k - c(p)\,. \tag{5}$$

Thus, it follows immediately from 4.(5), 4.(6), and (3c) that

$$\frac{\partial \phi}{\partial p} \equiv 0\,, \tag{6}$$

$$\frac{\partial \phi}{\partial k} = -\frac{(f_{pp}f_{gg} - f_{pg}^2)}{f_{pp} + f_{gg} - 2f_{gp}} > 0\,. \tag{7}$$

From (5) and (1a),

$$\frac{\partial \psi}{\partial p} = -\frac{1}{U_{cc}} > 0\,. \tag{8}$$

From (5), (1b), and 3.(2f),

$$\frac{\partial \psi}{\partial k} = f_p - \gamma\,. \tag{9}$$

Thus, the phase diagram in this case is rather simple, in fact identical with that of the one-sector model of chapter III (see figure 2). The curve

$\phi = 0$ is attained simply by solving the equations $f_p[k_p(k), k_g(k)] = \omega$ which, in view of (4) and (7), must have a unique solution $k^\infty$. Moreover, the stationary point must lie on the negatively-sloped segment of the $\psi = 0$ curve [from (9), (8), and the assumption that $\omega > \gamma$], and thus it is unique. The optimal path has the saddle point property.

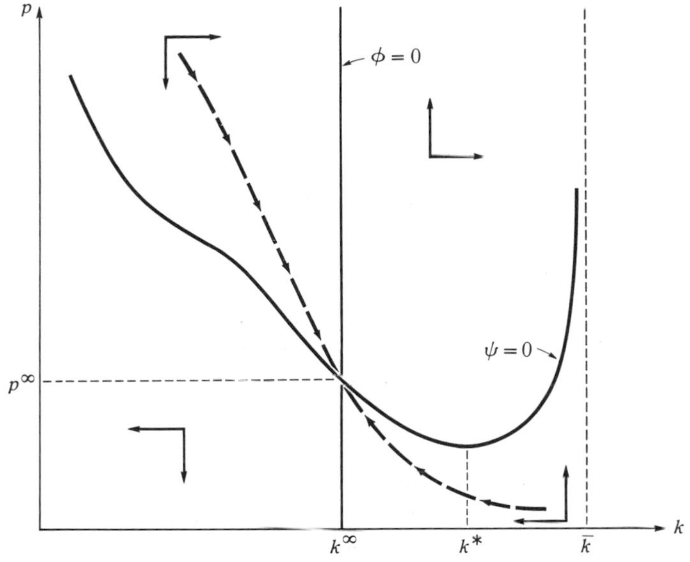


**Figure 10**

Note that we have designated by $k^*$ the point at which the curve $\psi = 0$ reaches its minimum. This is justified by the fact that

$$\left.\frac{dp}{dk}\right|_{\psi = 0} = U_{cc}(f_p - \gamma). \tag{10}$$

Thus, the curve $\psi = 0$ yields a monotonic relation between $p$ and $k$ over the two intervals $(0, k^*)$ and $(k^*, \infty)$. At $k^*$ we must have

$$f_p[k_p(k^*), k_g(k^*)] = \gamma,$$

so that at $k^*$ we attain the equality between the rate of interest and the natural growth rate.

It may be of some interest to show that the case $U_g = 0$ may be reduced to the Ramsey case of chapter III in spite of the presence of two stocks: $k_g$ and $k_p$. To see this, we write the current-value Hamiltonian as

$$H = U(c) + p[f(k_p, k_g) - \gamma k - c],$$

and we wish to maximize $H$ with respect to $c$, $k_g$, and $k_p$ subject to the restriction $k_p + k_g = k$. Thus,

$$\max_{c,k_p,k_g} H = \max_{c} \max_{k_p+k_g=k} H$$
$$= \max_{c} \{U(c) - pc - \gamma pk + p \max_{k_p+k_g=k} f(k_p, k_g)\}.$$

If we recall the definition of $g(k)$ in 4.(8), we see that $g(k)$ can be viewed as a production function which is attained by allocating any $k$ in such a way that $f_p = f_g$. The Hamiltonian then takes the conventional form:

$$H = U(c) + p[g(k) - c - \gamma k],$$

where the only state variable is $k$ and the only control is $c$.

## 7. Irreversible Investment Decisions

As we have indicated in section 1, the irreversibility assumption means the additional constraints $I_p \geqq 0$, $I_g \geqq 0$. These constraints lead to the appearance of two prices, $p_p$ and $p_g$, associated with these constraints, and the investment strategy depends on $p_p - p_g$.

In general, the asymptotic behavior of the optimal program is the same as in the case of the economy with reversible investment decisions. The difference arises in the transition from any arbitrary initial conditions to the asymptotic values of the variables. Two types of constraints may become binding under the irreversibility assumption. The first is a case in which there is a specialization of investments; in this case $I_p = 0$, $I_g > 0$, or $I_p > 0$, $I_g = 0$. The second is the specialization to consumption where $I_p = I_g = 0$, while $C > 0$. There could be various intervals on the time axis along which one or the other type of situation could arise. As has already been seen in discussion of a simpler model (chapter III, end of section 4), practically any sequence of such alternating intervals is possible along the optimal path. For this reason we shall not discuss this case further.

## 8. Increasing Returns to Scale

In chapter I we discussed the question of increasing returns to scale resulting from public investments. It was argued that public capital may yield externalities in the economic system that will give rise to increasing returns in production. In the pure public good case, government capital increases the productivity of each individual worker to an extent independent of the number of workers. Such capital is a prime candidate for government policy since it cannot possibly be allocated efficiently by any competitive pricing scheme. An excellent example is investment in research and development; such investment raises productivity, and the results are applicable to an economy of arbitrary size. It may well be that the marginal productivity that research imparts to any one individual will diminish with the volume of research but not with the size of the labor force.

The pure public good case is extreme. More generally, there may be some degree of diminishing returns in the effect of a given volume of government capital on the productivity of labor, but not enough to prevent increasing returns in all factors; public education and transportation are frequently thought to exemplify this condition. We do require, however, that there be diminishing returns to scale (more strictly speaking, concavity) in the two kinds of capital for a fixed labor force.

In this section we shall analyze a model which incorporates these ideas. We shall first present a general formulation of the model and later specify some additional assumptions that will simplify the analytic developments.

The production function is assumed, then, to display increasing returns to all factors:

$$F(\lambda K_p, \lambda K_g, \lambda L) > \lambda F(K_p, K_g, L).$$

Specifically, we assume that government capital acts solely in a labor-augmenting fashion; government capital and labor together produce "trained labor," which in turn enters a constant-returns production function as a factor cooperating with private capital.

$$Y = F(K_p, K_g, L) = G(K_p, L') = G[K_p, H(K_g, L)], \tag{1}$$

where $L' = H(K_g, L)$ is trained labor and $G(K_p, L')$ is assumed homogeneous of degree 1, concave, and twice differentiable. Then $F(K_p, K_g, L)$ shows increasing returns if and only if $H(K_g, L)$ shows increasing returns. For $F$ to be concave in $K_p$ and $K_g$ for fixed $L$, it is sufficient that $H$ be concave in $K_g$.

So far we have not considered exogenous technological change. We shall assume, as before, that it takes only a labor-augmenting form; i.e., we replace $L$ in (1) by

$$L_E(t) = e^{\tau' t}L(t),$$

where $\tau'$ is now the rate of labor-augmenting exogenous technological progress. Since $L(t)$ is itself growing at the rate $\pi$, the effective labor force is growing at the rate $\pi + \tau'$.

Let us now consider a few problems related to the existence of paths of balanced growth. Along such paths all stocks of capital and flows of output and consumption grow at the same relative rate, and the interest rate is constant. There is nothing intrinsically important about such paths and there are many economic models that do not possess balanced growth paths. However, economic systems that do possess a balanced growth path (for all values of the parameters) have important properties that make their analysis elegant. In addition, the mathematical tools of control theory are better equipped to deal with systems that do possess balanced growth paths; in most other cases these tools do not seem to yield interesting results.

The formulation of our problem so far is too general to enable us to proceed much further. From the general theory of growth we know that only a restricted class of increasing-returns-to-scale production functions will indeed possess balanced growth paths (see chapter I, section 5; chapter III, section 5; Levhari and Sheshinski 1969). Suppose that output and the two kinds of capital are growing at a constant rate, $\gamma$. Since $Y$ and $K_p$ are growing at this rate and $G$ is homogeneous of degree 1, it follows from (1) that $H(K_g, L_E)$ must also be growing at the rate $\gamma$ when $K_g$ grows at that rate and $L_E$ grows at the rate $\pi + \tau'$. But if $H(K_g, L_E)$ grows at the rate $\gamma$ and $K_g$ grows at the same rate, it follows from Levhari and Sheshinski (1969, Theorem 1) that the function $H(K_g, L_E)$ must be of the special form:

$$H(K_g, L_E) = \tilde{H}[K_g, L_E^{\gamma/(\pi+\tau')}],$$

where $\tilde{H}$ is homogeneous of degree 1 and for a fixed $L_E$ has the same concavity properties as $H$. This means that for a balanced growth to exist, we must have

$$F(K_p, K_g, L_E) = G\{K_p, \tilde{H}[K_g, L_E^{\gamma/(\pi+\tau')}]\}$$

and, for any fixed $L_E$, $G$ is concave in the two variables $K_p$ and $K_g$.

We thus replace assumption 1.A.1 by

(A.1)′
$$\begin{aligned} Y(t) &= F[K_p(t), K_g(t), L(t), t] \\ &= G(K_p(t), \tilde{H}\{K_g(t), [L_E(t)]^{\delta}\}), \end{aligned}$$

*for some $\delta > 0$, where both $G(K_p, L')$ and $\tilde{H}(K_g, L_E^{\delta})$ are homogeneous of degree 1, concave and twice differentiable.*

We retain assumptions 1.A.2 and 1.A.3.

The natural rate of growth is

$$\gamma = \delta(\pi + \tau'). \tag{2}$$

Since $G$ and $\tilde{H}$ are homogeneous of degree 1, $F$ displays increasing returns if and only if $\delta > 1$.

Since $\gamma$ is the rate of growth of all aggregate magnitudes, and $\pi$ is the growth rate of population, per capita magnitudes will grow at the rate

$$\tau = \gamma - \pi. \tag{3}$$

From (2),

$$\tau = \delta(\pi + \tau') - \pi = (\delta - 1)\pi + \delta\tau'.$$

Hence, if $\delta > 1$, $\tau$ must certainly be positive, even if $\tau' = 0$ (no exogenous technological progress); per capita magnitudes will grow because of increasing returns alone.

A special function which satisfies all the conditions above is the power function,

$$H(K_g, L_E) = K_g^{\epsilon} L_E^{\delta(1-\epsilon)}.$$

In this case the elasticities are constant. Increasing returns to scale occur when $\delta > 1$, while decreasing returns hold when $\delta < 1$. The concavity of $H$ in $K_g$ (for a fixed $L_E$) is insured by the condition $0 < \epsilon < 1$.

We have now developed all the tools needed for the final step of the analysis. It is our purpose to reduce the problem of optimal growth under conditions of increasing returns to a more familiar and manageable form.

We introduce the familiar transformations, 2.(2), 2.(5), and 2.(6):

$$\begin{aligned} k &= Ke^{-\gamma t}, \qquad k_p = K_p e^{-\gamma t}, \\ k_g &= K_g e^{-\gamma t} = P(t)\bar{k}_g(t)e^{-\gamma t} = P(0)\bar{k}_g(t)e^{-\tau t}, \\ c(t) &= P(t)\bar{c}(t)e^{-\gamma t} = P(0)\bar{c}e^{-\tau t}. \end{aligned} \tag{4}$$

Then, exactly as in section 2, the maximand 1.(5a) can be written as 2.(8):

$$\max \int_0^\infty e^{-\lambda t} U[c(t), k_g(t)]dt, \tag{5}$$

where

$$\lambda = \omega - \gamma, \qquad \omega = \rho + \sigma\tau, \tag{6}$$

From (4),

$$\dot{k} = \dot{K}e^{-\gamma t} - \gamma K e^{-\gamma t}.$$

But the capital accumulation equation 1.(5b) can be written

$$\begin{aligned} \dot{K}e^{-\gamma t} &= e^{-\gamma t}F[K_p(t), K_g(t), L(t), t] - P(t)\bar{c}(t)e^{-\gamma t} \\ &= e^{-\gamma t}G(K_p(t), \tilde{H}\{K_g(t), [L_E(t)]^{\delta}\}) - c(t) \\ &= G\{e^{-\gamma t}K_p(t), \tilde{H}[K_g(t)e^{-\gamma t}, L_0^{\delta}e^{(\pi+\tau')\delta t}e^{-\gamma t}]\} - c(t) \\ &= G\{k_p(t), \tilde{H}[k_g(t), L_0^{\delta}]\} - c(t), \end{aligned}$$

where use has been made of A.1′, the homogeneity of degree 1 of $G$ and $\tilde{H}$, and (2).

Now let

$$f(k_p, k_g) \equiv G[k_p, \tilde{H}(k_g, L_0^{\delta})]. \tag{7}$$

Since $G$ is concave in $k_p$ and $k_g$, it follows that $f(k_p, k_g)$ is also. Assembling the calculations, we have

$$\dot{k} = f(k_p, k_g) - \gamma k - c, \tag{8}$$

with $f(k_p, k_g)$ concave. But the maximization of (5) subject to (8) is formally identical with that of 2.(8) subject to 2.(10); the only difference in interpretation is that in the constant returns model the rate of per capita balanced growth is solely due to exogenous factors, whereas now per capita growth can be positive even in the absence of exogenous technological progress.

PROPOSITION 3. *Propositions 1 and 2 remain valid if the assumed constraint on the two types of capital accumulation and consumption is replaced by the following:*

(a) $\dot{K}_p(t) + \dot{K}_g(t) + P(t)c(t) = G\{K_p(t), H[K_g(t), L_E(t)]\}$

*where*

(a.1) $L_E(t) = e^{\tau' t}L(t)$

(a.2) $H(K_g, L_E)$ *has the special form*

$$H(K_g, L_E) \equiv \tilde{H}(K_g, L_E^{\delta})$$

*and* $\tilde{H}$ *is homogeneous of degree 1, concave, and twice differentiable.*

(a.3) $G(K_p, L')$ *is homogeneous of degree 1, concave, and twice differentiable.*

(b) *The natural rate of aggregate growth is*

$$\gamma = \delta(\pi + \tau').$$

(c) *The natural per capita growth rate is*

$$\tau = \gamma - \pi.$$

*Remark.* Of course, since there are increasing returns, it is impossible that each factor, including government capital, be paid its marginal product. Hence, in a decentralized economy, government capital must be underpriced economically if the other factors are paid their marginal products.

# V

# OBJECTIVES, MARKETS, AND PUBLIC INSTRUMENTS

## 0. Introduction

In a centralized society, the problem of optimal public investments is rather simply defined: the central planning board sets up its objectives and then seeks those investment criteria that will maximize these objectives subject to the technological constraints and resource availability. This kind of procedure has been employed in most recent work in the theory of optimal growth; indeed, this is the procedure that we have employed in chapters III and IV. Thus, the results of these chapters can be interpreted as applicable to a central planning organization.

In a decentralized society, where individuals and firms are free to maximize their own objectives subject to their own private constraints, the investment and financing behavior of the public sector becomes a more delicate matter. The government no longer makes all allocation decisions itself. Instead, it has the choice of values of a limited range of instruments. Some of these may be allocative decisions; for example, government investment. Others may be decisions which are intended to influence the resource allocations made by the private sector, for example, taxes. The problem, as formulated by Tinbergen (1952, chapter II; see also chapters IV and V), is to determine what policies the government can achieve by its choices of instruments. The complexity of the situation originates from three sources: (a) there might be a basic divergence between private and social objectives; (b) in order to achieve its goals, society has to define the instruments of public policy and their application may entail substantial political difficulties; and (c) the application of policy instruments must take into account the conditions of the market mechanism in which they are applied.

This chapter will provide basic introductory remarks to explain and justify the general notion of controllability by public instruments studied in the following chapters.

## 1. Private and Social Objectives

It has already been noted (section I.2, subsection headed *Social and Private Rates of Time Preference*) that a case can be made for a divergence between social and private benefits from the future, on the grounds that there is a collective benefit from future (especially unborn and therefore unrepresented) generations. In order to accommodate this point of view, we shall frequently use two objective functions: "public,"

$$\int_0^{\infty} e^{-\rho_g t} U^g[\tilde{c}(t), \tilde{k}_g(t)]dt, \tag{1}$$

and "private,"

$$\int_0^{\infty} e^{-\rho_p t} U^p[\tilde{c}(t), \tilde{k}_g(t)]dt, \tag{2}$$

where $\tilde{c}(t)$ and $\tilde{k}_g(t)$ are per capita consumption and public capital, while

$$\begin{aligned} \rho_g &= \text{public discount factor}, \\ \rho_p &= \text{private discount factor}, \\ U^g(\tilde{c}, \tilde{k}_g) &= \text{public felicity function}, \\ U^p(\tilde{c}, \tilde{k}_g) &= \text{private felicity function}. \end{aligned}$$

We generally assume these felicity functions to be homogeneous; more specifically we assume

$$U^g(\lambda c, \lambda k_g) = \lambda^{1-\sigma_g} U^g(c, k_g) \qquad 0 < \sigma_g \tag{1'}$$

$$U^p(\lambda c, \lambda k_g) = \lambda^{1-\sigma_p} U^p(c, k_g) \qquad 0 < \sigma_p. \tag{2'}$$

The notion of "public objective function" is understood in terms of the "collective" objective that is based on some kind of interaction among individual benefits. The notion of "private objective function" is clearly a theoretical fiction and attempts to represent the objectives of the selfish, decentralized collection of decision makers. One view assumes that all individuals are alike; alternatively this function can be seen as representing the "average individual." This is clearly an abstraction from the standard problems of aggregation; however, it is hoped that this abstraction will help to clarify the basic problems of public policy in a decentralized economy.

Thus, according to our view, the path analyzed in chapter IV is optimal according to the public criterion. In chapter VII we shall analyze the path resulting from "private optimization." These two paths are not necessarily consistent with each other and a basic divergence between private decisions and social goals may occur. In order to counter such divergence, the public sector needs instruments for the implementation of its programs. These instruments represent in most societies indirect intervention in the market mechanism. The range of paths that can be achieved depends upon the range of instruments available to the government, the divergence between private and public objectives, and the imperfections of the markets in which the instruments are employed.

## 2. Market Conditions

The most important market with which we are concerned here is the capital market. The view that the capital market is imperfect is immediately derived from the observation that many different rates of return appear to be available in our economy. The opportunities for investment range from cash, with zero return, up through various forms of time deposits, government bonds, personal finance loans, consumer installment credit, and direct investments—a wide range indeed. In addition, while some of these rates are market prices in a reasonably strict sense, others have to be imputed, sometimes by methods of such subtlety that experts find themselves in sharp disagreement. We particularly have in mind the discussion of the rate of return on human capital; e.g., Becker (1965).

It is, of course, not sufficient merely to look at these rather general facts; their interpretation requires more analysis of the different services rendered by different capital markets than would be consistent with the scope of this work. But it is crucial in welfare evaluation to examine the extent to which observed rates of interest reflect time preference, and this question will be briefly discussed now.

The welfare interpretation of interest rates requires that they correspond to time preference on the part of individuals. Thus, if an observed interest rate is to be used for discounting investments, it ought to be true that individuals make their choice between saving and spending on the basis of that rate. Under perfectly competitive conditions, the consumption of an individual should be a function of this wealth and of the rate of interest, wealth itself being defined in turn as the sum of discounted returns to both currently held material assets and personal skills and qualities. The present and future values of the rate of interest thus enter both directly and through the measurement of wealth.[1]

[1] It is possible for consumption to depend only on wealth (as defined above) if the individual is maximizing a discounted sum of utilities of consumption at the successive time points in the future, where the utility of consumption at any given time point is its logarithm. But even then the wealth must in general depend on present and future rates of interest, through the discounting of future returns. It can be shown that, in general, consumption (or savings) can never be independent of the rate of interest under perfectly competitive conditions.

Although there have been many empirical investigations of savings behavior, none to our knowledge has been completely compatible with this hypothesis. Among the innumerable time series analyses of the consumption function, none that we know of has introduced any version of the rate of interest as an explanatory variable. Further, the very concept of a consumption function, especially in its original Keynesian form, is a denial of a purely competitive theory, for it relates consumption to current income rather than to wealth in any form; indeed, the explanatory power of the consumption function for business cycles (and for employment policy) depends on its sensitivity to current income. More modern analysis, particularly the vital investigations of Modigliani and Brumberg (1954) and Friedman (1957), have placed greater emphasis on some kind of lifetime average of income, a concept more closely related to wealth. But when Friedman makes explicit use of time series analysis, "permanent income" turns out to be an average of about three or four years' previous income (with adjustment for trends in income) (see Friedman 1957, pp. 142–52, especially p. 150).

In any case, the evidence from time series data of aggregate consumption and income does not cast much light on the way individuals allocate their resources over time. The perfectly competitive hypothesis would imply that two individuals with the same wealth (human and material) would consume the same amount at a given age regardless of the way income is distributed over one's lifetime. More strongly, if we assume that the utility function for consumption does not vary with age, then consumption should be either steadily increasing or steadily decreasing as a function of time (see Yaari 1964*a*, p. 309). Casual observation suggests that neither of these statements is valid, at least for individuals whose primary wealth is derived from wages and salaries; on the contrary, consumption profiles over time bear a distinct relation to income profiles. Medical students with high expected incomes do not typically live as well as they will when in practice, though the perfectly competitive hypothesis would imply that they could borrow for current consumption against their future incomes.

The inapplicability of the perfectly competitive hypothesis is also suggested by the variety of interest rates facing the individual. He may receive 4 or 5 per cent in time deposits and government bonds, and perhaps double (after taxes) by investing in stocks; but he may have to pay 30 per cent or more for personal finance or consumer credit. We may also compare these rates with some computed in various indirect fashions. Certain writers on the consumption function have attempted to infer the rate of interest implicit in their estimates. Hamburger (1955, p. 10) found a rate of 16-2/3 per cent for discounting future wages and salaries, which he attributes to "interest, uncertainty discount, and the effect of the illiquidity of human wealth." Friedman has, by different methods, found the even higher rate of 33-1/3 per cent (1963, p. 23). Perhaps even more relevant are the rates of return on investment in human capital in the form of education. For college education, Becker (1965, p. 114) finds a rate of 12 per cent, to which must be added the considerable nonpecuniary consumption benefits to the student.

There is no pretense here of a complete reanalysis of the empirical evidence on consumption and savings from the viewpoint of the perfectly competitive hypothesis. Enough has been said, one hopes, to make plausible the observation that in our real capital markets, borrowing against future earnings cannot in general be carried out at the usual rates of interest. For the theorist this does not remove the normative value of studying the behavior of the economy under the condition of perfect capital market; it does, however, mean that in order to carry out a theoretical study of optimal fiscal policy under decentralization of private decisions, one should study the problem in both perfect and imperfect capital markets.

To express the assumption of imperfect capital markets in a simple manner, one can follow the simple Keynesian assumption in the form Harrod and others have applied to growth theory; namely, to make consumption simply proportional to disposable income. In the chapters to follow we shall examine two basic models of market behavior: imperfect capital markets, expressed by the fact that consumers choose a constant savings ratio; and perfect capital markets, where the consumer's choice between consumption and savings is determined by an intertemporal optimization in which decisions are sensitive to market prices and public instruments. The optimization problem under the assumption of perfect capital markets gives rise to "incentive effects." The problem arises because various taxes influence market prices and the consumer's optimization, thus leading to a reaction by the consumer to changes in the values of the instruments employed. We thus consider next the various instruments which will be employed and our conceptual approach to the problem.

## 3. Controllability by Public Instruments

We shall consider in this work six types of public instruments: (a) a single income tax, its rate denoted by $x(t)$, to be imposed on private incomes; (b) a tax on consumption, its rate denoted by $x_c(t)$, to be imposed on planned consumption; (c) a tax on savings, its rate denoted by $x_s(t)$, to be imposed on planned savings; (d) a tax on wages, its rate denoted by $x_w(t)$; (e) a tax on interest income, its rate denoted by $x_r(t)$;

(f) national borrowing, denoted by $\dot{D}(t)$, which is the net change in the national debt $D(t)$.

These instruments will be utilized by the public authorities in order to try to direct the economy towards its optimal path. This notion by itself raises an immediate question: Which path are we aiming for? We will regard *the publicly optimal path* to be the one characterized in chapter IV where the objective function is understood to be the *public* objective function. Then the question arises: What will guarantee that the public sector can steer the economy to that optimal path?

Actually, the theory to be developed will be more general. Though the primary aim of this whole study is the achievement of publicly optimal paths, the theory will give conditions on the range of instruments available under which the government can achieve almost any given desired and feasible allocation.

This leads to the notion of controllability.

DEFINITION 1. *A policy is said to be controllable by a given set of instruments if there exist values of the instruments, varying over time in general, which cause the private and government sectors together to realize that policy.*

*Remark.* The controllability of a policy with respect to a given set of instruments may depend on the exact values of the parameters of the economic system (e.g., a given policy may be controllable for one production function but not for another) or of the initial conditions (e.g., controllability may depend on the initial capital stocks or on the initial level of government debt).

In general, in the development of the theory of controllability we shall use some general asymptotic and boundedness assumptions on the policies to be controlled but make relatively less use of the precise nature of optimal paths when we aim for them. In this sense, the theory of controllability developed below is more general than the analysis, which will use the explicit properties of the optimal path.

Upon reflection it is clear that for any economy one can always find sufficient instruments which will make it controllable. Moreover, if we allow some instruments to be completely unrestricted in their values, then it is always possible to introduce such instruments, which can expropriate all private capital and transfer it into public hands. We do not have an explicit theory of the political and economic cost of any given instrument, but both the instruments and variations in them involve real cost and are politically difficult to accomplish. This is particularly true of a world of uncertainty where changes in the values of the instruments lead to changes in the structure of private anticipations and may disrupt the smooth functioning of the economic system. So it is clear that instruments which change little and continuously are less costly than and politically superior to instruments which fluctuate widely over time and may even move discontinuously. Without being prepared to incorporate explicit costs of instrument changes in our formal model, we would regard it as desirable to reduce the number of instruments and to narrow down the range of each of them. Thus, the theory of controllability aims at the examination of every system of instruments in order to establish whether a given set is too small, unnecessarily extensive, or unstable in its behavior over time.

To give more precise meaning to the "stability" property mentioned above, we note first that the values of the instruments change with the changing conditions of the economy. It may be that the economy is controllable only by values of the instruments which behave in an extreme fashion. This may arise in a controllable economy where the tax rates or the ratio of debt to national income tends to $\pm\infty$. Thus we introduce the notion of "stability of public instruments":

DEFINITION 2. *A policy is said to be controllable with stable instruments if the policy is controllable, the values of the tax rates that achieve control converge to finite values, and the value of the ratio of debt to national income* $(D/Y)$ *also converges to a finite value.*

In a completely formulated model we would not be interested in stability of instruments but only in controllability of policy. But if we do not have a proper theory of the constraints on public instruments, we can develop the theory of controllability for the unconstrained case and then examine the stability properties of the instruments. An unstable set of instruments may lead to a required policy that is politically or economically unacceptable for reasons outside the model. Thus, an unstable system usually becomes uncontrollable at ranges of the instruments that are not necessarily known to us in advance.

The theory of controllability aims at answering the question of whether the target policy is attainable, while the theory of the stability of public instruments aims at understanding the dynamic properties of the instruments after having established the controllability of the policy.

## 4. Second-Best Policy

A serious problem arises when the publicly optimal or some other specified policy is not controllable by a given set of public instruments. By comparing alternative fiscal systems one can always find additional instruments that will make the target policy controllable; indeed there are usually a great many alternative ways of expanding the fiscal system in order to achieve controllability.

An alternative approach to uncontrollable policies is to regard the public sector as operating under constraints that prevent attainment of the publicly optimal policy of chapter IV. Note that here we specify the target policy not by general boundedness conditions but rather by specification of the policy resulting from the optimization problem of chapter IV. Thus, when specific public instruments are introduced and are insufficient to control the optimal policy of chapter IV, a "second-best" policy is followed, which is the best that can be achieved with the given set of instruments. This means that the analysis of the noncontrollable cases is in essence a dynamic theory of second best. [Meade's corresponding static theory of the "second best" (1955, vol. 2, chapter VI) is identical with Tinbergen's theory of economic policy (1952) when the instruments are insufficient.]

It is clear that failure to control the optimal policy can result either from failure to allocate capital optimally between public and private uses or from failure to allocate optimally the available output between consumption and investment. The first kind of misallocation is familiar from the static theory of second best. It leads to the existence of different shadow prices for public and private capital, and the difference between these two prices is a measure of the deviation of the second-best solution from the optimal policy. Similarly, when the second-best solution leads to a nonoptimal allocation between consumption and investment, the shadow prices of investment and consumption differ from each other.

The derivation of a second-best policy uses the standard Pontryagin techniques of chapter II. However, unlike the situation in chapters III and IV, the number of state variables exceeds one and graphic analysis of the dynamics is no longer possible. It is conjectured that the optimal solutions do exhibit stable behavior in that the state variables converge to asymptotic values. As in the case where publicly optimal policies are controllable, the question of whether the dynamic behavior of the instruments is stable or explosive remains to be investigated.

## 5. The Accounting Identities of Resource Allocation and Public Policy

We turn now to the formulation of the basic equations relating the formation of private and government capital to consumption and the public instruments—borrowing and taxes.

The basic assumption is made throughout that the individual is indifferent between holding private capital and holding government debt at the same rate of return. Hence, from the private point of view, we are interested in the total material assets held by an individual; but, from the viewpoint of the general equilibrium, material assets equal the sum of private capital and government debt. In what follows, let

$A^M(t)$ = private sector's stock of material assets,
$r(t)$ = rate of return on material assets,
$D(t)$ = government debt,
$W(t)$ = income of the private sector from sources other than interest on material assets.

Then,

$$A^M(t) = K_p(t) + D(t), \tag{1}$$

and the equality of returns on the two forms of material assets can be written

$$f_p = r(t), \tag{2}$$

where $f_p$ is, as in chapter IV, the marginal productivity of private capital.

The possibility that either $A^M$ or $D$ may be negative at some point of time is not excluded. In seeking an optimum consumption stream, an individual may well borrow in anticipation of wages or other exogenous income, and the government may be a net creditor of the economy.

With this notation, the individual's total income in the absence of taxes would be

$$r(t)A^M(t) + W(t). \tag{3}$$

For clarity, it is important to discuss the nature of the income denoted by $W(t)$. The definition depends on which of our two models of production is being considered and—a point not discussed before—the extent to which the return to government capital is appropriated by the government.

In any case, output is a function, $F(K_p, K_g, L)$, of private capital, government capital, and labor. In the first case (see sections IV.1 and IV.2), we assume that $F$ is a function homogeneous of degree one in all the variables. Then, in the usual way, the total output can be decomposed into the imputed shares of private capital, $F_pK_p$; government capital, $F_gK_g$; and labor, $F_LL$. Since private capital is owned by private individuals, the share of private capital is included in the return to material assets, along with interest on the government debt. The share of labor is also received by private individuals, and forms part of $W(t)$.

With regard to the imputed share of government capital, there are two extreme possibilities. One is that the government prices the services of its capital goods so as to recover its full share. The other is that the government supplies the services of its capital free of charge. In the latter case, we assume that private individuals have some way of appropriating these benefits and converting them into rents. Thus, a highway may be operated at no price, but use of it requires adjacent privately owned land, which thereby acquires a scarcity value yielding a rent on the open market. If the government receives the imputed share of its capital, then $W(t)$ consists only of wage income. If, on the contrary, the government supplies its services free of charge, then $W(t)$ is taken to include both wages and rents and therefore equals the sum of the shares of labor and government capital.

More generally, the government may appropriate some but not all of the marginal productivity of government capital. Thus, a service such as police or defense may be supplied free; but still the government has the option of substituting capital for labor in the production of these services, and any resulting cost savings are realized by the government. Let $r_g$ = rental charged on government capital. Since the marginal productivity of private capital, $f_p$, is also its rental, we define $W$ as the difference between total output and the rental payments on the two kinds of capital:

$$Y = f_p K_p + r_g K_g + W \,, \tag{4}$$

where $Y$ is total output and $W(t)$ is the sum of wages and that portion of the imputed government share that is not appropriated by the government.

The alternative assumption (see section IV.8) about the production function is that it displays increasing returns to all variables. In this case it is impossible that the returns to government capital are fully appropriated; $r_g < f_g$. Equation (4) again holds; this time $W$ falls short of the sum of the imputed shares of labor and government capital, though it at least equals labor's share.

Under either of these alternatives we shall always assume that $W(t) \geqq 0$, but for large enough $\bar{t}$, $W(t) > 0$, $t > \bar{t}$. Thus, the economy may be in an initial state of oversupply of labor, but in finite time $W(t)$ becomes positive and stays so.

Since the total income of the individual in the absence of taxes is given by (3), this is the amount available for allocation between consumption and the acquisition of more material assets.

$$\dot{A}^M = r(t) A^M + W(t) - C(t) \,. \tag{5}$$

For any given consumption policy, (5) defines the evolution of $A^M$, since $A^M(0)$ is given.

We now introduce taxes; primarily, we consider taxes on consumption and savings. Let $x_c$ and $x_s$ be the tax rates on *expenditures* on consumption and savings, respectively; in general, both may be functions of time. Thus, if $C_E$ is the expenditure on consumption, actual consumption becomes $C = (1 - x_c)C_E$, or

$$C_E = C/(1 - x_c). \tag{6}$$

This is a somewhat unconventional way of representing consumption taxes. A more standard approach would be to assume a specific tax on real consumption; if the tax rate were $\bar{x}_c$, say, then $C_E = (1 + \bar{x}_c)C$. The two descriptions of consumption taxes are completely equivalent, with $1 + \bar{x}_c = 1/(1 - x_c)$. The convention used here permits slightly simpler formulas in the sequel. In particular, note that an income tax can be identified with the special case, $x_s = x_c = x$.

From (3) and (6), the volume of resources available for saving (accumulation of material assets) is

$$rA^M + W - [C/(1 - x_c)].$$

However, because of the tax on saving,

$$\dot{A}^M = (1 - x_s)\{rA^M + W - [C/(1 - x_c)]\}.$$

To lighten the notation, introduce the following *tax parameters*, any of which may vary in time:

$$z_s = 1 - x_s, \qquad z_c = 1 - x_c, \qquad v = z_s/z_c. \tag{7}$$

Then, with taxes on consumption and saving, the accumulation of material assets is governed by the equation:

$$\dot{A}^M = z_s rA^M + z_s W - vC. \tag{8}$$

For generality, we also consider an alternative possibility for taxes; namely, differing tax rates on wages and interest. Let $x_w$, $x_r$ be the respective rates, and

$$z_w = 1 - x_w, \qquad z_r = 1 - x_r. \tag{9}$$

Then the accumulation equation is

$$\dot{A}^M = z_r rA^M + z_w W - C. \tag{10}$$

Finally, we can consider all four taxes simultaneously. For convenience, let $z_{ab} = z_a z_b$, where $a$ and $b$ can be any of the subscripts $c$, $s$, $w$, $r$,

$$A^M = z_{sr} rA^M + z_{sw} W - vC. \tag{11}$$

The four tax rates give rise to only three independent combinations; to illustrate, a pure income tax can be represented either by an equal tax on savings and consumption, with no tax on wages or interest, or by an equal tax on wages and interest, with no tax on savings and consumption.

From (1), we can rewrite (11) to bring out the dependence of private capital formation on public instruments and on consumption:

$$\dot{K}_p = z_{sr}r(K_p + D) + z_{sw}W - vC - \dot{D}. \tag{12}$$

For future reference, these identities will be collected into the following proposition.

Proposition 1. *Let $r_g$ = the rental price of government capital; $W$ = total noninterest income of the private sector; $A^M$ = total material assets held by the private sector; and $D$ = government debt. Then, $W$ and $A^M$ are defined by the following equations:*

(a) $$Y = f_pK_p + r_gK_g + W,$$

*and*

(b) $$A^M = K_p + D.$$

*Let $x_c$, $x_s$, $x_r$, and $x_w$ be the tax rates (possibly negative) on consumption expenditures, savings expenditures, interest income, and noninterest income, respectively. For any subscript a—which may be c, s, r, or w—let $z_a = 1 - x_a$; for any pair of subscripts, a, b, among these four, let $z_{ab} = z_a z_b$. Let $v = z_s/z_c$, and let r be the rate of return for material assets. Then the accumulation of the private sector satisfies the condition*

(c) $$\dot{A}^M = z_{sr}rA^M + z_{sw}W - vC.$$

*The indifference of the private sector between the two forms of material assets implies*

(d) $$r = f_p.$$

Suppose the government has, on one criterion or another, designated a feasible allocation policy which it desires to see established. Suppose further that it can, through its choice of instruments, cause the private sector to choose the consumption part of this policy, $C(t)$. Then, if the government engages in government investment in accordance with the desired policy, it follows from Walras's Law that the demand for material assets by the private sector will exactly equal the sum of the debt needed by the government to carry out its investment policy and the amount of private capital which the government desires to be held. To see this, let $X$ represent tax collections, plus payments to the government for the rental of government capital, less interest on the public debt. Then private disposable income is $Y - X$, where $Y$ is total national income. The private sector allocates its disposable income between consumption and accumulation of material assets: $Y - X = C + \dot{A}^M$. On the other hand, the government has to borrow (increase its debt) by the difference between its desired program of public capital formation and $X$; $\dot{D} = \dot{K}_g - X$. Finally, feasibility for the desired program means that $Y = C + \dot{K}_p + \dot{K}_g$. From these budget and feasibility conditions, we deduce immediately that $\dot{A}^M = \dot{K}_p + \dot{D}$; i.e., private savings will automatically just balance the needs for private capital formation and government borrowing. Since Proposition 1(b) holds at $t = 0$, integration of the last result shows that it holds for all $t$ as an identity.

PROPOSITION 2. *Let $C(t)$, $K_p(t)$, and $K_g(t)$ together constitute a desired allocation policy. If the government by its choice of instruments can induce the private sector to choose $C(t)$ as its desired policy, then the policy is controllable.*

In the following chapters we will consider various combinations of the instruments discussed here. Each combination of public instruments is viewed as a fiscal system. In chapters VI and VIII, different models of the choice behavior of consumers are used to examine the degree to which the government can induce the private sector to choose its desired consumption policy. In effect, the public sector has two targets: (a) the achievement of a given total amount of savings; (b) the attainment of a given allocation of capital between the two sectors. Thus, following Tinbergen's suggestion, we should expect to control the economy with two instruments. We shall study this proposition extensively in chapters VI and VIII. One should note, however, that it is not possible in general to identify any instrument with a target since the natural economic interdependence makes all variables, including the optimal values of the instruments, depend upon all other variables.

# VI

# OPTIMAL POLICY AND CONTROLLABILITY WITH IMPERFECT CAPITAL MARKETS

## 0. Introduction

In chapter V, we distinguished between perfect and imperfect capital markets. This chapter is devoted to an examination of the determination and controllability of optimal policy when the capital market is assumed to be imperfect, in the specific sense that the ratio of private savings to private disposable income is a constant.

We shall consider alternative assumptions on the range of public instruments available. If there is a sufficient number of these instruments and if they are powerful enough, the publicly optimal policy (as studied in chapter IV) and, indeed, virtually any feasible policy, is controllable, in general with stable instruments. If the public instruments are few and ineffective, then the publicly optimal policy is not controllable, and analytic interest shifts to the determination of the second-best optimal policy (see section V.4) and to the stability of the instruments needed to achieve it.

In most of this chapter, it is assumed that the services of government capital are completely inappropriable; no charge can be made for them. In section 9, it is shown that the previous results are not qualitatively changed by the introduction of some charge by the government for the use of its capital.

## 1. The General Framework of Fixed-Savings-Ratio Models

It is assumed that both the utility functional for choosing among allocation policies and the production conditions are as described in chapter IV. We considered there two possible assumptions about production: constant returns in section IV.2 and increasing returns in section IV.8.

A natural rate of growth, $\gamma$, was associated with each model [see IV.2.(4) and IV.8.(2), respectively] and it was then useful to normalize all the magnitudes on growth by multiplication by $e^{-\gamma t}$. Then the aim of the economy, according to the analysis in those two sections, is the maximization of

$$\int_0^{\infty} e^{-\lambda t} U[c(t), k_g(t)] dt, \tag{1}$$

and the total output is

$$y = f(k_p, k_g), \tag{2}$$

where $f$ is strictly concave. Here, $y$, $k_p$, $k_g$ are total output ($Y$), total private capital ($K_p$), and total government capital ($K_g$) normalized for growth, and $c$ is total consumption normalized for growth.

To complete the model, it is necessary to specify the relations that govern the allocation of total output among consumption, private capital formation, and government capital formation. These relations are determined partly by private savings behavior, which is a datum to the government, and partly by the choice of government instruments: taxes and borrowing. The exact nature of these relations is different in each of the models studied, but in general they take the following form. Given total output, $Y$, and government debt, say $D$, a quantity of *personal income* is defined:

$$Y_p = Y + \text{interest on government debt}. \tag{3}$$

Given $Y_p$, taxes, and the savings behavior of the private sector, it is possible to define personal savings, $S_p$; consumption, $C$; and total tax collections, $X^*$. Personal savings are allocated between private capital formation and government borrowing, $B$, so that

$$\dot{D} = B, \tag{4}$$

and

$$\dot{K}_p + B = S_p. \tag{5}$$

Finally, the budget constraint for the government is written,

$$\dot{K}_g = B + X^* - \text{interest on government debt}. \tag{6}$$

From V.5.(2), interest on government debt is $f_p D$. Normalize all variables on growth; in particular, introduce the new definitions,

$$s_p = S_p e^{-\gamma t}, \qquad d = De^{-\gamma t}, \qquad b = Be^{-\gamma t}, \qquad x^* = X^* e^{-\gamma t}. \tag{7}$$

Then (4)–(6) and (3) can be written

$$\dot{d} = b - \gamma d, \tag{8}$$

$$k_p = s_p - b - \gamma k_p, \tag{9}$$

$$k_g = x^* + b - f_p d - \gamma k_g, \tag{10}$$

$$y_p = y + f_p d. \tag{11}$$

The models presented in subsequent sections differ according to the restrictions placed on borrowing (in models that insist on a balanced budget, $b$ must be zero) and the types of taxes which determine $x^*$. The policy problem is the optimization of (1), subject to the conditions (2) and (8)–(11), with respect to the allowable borrowing and tax instruments; the time path for $d$ implied by (8) is then studied for possible instability. The first step in the analysis is to test the model for controllability of the publicly optimal policy; in practice, this is done by testing for controllability of any arbitrary feasible policy. If the instruments are sufficient for controllability, then their stability, and that of $d$, is tested. If the instruments are insufficient for controllability, then a second-best optimum (see section V.4) is determined and the stability of taxes and debt along this path studied.

## 2. Financing by Income Tax Alone: Controllability

A model that is especially interesting because it roughly reflects actual practice is one in which the financing of government investment is accomplished through the income tax alone. Borrowing, at least in peacetime, is relatively small compared with the total budget, and is primarily motivated by considerations of employment, rather than allocation, policy. This model has been studied by Eckstein (1958, pp. 94–104) and subsequently by Steiner (1959) and Marglin (1963*c*). Some of the present analysis was earlier presented by Arrow (1966, section 4).

In this case, in the notation of section 1, $b = 0$. For simplicity of exposition, assume $d = 0$ (absence of debt); this is a minor assumption because, with $b = 0$, it follows from 1.(8) that $d$ decays exponentially to zero.

Let $x$ be the rate of income tax, $z = 1 - x$. (Note the difference between $x$, the tax *rate*, and $x^*$, *total* taxes normalized for growth.) Then $X^* = xY$, $x^* = xy$. In this case, the hypothesis of a fixed savings ratio implies that, for some fixed $s (0 < s < 1)$, private savings is a fixed fraction of disposable income,

$$y_d = zy, \tag{1}$$

and consumption the remainder.

$$s_p = s y_d, \tag{2}$$

$$c = (1 - s) y_d. \tag{3}$$

If (2), (3), and the assumptions $b = d = 0$ are substituted into 1.(9)–(10), then the optimal policy is that which maximizes 1.(1),

$$\int_0^\infty e^{-\lambda t} U[c(t), k_g(t)] dt, \tag{4}$$

subject to the constraints

$$\dot{k}_p = s y_d - \gamma k_p, \tag{5}$$

$$\dot{k}_g = x y - \gamma k_g, \tag{6}$$

where, by 1.(2),

$$y = f(k_p, k_g). \tag{7}$$

First, we observe that the publicly optimal policy is not controllable except by chance. For, from (2), (3), and (5), we find

$$(\dot{k}_p + \gamma k_p)/c = s/(1 - s). \tag{8}$$

The right-hand side is a constant; from Proposition IV.2 or IV.3, $k_p$ and $c$ approach definite limits; further, since $k_p$ is a component of the solution of a system of autonomous differential equations, it follows by a well-known theorem on differential equations (see, for example, Bellman 1953, chapter 4, Lemma 1, p. 77) that $\dot{k}_p$ approaches zero if the variables of the system approach a limit. Hence,

$$\gamma k_p^\infty / c^\infty = s/(1 - s),$$

an equation which will be valid for only one possible value of $s$.

The argument did not make any use of the special properties of the publicly optimal policy other than that $k_p$ and $c$ converged to limits and $\dot{k}_p$ to zero. Indeed, more generally, the statement that the left-hand side of (8) is constant at any value, and certainly that it is constant at a prescribed value, is a condition of possible allocation policies that would hold only by chance.

PROPOSITION 1. *If private savings are a fixed proportion of disposable income and the government balances its budget and imposes only an income tax, then neither the publicly optimal policy nor any other given feasible allocation policy is controllable in general.*

## 3. Financing by Income Tax Alone: General Analysis of the Second-Best Policy

We now turn to the determination of the second-best policy. The current-value Hamiltonian is

$$H = U(c, k_g) + p_p(s y_d - \gamma k_p) + p_g(x y - \gamma k_g), \tag{1}$$

where $p_p$ and $p_g$ are the auxiliary variables corresponding to the transition equations, 2.(5) and 2.(6) respectively, and $c$ is understood to be defined by 2.(3). From 2.(1) and 2.(7), it will immediately be seen that

$$\partial y_d/\partial x = -y, \qquad \partial y_d/\partial k_p = zf_p, \qquad \partial y_d/\partial k_g = zf_g. \tag{2}$$

Let

$$\phi(y_d, k_g, p_p) = U(c, k_g) + p_p s y_d, \tag{3}$$

$$q = \partial\phi/\partial y_d = U_c(1 - s) + p_p s. \tag{4}$$

We can interpret $p_p$ and $p_g$ as the shadow prices (in terms of utility) of private and government savings, respectively, while $U_c$ is necessarily the shadow price of consumption. Since disposable income is allocated between consumption and private investment in the proportions $1 - s$, $s$, respectively, it is natural to interpret $q$ as the *shadow price of disposable income.*

Also observe that

$$\partial\phi/\partial k_g = U_g. \tag{5}$$

From (3), (1) can be rewritten

$$H = \phi(y_d, k_g, p_p) + p_g xy - \gamma(p_p k_p + p_g k_g). \tag{6}$$

The sole instrument, $x$, the rate of income tax, is so chosen as to maximize $H$.

$$\partial H/\partial x = (\partial\phi/\partial y_d)(\partial y_d/\partial x) + p_g y = (p_g - q)y,$$

from (2) and (4). The choice of $x$ is constrained only by the condition that consumption, $c$, be nonnegative; from 2.(3) and 2.(1), this means that $x \leqq 1$; i.e., that the income tax rate not exceed 100 per cent. Then $x = 1$ is optimal only if $\partial H/\partial x \geqq 0$ there; but for $x = 1$, $c = 0$, so that $U_c(0, k_g) = +\infty$, by assumption IV.4.A.5, and then $q = +\infty$ and $\partial H/\partial x = -\infty$, a contradiction.

If we assume for the time being that $H$ is maximized at a finite value of $x$, we can conclude that

$$p_g = q, \tag{7}$$

$$x < 1. \tag{8}$$

From (4), 2.(3), and 2.(1), (7) can be written more explicitly

$$(1 - s)U_c[(1 - s)(1 - x)f(k_p, k_g), k_g] = p_g - sp_p. \tag{9}$$

Since $U$ is concave, $U_c$ is decreasing in $c$ and therefore increasing in $x$, so that (9) has a unique solution for $x$ as a function of $k_p$, $k_g$, $p_p$, and $p_g$. The concavity of $U$ also ensures that the chosen value of $x$ indeed maximizes $H$.

The differential equations which govern the movement of the auxiliary variables are, from Proposition II.7(e),

$$\dot{p}_p = \lambda p_p - (\partial H/\partial k_p), \qquad \dot{p}_g = \lambda p_g - (\partial H/\partial k_g).$$

From (6), (4), (2), and (5),

$$\partial H/\partial k_p = (qz + p_g x) f_p - \gamma p_p,$$

$$\partial H/\partial k_g = (qz + p_g x) f_g + U_g - \gamma p_g.$$

But from (7), $qz + p_g x = p_g(z + x) = p_g$. Recall that $\omega = \lambda + \gamma$; then

$$\dot{p}_p = \omega p_p - p_g f_p, \tag{10}$$

$$\dot{p}_g = \omega p_g - p_g f_g - U_g. \tag{11}$$

The movement along the optimal path is governed by the differential equations for the state variables 2.(5) and 2.(6) and those for the auxiliary variables, (10) and (11), with the instrument (the income tax rate, $x$) being determined by (9). From chapter II, these conditions are necessary for optimality (second-best optimality in this case). It is sufficient for optimality that the path satisfy these equations for a set of initial values of the auxiliary variables, $p_p(0)$, $p_g(0)$, so chosen that the state and auxiliary variables converge to a stationary solution, provided also that $H^0 = \max_x H$, is concave in the state variables, $k_p$, $k_g$, for given values of $p_p$, $p_g$ (see Proposition II.10). To see that this last condition is satisfied, it is convenient to take the instrument to be $x^* = xy$, rather than $x$ itself; since $y$ is a function of the state variables, there is a unique correspondence between $x^*$ and $x$ for any fixed values of the state and auxiliary variables. The constraint that $c \geqq 0$, and therefore $x \leqq 1$, is now written $x^* \leqq y$. The current-value Hamiltonian is

$$H(k_p, k_g, p_p, p_g, x^*) = U(c, k_g) + p_p[s(y - x^*) - \gamma k_p] + p_g(x^* - \gamma k_g),$$

where

$$c = (1 - s)(y - x^*), \qquad y = f(k_p, k_g).$$

Since $U$ and $f$ are concave functions, it follows easily that $H$ is a concave function of the three variables $k_p$, $k_g$, $x^*$, for fixed values of the auxiliary variables. Since

$$H^0(k_p, k_g, p_p, p_g) = \max_{x^*} H(k_p, k_g, p_p, p_g, x^*),$$

it can be easily seen that $H^0$ is concave in the state variables as was to be proved.

## 4. Financing by Income Tax Alone: Balanced Growth

A stationary solution is found by setting $\dot{k}_p$, $\dot{k}_g$, $\dot{p}_p$, and $\dot{p}_g$ equal to 0 in 2.(5), 2.(6), 3.(10), and 3.(11), respectively, and then using the maximum principle, 3.(9), and the definitions 2.(3), 2.(1), and 1.(2). As usual, the stationary values of the instruments and state variables are distinguished by the superscript $^\infty$.

$$s(1 - x^\infty) y^\infty = \gamma k_p^\infty, \tag{1}$$

$$x^\infty y^\infty = \gamma k_g^\infty, \tag{2}$$

$$f_p^\infty = (p_p^\infty / p_g^\infty) \omega, \tag{3}$$

$$f_g^\infty = \omega - (U_g^\infty / p_g^\infty), \tag{4}$$

$$(1 - s) U_c^\infty = p_g^\infty - s p_p^\infty, \tag{5}$$

$$c^\infty = (1-s)(1 - x^\infty) y^\infty, \tag{6}$$

$$y^\infty = f(k_p^\infty, k_g^\infty). \tag{7}$$

Eliminating $x^\infty$ between (1) and (2) and substituting for $y^\infty$ from (7) yields

$$s f(k_p^\infty, k_g^\infty) = \gamma(k_p^\infty + s k_g^\infty), \tag{8}$$

which is the analog of the Harrod-Domar relation in this model. As will be discussed in more detail below, the magnitude $k_p + s k_g$ is the amount to which private capital would be raised if the government were to liquidate all its capital and turn the proceeds over to the private sector.

A detailed discussion of the stationary solution will be given for the special case where government capital does not enter the utility function, $U_g = 0$ for all $k_p$ and $k_g$. In particular, $U_g^\infty = 0$, and (4) simplifies to

$$f_g^\infty = \omega. \tag{9}$$

Equations (8) and (9) involve only $k_p^\infty$ and $k_g^\infty$. Note that any solution to them uniquely defines a stationary solution. This is so because $y^\infty$ is defined by (7) and then $x^\infty$ is defined by either (1) or (2), the other being automatically satisfied by (8). Then $c^\infty$ is defined by (6), and thereby $U_c^\infty$, so that $p_p^\infty$ and $p_g^\infty$ are then defined by (3) and (5). As in the Ramsey model, the stationary point is completely determined by technology if $U_g = 0$.

Thus, the existence and uniqueness of the stationary solution are determined by the existence and uniqueness of the solution to (8) and (9). We shall first present some conditions to ensure the existence of a stationary solution.

PROPOSITION 2. *Suppose that private savings constitute a fixed proportion of disposable income and that the government balances its budget and imposes only an income tax. Suppose further that $U_g$ is identically zero and that the production function, $f(k_p, k_g)$, is strictly concave and differentiable and satisfies the following conditions:*

(a) $f_g(k_p, 0) = \infty$, $f_g(k_p, \infty) = 0$ *for all* $k_p > 0$;

(b) $f(k_p, k_g)/(k_p + k_g)$ *can be made arbitrarily small for* $k_p + k_g$ *large;*

(c) *one of the following conditions holds: (1)* $f_p(0, 0) > \gamma/s$; *(2) if* $k_p$ *approaches* 0 *and* $(k_p, k_g)$ *vary along the curve* $f_g = \omega$, *then* $k_p/k_g$ *approaches* 0; *(3)* $f_g(0, k_g) = \omega$, *some* $k_g > 0$.

*Then there exists a positive stationary solution, defined by (1)–(7), to the dynamic system describing the second-best policy.*

*Remark.* Conditions (a) and (b) have already been used in chapter IV; see Proposition IV.2(b)–(c) or conditions IV.4.A.6, IV.4.A.7.

*Proof:* Define $k_g^*(k_p)$ as the solution of the equation

$$f_g[k_p, k_g^*(k_p)] = \omega. \tag{10}$$

From (a), such a solution exists; from the strict concavity of $f$, $f_g$ is strictly decreasing in $k_g$ for fixed $k_p$, so that $k_g^*(k_p)$ is uniquely defined for $k_p > 0$.

The solution of (8)–(9) is equivalent to a solution in $k_p$ for the equation

$$sf[k_p, k_g^*(k_p)] = \gamma[k_p + sk_g^*(k_p)]. \tag{11}$$

Since $k_g^*(k_p) \geqq 0$, $k_p + k_g^*(k_p)$ is large if $k_p$ is large. From (b), $sf[k_p, k_g^*(k_p)] < \gamma s[k_p + k_g^*(k_p)] < \gamma[k_p + sk_g^*(k_p)]$ for all $k_p$ sufficiently large. To find a solution for (11), it then suffices to show that

$$sf[k_p, k_g^*(k_p)] > \gamma[k_p + sk_g^*(k_p)] \text{ for some } k_p. \tag{12}$$

Since $f$ is concave, we have the well-known inequality

$$f(0, 0) - f[k_p, k_g^*(k_p)] \leqq f_p[k_p, k_g^*(k_p)](0 - k_p) + f_g[k_p, k_g^*(k_p)][0 - k_g^*(k_p)],$$

or, since $f(0, 0) \geqq 0$ and $f_g[k_p, k_g^*(k_p)] = \omega$ by (10),

$$f[k_p, k_g^*(k_p)] \geqq f_p k_p + \omega k_g^*(k_p).$$

Then it is sufficient for (12) to hold that

$$s(\omega - \gamma)k_g^*(k_p) \geqq (\gamma - sf_p)k_p,$$

or

$$s(\omega - \gamma) \geqq (\gamma - sf_p)[k_p/k_g^*(k_p)].$$

Since $s > 0$ and $\omega > \gamma$, the left-hand side is positive, so that a sufficient condition for (12) is that

$$\limsup_{k_p \to 0}(\gamma - sf_p)[k_p/k_g^*(k_p)] \leqq 0. \tag{13}$$

We now divide the proof according to which of the assumptions under (c) holds.

- Suppose that (c)(1) holds. To start with, suppose in addition that, as $k_p$ approaches zero, $k_g^*(k_p)$ has a nonzero limit point, say, $k_g^0$. Then, by (10) and the continuity of $f_g$, $f_g(0, k_g^0) = \omega$, and the problem is reduced to case (3). Hence, suppose that $k_g^*(k_p)$ approaches zero.

Since $f$ is concave, $f_p$ is decreasing; particularly for any $h > 0$,

$$f_p[k_p + \theta h, k_g^*(k_p)] \leqq f_p[k_p, k_g^*(k_p)], \qquad 0 \leqq \theta \leqq 1,$$

and, by integration,

$$f[k_p + h, k_g^*(k_p)] - f[k_p, k_g^*(k_p)] \leqq f_p[k_p, k_g^*(k_p)]h.$$

For fixed $h$, let $k_p$ approach 0;

$$f(h, 0) - f(0, 0) \leqq h \liminf_{k_p \to 0} f_p[k_p, k_g^*(k_p)].$$

Divide through by $h$ and let $h$ approach 0.

$$\liminf_{k_p \to 0} f_p[k_p, k_g^*(k_p)] \geqq f_p(0, 0) > \gamma/s,$$

by (c)(1). Then (13) certainly holds if $k_p$ is sufficiently small.

- Now suppose (c)(2) holds. Since $f_p \geqq 0$, $\gamma - sf_p \leqq \gamma$, and

$$(\gamma - sf_p)[k_p/k_g^*(k_p)] \leqq \gamma[k_p/k_g^*(k_p)] \to 0,$$

by (c)(2).

- If (c)(3) holds, then $k_g^*(0)$ is defined and positive, so that certainly $k_p/k_g^*(k_p)$ approaches 0 as $k_p$ approaches 0, and (c)(2) holds.

It is useful to show, by a counterexample, that existence need not hold if conditions like (c) are not imposed. Let the production function be

$$f(k_p, k_g) = (1 + k_p^{-1/2} k_g^{-1/2})^{-1}.$$

Then, by straightforward calculations, it can be shown that, if $s$ is chosen sufficiently small,

$$sf[k_p, k_g^*(k_p)] < \gamma[k_p + sk_g^*(k_p)] \text{ for all } k_p > 0,$$

so that (11) never holds.

We have no corresponding theorem for uniqueness of the stationary point. It can indeed be shown that a sufficient condition for uniqueness is that $f_{gp}k_p + f_{gg}k_g < 0$ (i.e., that $f_g$ is decreasing as $k_p$ and $k_g$ increase in any fixed proportion), but this condition will not be satisfied typically if there are increasing returns.

One very interesting aspect of the stationary solution deserves to be stressed. The relation governing the rate of return on government investment, (4), has exactly the same *form* as in the publicly optimal policy studied in chapter IV [see IV.5.(3)]. This point is seen even more strongly in the special case, (9), where government capital does not enter the utility function.

PROPOSITION 3. *Suppose that private savings constitute a fixed proportion of disposable income, that the government balances its budget and imposes only an income tax, and that $U_g$ is identically zero. Then at any stationary point of the second-best policy the rate of return on government investment is simply $\omega$; i.e., the asymptotic consumption rate of interest.*

The government's choice of interest rate is, in the long run, the same as it would be if it could completely control savings; the second-best features of the solution might be said to disappear in the long run. It may be useful to give an intuitive explanation of this somewhat surprising result.

The fundamental point is that the benefits from a government investment project increase national income and therefore are partly saved. Hence, indirectly, the returns from government investment include some benefit from private investment projects. It turns out that in balanced growth this benefit exactly offsets the loss of private investment caused by the initial act of government investment.

To see this, consider first any dollar added to the disposable income of the private sector. Some of these will be consumed immediately, the rest saved. The earnings from the amount saved will again be split between savings and investment, and the process continued. In our notation, $f_p^\infty$ is the rate of return available at all times in the private sector (a constant along the path of steady growth). Then at any instant the individual earns a return of $f_p^\infty$ on his present capital, of which $sf_p^\infty$ constitutes an increase of capital. Thus, the stock of capital grows at the rate $sf_p^\infty$; at a constant rate of return, income rises at the same rate, and hence so does consumption. Under the assumption that $\omega > sf_p^\infty$, this exponential increasing stream of consumption will have a finite social value (i.e., when discounted at the consumption rate of interest), say $v$. Thus, the addition of a dollar to disposable income is equivalent to a single act of consumption of value $v$. Now consider that a government project costing a dollar, and yielding a constant perpetual income of $r$, is contemplated. The welfare loss to the private sector for the cost is $v$. In each subsequent time period, however, $r$ dollars are added to the private sector and hence yield a welfare increase of $rv$. Thus, taking account of all interactions, the rate of return of the government project to the economy is still $r$, and it should, of course, be undertaken if and only if $r \geqq \omega$. Thus, we conclude that $f_g = \omega$ along a balanced growth path.

On the other hand, it is not necessary that the rate of return on private capital should also equal $\omega$ along the balanced growth path, as it would for a publicly optimal policy. On the contrary, the two rates will necessarily differ unless the stationary solution for the second-best policy happens also to be the stationary solution of a publicly optimal policy. To see this, suppose $f_p^\infty = \omega$. From (3), $p_p^\infty = p_g^\infty$. Let $p^\infty$ be the common value. Then (5) simplifies to $U_c^\infty = p^\infty$. If we let $k^\infty = k_p^\infty + k_g^\infty$, it follows from (1), (2), and (6), that $y^\infty - c^\infty = \gamma k^\infty$. But these conditions, with (4), are precisely those that define the stationary solution of a publicly optimal policy (section IV.5).

Proposition 4. *Suppose that private savings constitute a fixed proportion of disposable income and that the government balances its budget and imposes only an income tax. Then, at a stationary point of the second-best policy, the rate of return on private capital is equal to $\omega$, the asymptotic consumption rate of interest, if and only if the capital stocks are also stationary values for a publicly optimal policy.*

The inequality between the rates of return to the two kinds of capital (in the case $U_g = 0$) is an indicator of the failure to achieve the optimum possible in a perfectly planned or perfectly competitive world. Essentially, to use Tinbergen's terminology again, there are now two targets, the rates of capital accumulation in the two sectors, and only one instrument, the tax policy.

*Remark.* If $U_g = 0$, then at a stationary point the shadow prices of private and government capital are in the same proportion as their rates of return. This can be seen from (3) and (9).

## 5. Financing by Income Tax Alone: Dynamic Analysis

In this section we shall complete the study, begun in section 3, of the movement along the second-best path. The analysis can be completed on one important point: the possibility of infinitely high subsidies (since $x$ is necessarily less than or equal to 1 to insure nonnegative consumption). The discussion is unfortunately rather technical; results are summarized in Proposition 5 at the end of the section.

The discussion here is based on the theory of optimal control when jumps in some state variables are permitted; see section II.7. The method used here seems capable of generalization. In particular, the determination of the publicly optimal policy in chapter IV could have followed the same lines; $k_p$ and $k_g$ would be treated as two state variables, and borrowing, $b$, as the instrument; with infinitely high values of $b$ meaning an upward jump in $k_g$ with an equal downward jump in $k_p$, and the reverse for infinitely low values of $b$. The results would have been the same; the approach actually used of treating $k_p$ and $k_g$ themselves as instruments was simpler in the case treated but does not generalize as well.

If we refer to the transition equations for the state variables, private and government capital, 2.(5) and 2.(6), we see that as $x$ approaches $-\infty$, $\dot{k}_g$ approaches $-\infty$ while $\dot{k}_p$ approaches $+\infty$. This mathematical process has a perfectly definite economic interpretation; it can be regarded as the instantaneous transfer of a *stock* of government capital to the private sector. We have already encountered such a possibility in the publicly optimal policy (see section IV.2, especially the remark to Proposition IV.1); in fact, since capital could, in that model, be freely transferred between the two sectors, the two state variables, $k_p$ and $k_g$, could be collapsed into one, their sum, $k = k_p + k_g$. The situation in the present model is more complicated because of the strict relation between consumption and private capital formation. In the first place, as we have already seen, the transfer can take place in only one direction. In the second place, the (infinite) increase in disposable income accompanying the infinite subsidy produces an infinitely high rate of consumption which dissipates a fraction, $1 - s$, of the capital transferred. To see this in more detail, define *available capital*, $k_a$, by

$$k_a = k_p + sk_g. \tag{1}$$

If we multiply 2.(6) by $s$ and add to 2.(5), we see, from 2.(1), that

$$\dot{k}_a = sy - \gamma k_a. \tag{2}$$

The instrument, $x$, does not appear in (2); hence, $\dot{k}_a$ cannot take on infinite values, and there can be no jump in $k_a$. Thus, any downward jump in $k_g$ implies a corresponding upward jump in $k_p$ in the ratio $s$:1.

It is then convenient for the purpose of analyzing possible jumps in the optimal policy to use $k_a$ and $k_g$ as the state variables, instead of $k_p$ and $k_g$. The range of $k_g$ for fixed $k_a$ is defined by the conditions $k_g \geqq 0$, $k_p \geqq 0$. Thus the range is $0 \leqq k_g \leqq k_a/s$. Now write

$$y = f(k_p, k_g) = f(k_a - sk_g, k_g) = g(k_a, k_g), 0 \leqq k_g \leqq k_a/s; \tag{3}$$

$g$ is a concave function of its arguments. The aim is to maximize 2.(4) subject to (2) and 2.(6). In this form, the current-value Hamiltonian is

$$H = U(c, k_g) + \bar{p}_a(sy - \gamma k_a) + \bar{p}_g(xy - \gamma k_g)$$
$$= U(c, k_g) + \bar{p}_a(sy_d - \gamma k_p) + (\bar{p}_g + s\bar{p}_a)(xy - \gamma k_g), \tag{4}$$

where $\bar{p}_a$ and $\bar{p}_g$ are the auxiliary variables for the transition equations (2) and 2.(6), respectively. Comparison of (4) with 3.(1) shows that

$$\bar{p}_a = p_p, \qquad \bar{p}_g + s\bar{p}_a = p_g,$$

so that

$$\bar{p}_g = p_g - sp_p, \qquad \bar{p}_a = p_p. \tag{5}$$

At any instant of time, as we have seen, there can be no jump in $k_a$, while $k_g$ can jump down but not up. For any time, $t$, let $k_g^-(t)$ be the value arrived at by past history, while $k_g^+(t)$ is the value to which $k_g$ is made to jump;

$$k_g^+(t) \leqq k_g^-(t) \tag{6}$$

The optimization problem is in the general form of that studied in section II.7, but we still have to establish the effect, if any, of a jump in $k_g$ on utility. In the notation of section II.7, we need a determination of $\bar{U}_g(t)$. Note that consumption, $c$, is forced to infinity when there is an infinite subsidy on income, and it would seem to be possible that there might be a finite contribution to utility over an infinitesimal interval. In fact, we shall show that, because the marginal felicity declines to zero as $c$ approaches infinity, the contribution to utility due to a jump must be zero.

To this end, imagine that the jump is replaced by a corresponding change in $k_g$ over a time interval of length $\epsilon$. Suppose first that at time $t_0$, $k_g^-(t_0) = k_g^0$, $k_g^+(t_0) = k_g^1 < k_g^0$. Now suppose that instead we constrain this transition to take place over an interval, $\langle t_0, t_0 + \epsilon\rangle$.

$$k_g(t_0) = k_g^0,\ k_g(t_0 + \epsilon) = k_g^1 < k_g^0. \tag{7}$$

Consider the optimal solution to the original problem with the additional constraint (7). Then the contribution to utility over the interval $\langle t_0, t_0 + \epsilon\rangle$ is

$$\int_{t_0}^{t_0+\epsilon} e^{-\lambda t} U[c(t), k_g(t)]dt.$$

It is natural therefore to define $\bar{U}_g(t_0)$ as the limit of this expression as $\epsilon \to 0$. We seek to prove that $\bar{U}_g(t_0) = 0$ for all $t_0$, or, equivalently, that $e^{-\lambda t_0} U_g(t_0) = 0$, that is

$$\lim_{\epsilon \to 0} \int_{t_0}^{t_0+\epsilon} e^{-\lambda(t-t_0)} U[c(t), k_g(t)]dt = 0. \tag{8}$$

The proof of (8) is divided into two parts: (a) for any policy, optimal or not, we show that

$$\limsup_{\epsilon \to 0} \int_{t_0}^{t_0+\epsilon} e^{-\lambda(t-t_0)} U[c(t), k_g(t)]dt \leqq 0. \tag{9}$$

(b) We then exhibit a policy for each $\epsilon$ such that

$$\liminf_{\epsilon \to 0} \int_{t_0}^{t_0+\epsilon} e^{-\lambda(t-t_0)} U[c(t), k_g(t)]dt \geqq 0. \tag{10}$$

Since (9) holds for any policy, it holds for the optimal policy for each $x$. If (10) holds for some policy, it must also hold for the optimal policy, so that (8) will be demonstrated.

(a) First, we shall prove (9). We note to begin with that $k_a(t)$ is bounded in a right-hand interval uniformly in the policy. The function $g(k_a, k_g)$, defined in (3), has a maximum over the compact set $0 \leqq k_g \leqq k_a/s$ for any fixed $k_a$; call the maximum $h(k_a)$.

$$0 \leqq g(k_a, k_g) \leqq h(k_a).$$

The state variable $k_a$ satisfies the differential equation (2), with $y$ defined by (3). Let $k_a^*$, $k_a^{**}$ satisfy the differential equations

$$\dot{k}_a^* = -\gamma k_a^*, \qquad \dot{k}_a^{**} = sh(k_a^{**}) - \gamma k_a^{**},$$

with the initial conditions, $k_a^*(t_0) = k_a^{**}(t_0) = k_a^0$. Then, clearly,

$$k_a^*(t) \leqq k_a(t) \leqq k_a^{**}(t), \qquad t_0 \leqq t \leqq t_0 + \epsilon, \tag{11}$$

and $k_a^*(t)$ and $k_a^{**}(t)$ are continuous functions. From (11), $k_a(t)$ is bounded above uniformly in every interval $\langle t_0, t_0 + \epsilon\rangle$, for $\epsilon$ sufficiently small. Since $k_g \leqq k_a/s$, for some $\bar{k}_g$,

$$k_g(t) \leqq \bar{k}_g \text{ for all policies and all } t,$$
$$t_0 \leqq t \leqq t_0 + \epsilon, \ \epsilon \text{ sufficiently small.} \tag{12}$$

Since $y \leqq h(k_a)$, it also follows from the boundedness of $k_a$ that $(1 - s)y$ is bounded from above. Choose $\bar{c}$ so that

$$\bar{c} > (1 - s)y, \qquad t_0 \leqq t \leqq t_0 + \epsilon, \ \epsilon \text{ sufficiently small.} \tag{13}$$

If, as in section 1, we use $x^*$ to represent tax collections normalized for growth, then, from 2.(6), 2.(3), and 2.(1),

$$x^* = \dot{k}_g + \gamma k_g, \qquad c = (1 - s)(y - x^*), \tag{14}$$

and, with the aid of (13),

$$c < \bar{c} - (1 - s)(\dot{k}_g + \gamma k_g). \tag{15}$$

Since $U(c, k_g)$ is monotone increasing in both its arguments, it follows from (12) and (15), plus the standard differential inequality for concave functions, that

$$\begin{aligned} U[c(t), k_g(t)] &\leqq U[\bar{c} - (1 - s)(\dot{k}_g + \gamma k_g), \bar{k}_g] \\ &\leqq U(\bar{c}, \bar{k}_g) - U_c(\bar{c}, \bar{k}_g)(1 - s)(\dot{k}_g + \gamma k_g). \end{aligned} \tag{16}$$

Also, by integration by parts,

$$\int_{t_0}^{t_0+\epsilon} e^{-\lambda(t-t_0)} \dot{k}_g(t)dt = e^{-\lambda\epsilon} k_g(t_0 + \epsilon) - k_g(t_0) + \lambda \int_{t_0}^{t_0+\epsilon} e^{-\lambda(t-t_0)} k_g(t)dt.$$

Since $k_g(t_0 + \epsilon) = k_g^1$, $k_g(t_0) = k_g^0$, by (7), it follows from (16), that

$$\begin{aligned} \int_{t_0}^{t_0+\epsilon} e^{-\lambda(t-t_0)} U[c(t), k_g(t)]dt &\leqq U(\bar{c}, \bar{k}_g) \int_{t_0}^{t_0+\epsilon} e^{-\lambda(t-t_0)} dt \\ &- U_c(\bar{c}, \bar{k}_g)(1 - s)\left[ e^{-\lambda\epsilon} k_g^1 - k_g^0 + (\lambda + \gamma) \int_{t_0}^{t_0+\epsilon} e^{-\lambda(t-t_0)} k_g(t)dt \right]. \end{aligned}$$

But, as $\epsilon \to 0$,

$$\int_{t_0}^{t_0+\epsilon} e^{-\lambda(t-t_0)} dt \to 0,$$

and, since $k_g(t)$ is bounded above, by (12),

$$\int_{t_0}^{t_0+\epsilon} e^{-\lambda(t-t_0)} k_g(t)dt \to 0.$$

Hence,

$$\limsup_{\epsilon \to 0} \int_{t_0}^{t_0+\epsilon} e^{-\lambda(t-t_0)} U[c(t), k_g(t)]dt \leqq -U_c(\bar{c}, \bar{k}_g)(1 - s)(k_g^1 - k_g^0).$$

But $\bar{c}$ was chosen only in order to satisfy (13), and does not enter on the left-hand side of the above relation. On the other hand, by choosing $\bar{c}$ arbitrarily large, $U_c(\bar{c}, \bar{k}_g)$ can be made arbitrarily close to 0, since $U_c$ is homogeneous of negative degree. Hence, (9) has been demonstrated.

(b) We shall now demonstrate (10). We shall choose a policy in which $k_g^\sigma$ is a linear function of $t$ for each $\epsilon$, specifically,

$$k_g^\sigma = a(\epsilon) - b(\epsilon)(t - t_0),$$

where $a(\epsilon)$ and $b(\epsilon)$ are chosen so that (7) is satisfied. Then, if $a = a(1)$, $b = b(1)$, we see immediately that for any $\epsilon$, $a(\epsilon) = a$, $b(\epsilon) = b/\epsilon$. Also, $b > 0$, clearly. By differentiation, we see that

$$k_g^{\sigma-1} \dot{k}_g = -b/\epsilon. \tag{17}$$

From (14) and (17), for this policy,

$$x^* = \dot{k}_g + \gamma k_g = k_g[\gamma + (\dot{k}_g/k_g)] = (1/\epsilon)k_g(\gamma\epsilon - bk_g^{-\sigma}),$$

so that

$$c/k_g = (1 - s)(y - x^*)x/k_g \geqq -(1 - s)x^*/k_g = [(1 - s)/\epsilon](bk_g^{-\sigma} - \gamma\epsilon)$$
$$\geqq [(1 - s)/\epsilon][b(k_g^0)^{-\sigma} - \gamma\epsilon].$$

The last bracket is positive for $\epsilon$ sufficiently small. Hence, we can certainly choose $\underline{c} > 0$ so that for $\epsilon$ sufficiently small, $c/k_g \geqq \underline{c}$ for all $t$, $t_0 \leqq t \leqq t_0 + \epsilon$.

Since $U(c, k_g)$ is increasing in $c$ and homogeneous of degree $1 - \sigma$,

$$U(c, k_g) = k_g^{1-\sigma}U(\underline{c}/k_g, 1) \geqq k_g^{1-\sigma}U(\underline{c}, 1).$$

$$\int_{t_0}^{t_0+\epsilon} e^{-\lambda(t-t_0)}U(c, k_g)dt \geqq U(\underline{c}, 1)\int_{t_0}^{t_0+\epsilon} e^{-\lambda(t-t_0)}k_g^{1-\sigma}dt$$
$$\geqq m\int_{t_0}^{t_0+\epsilon} k_g^{1-\sigma}dt, \qquad (18)$$

where

$$m = \begin{cases} U(\underline{c}, 1)\, e^{-\lambda\epsilon} & \text{if } U(\underline{c}, 1) \geqq 0, \\ U(\underline{c}, 1) & \text{if } U(\underline{c}, 1) < 0. \end{cases}$$

Note that in either case $m$ approaches the finite limit $U(\underline{c}, 1)$ as $\epsilon$ approaches zero.

By a change of variables and substitution from (17),

$$\int_{t_0}^{t_0+\epsilon} k_g^{1-\sigma}dt = \int_{k_g^1}^{k_g^0}(-k_g^{1-\sigma}/\dot{k}_g)dk_g = (\epsilon/b)(k_g^0 - k_g^1),$$

which approaches zero with $\epsilon$. Then (10) follows from (18), and therefore (8) is confirmed.

We can therefore apply Propositions II.11–12. The only variable in which a jump can take place is $k_g$. The permissible jumps are downward, rather than upward, which implies only that the inequality in Proposition II.11(d) is reversed. In the formulas, we now take $\bar{U}_g = 0$ for all $t$. Then by Proposition II.12, a jump can take place only at $t = 0$. From Proposition II.11(d), $\bar{p}_g(t) \geqq 0$ everywhere, while from (e) of the same proposition $\bar{p}_g(0) = 0$ if there is a jump at $t = 0$. From (5), these statements can be written

$$p_g \geqq sp_p \text{ everywhere}, \; p_g(0) = sp_p(0) \text{ if there is a jump at } t = 0.$$

Proposition 5. *Suppose that private savings constitute a fixed proportion of disposable income and that the government balances its budget and imposes only an income tax, at rate $x(t)$. Suppose, further, that the* *production function and the government's utility function satisfy all the conditions of Propositions IV.1 and IV.2 or IV.3. Then, in the second-best policy, there may be an initial immediate decrease in $k_g$, with $k_p$ increasing so that $k_p + sk_g$ is constant. After time 0, the second-best policy satisfies the differential equations*

(a) $$\dot{k}_p = s(1 - x)f(k_p, k_g) - \gamma k_p,$$

(b) $$\dot{k}_g = xf(k_p, k_g) - \gamma k_g,$$

(c) $$\dot{p}_p = \omega p_p - p_g f_p,$$

(d) $$\dot{p}_g = \omega p_g - p_g f_g - U_g;$$

*and $x$ is chosen so as to satisfy the equation*

(e) $$U_c[(1 - s)(1 - x)f(k_p, k_g), k_g] = (p_g - sp_p)/(1 - s).$$

*If the initial jump takes place, then*

(f) $$p_g(0) = sp_p(0).$$

*Conditions (a)–(e), and (f) if appropriate, are sufficient conditions for a second-best policy if $p_p(0)$, $p_g(0)$ can be so chosen that the time paths of the state and auxiliary variables converge to a stationary point.*

## 6. Financing Investment by Borrowing and Interest by Income Tax

It is sometimes suggested that the government should separate its capital and current budgets; public investment should be financed by borrowing, while other government expenditures, including interest on the government debt, should be paid for out of income taxation. While there would appear to be two instruments—borrowing and taxes—the latter is governed by the condition of a balanced budget on current account. Since we are abstracting from government expenditures other than investment and interest, it follows that taxes equal interest payments, or, in the notation of section 1,

$$x^* = f_p d. \tag{1}$$

From 1.(11), personal income is given by $y_p = y + f_p d$. Then, for an income tax at rate $x$, $x^* = xy_p$; from (1), taxes are not a freely disposable instrument but are determined as a particular function of the state variables. In effect, there is only one instrument, government borrowing. Disposable income here is defined as

$$y_d = (1 - x)y_p = y_p - x^* = y + f_p d - f_p d = y,$$

so that personal savings are defined by $s_p = sy$. The equations, 1.(8)–(10) become

$$\dot{k}_p = sf(k_p, k_g) - b - \gamma k_p, \tag{2}$$

$$\dot{k}_g = b - \gamma k_g, \tag{3}$$

$$\dot{d} = b - \gamma d. \tag{4}$$

Note first, from (3) and (4), that

$$d(k_g - d)/dt = -\gamma(k_g - d),$$

from which it follows that $k_g(t) - d(t)$ approaches 0. Hence, if $k_g(t)$ converges, so does $d(t)$. For the same reason, it follows from (1) that $x(t)$ converges. Also, $\dot{k}_g$ approaches 0 so that $b$ converges [from (3)]. Thus, if the state variables converge, the instruments are necessarily stable.

If we add (2) and (3), and define $k = k_p + k_g$, we have

$$\dot{k} = sf(k_p, k_g) - \gamma k. \tag{5}$$

Since $b$ can be made infinitely large positively or negatively, it follows, exactly as in sections IV.1–2, that $k_p$ and $k_g$ can be freely transformed into each other, provided that their sum, $k$, is constant. Hence, we can regard $k_p$ and $k_g$ themselves as instruments, subject to the constraint

$$k_p + k_g = k. \tag{6}$$

For a publicly optimal policy, from Proposition IV.1,

$$\dot{k} = f(k_p, k_g) - c - \gamma k.$$

If the publicly optimal policy were controllable, (5) would also hold, and we would have

$$c = (1 - s)f(k_p, k_g) = (1 - s)y.$$

The ratio $c/y$ certainly is not, in general, constant and need not have the specific value $1 - s$. Hence, in general, there is no controllability.

PROPOSITION 6. *If private savings constitute a fixed fraction of disposable income and the government finances investment by borrowing and interest payments by taxes, then the publicly optimal policy is not in general controllable.*

We shall now consider the second-best optimal policy. As in section 1, the aim is to maximize

$$\int_0^\infty e^{-\lambda t} U(c, k_g)dt,$$

subject here to (5) and (6). We apply Proposition II.7. The current-value Lagrangian is

$$L = U(c, k_g) + p[sf(k_p, k_g) - \gamma k] + \bar{q}(k - k_p - k_g)$$
$$= \phi(y, k_g, p) + (\bar{q} - p\gamma)k - \bar{q}k_p - \bar{q}k_g, \tag{7}$$

where

$$\phi(y, k_g, p) = U(c, k_g) + psy, \tag{8}$$

$$c = (1 - s)y. \tag{9}$$

Let

$$q = \partial\phi/\partial y = U_c(1 - s) + sp. \tag{10}$$

Also

$$\partial\phi/\partial k_g = U_g. \tag{11}$$

If we differentiate $L$ with respect to $k_p$ and $k_g$ and equate the derivatives to 0, we have, with the aid of (10) and (11),

$$qf_p = \bar{q}, \qquad qf_g + U_g = \bar{q},$$

or

$$f_p = f_g + (U_g/q). \tag{12}$$

Equations (10), (12), and (6) can be solved for $k_p$, $k_g$, $q$ as functions of $k$ and $p$.

The auxiliary variable, $p$, satisfies

$$\dot{p} = \lambda p - (\partial L/\partial k) = \lambda p - (\bar{q} - \gamma p) = \omega p - qf_p. \tag{13}$$

An optimal policy is one which satisfies (5), (6), (10), (12), and (13), and for which the starting value, $p(0)$, is such that the solution converges to a stationary value. As can be seen by comparison with sections IV.2–4, the model is formally rather similar to that of chapter IV, and the qualitative nature of the solution is the same. There may be more than one stationary value; if so, there are an odd number, with alternating saddle-points and totally unstable points.

Although the equations for the stationary values can easily be written down, there does not seem to be anything especially interesting about their properties.

Given the solution, $k_p$ and $k_g$ are determined as functions of time; hence, $b$ can be determined from (3). At time 0, the values of $k_p$ and $k_g$ determined by $k(0)$ and $p(0)$ need not be the historically given $k_p(0)$ and $k_g(0)$; thus, an initial jump is possible, to be financed by a corresponding jump (up or down) in the debt.

PROPOSITION 7. *Suppose that private saving is a fixed fraction of disposable income, that the government finances investment by borrowing and interest payments by taxes, and that the utility and production functions satisfy the hypotheses of Proposition IV.1–2 or IV.3. Then the second-best policy satisfies the following necessary conditions. Let* $k_p(k, p)$, $k_g(k, p)$, *and* $q(k, p)$ *be the solutions of the following equations:*

(a) $$f_p = f_g + (U_g/q),$$

(b) $$q = U_c(1 - s) + sp,$$

(c) $$k_p + k_g = k.$$

*Then* $k(t)$ *and* $p(t)$ *satisfy the differential equations:*

(d) $$\dot{k} = sf[k_p(k, p), k_g(k, p)] - \gamma k,$$

(e) $$\dot{p} = \omega p - q(k, p)f_g[k_p(k, p), k_g(k, p)].$$

*If* $\omega > \gamma$, *then any solution of (d)–(e) which converges to an equilibrium is an optimal policy.*

*There is at least one and, in general, an odd number of equilibria for the differential equations, (d)–(e); every other one, beginning with the one with the smallest value of* $k$, *is a saddle point, while the remaining are totally unstable. If the initial capital stock (normalized for growth) corresponds to one of the totally unstable equilibria, then the second-best policy calls for keeping it constant; otherwise, the growth-normalized capital stock converges to the value corresponding to one of the saddle points.*

*The instruments that generate the second-best policy are stable. At time 0, there may be equal and opposite adjustments in the stocks of government and private capital, with a corresponding change in public debt.*

The special case where government capital does not enter directly into the utility function reduces to the simple Solow-Swan growth model. In that case, $U_g = 0$, and $f_p = f_g$. Then the output from any given stock of capital is maximized. Equation (d) becomes completely determined, since it no longer involves $p$.

COROLLARY. *If the assumptions of Proposition 7 hold and, in addition,* $U_g = 0$, *then public policy is completely determined by the condition of equating rates of return of private and government capital; the motion of the system is determined by the single equation,*

$$\dot{k} = sg(k) - \gamma k,$$

*where*

$$g(k) = \max_{k_p + k_g = k} f(k_p, k_g).$$

## 7. Balanced Budget with Consumption and Savings Taxes

In this and the following sections, we shall increase the number of instruments and show that controllability is indeed attainable. First, we shall consider an economy where two tax rates are used as public instruments: a tax on consumption and a tax on savings. As in section V.5, let $x_c$ be the rate of taxation on consumption, $x_s$ that on savings. Also, let $z_c = 1 - x_c$, $z_s = 1 - x_s$.

The hypothesis of a fixed savings ratio is not unambiguous when savings and consumption are taxed at different rates. In effect, the price ratio between savings and consumption can vary. Then a fixed savings ratio might mean either that the "values" of savings and consumption are in constant proportion or that "real" savings and consumption are in constant proportion. We take here the former hypothesis. That is, we assume that the ratio of post-tax savings to total personal income is a constant. In this case, since there is no public debt and therefore no interest income from it, personal income is simply $Y$. Expenditures on personal savings are $sY$, but a fraction, $x_s$, is taken by the government, so that

$$S_p = z_s s Y ,$$

and similarly, consumption is

$$C = z_c(1 - s)Y .$$

It also follows that total taxes are

$$X^* = x_s s Y + x_c(1 - s)Y .$$

In the absence of borrowing and debt, then, the rates of private and government capital formation are, from 1.(9)–(10),

$$\dot{k}_p = s z_s y - \gamma k_p , \tag{1}$$

$$\dot{k}_g = [s x_s + (1 - s)x_c]y - \gamma k_g , \tag{2}$$

while

$$c = (1 - s)z_c y . \tag{3}$$

Consider *any* feasible allocation policy, which may be the publicly optimal one. Then $k_p$, $k_g$, and $c$ are specified as functions of time and, therefore, so are $y$ and $\dot{k}_p$. We can solve (3) for $z_c$, which must be positive, and hence $x_c < 1$ is determined; then $x_s$ can be solved for, from (1). Feasibility means that

$$\dot{K}_p + \dot{K}_g + C = Y ,$$

or

$$\dot{k}_p + {}_g\dot{k} + c = y - \gamma(k_p + k_g) ;$$

hence, once $x_s$ and $x_c$ are chosen to satisfy (1) and (3), (2) is automatically satisfied.

For any policy such that $k_p$ and $k_g$ converge to finite limits and $\dot{k}_g$ approaches 0, it is obvious that $x_s$ and $x_c$ converge to finite limits.

PROPOSITION 8. *Suppose that private savings constitute a fixed fraction of personal income and the government finances its investment by taxes on consumption and savings. Then any feasible allocation policy is controllable; if the policy is such that $k_p$ and $k_g$ converge and $\dot{k}_p$ approaches* 0, *then the instruments are stable. In particular, the publicly optimal policy is controllable by stable instruments.*

*Remark* 1. The feasible policy being controlled may, of course, have jumps in the two kinds of capital, though these cannot lead to an increase in $k = k_p + k_g$. The infinite taxes or subsidies needed to carry out the jumps may be interpreted as confiscation or gifts.

*Remark* 2. From (1) and (3), the role of the two kinds of taxes can be seen. The tax on consumption is designed to ensure that the correct amount of aggregate savings is forthcoming; the tax on savings then allocates this amount of savings between the two kinds of capital formation.

## 8. Financing by Borrowing and Taxes on Consumption and Savings

The public debt and the possibility of borrowing will now be introduced into our system. Of course, since we are simply extending the range of instruments, the system will certainly be controllable. We will, however, be interested in examining the effects on controllability of imposing constraints of one kind or another on the taxes.

If we introduce debt, then personal income [see 1.(3)] is now

$$Y_p = Y + f_p D.$$

If the fixed savings-ratio hypothesis is interpreted in the same way as in the last section, private savings and consumption are given by

$$S_p = z_s s Y_p, \qquad C = z_c(1 - s) Y_p,$$

and total taxes are

$$X^* = [x_s s + x_c(1 - s)] Y_p.$$

Then, in the presence of borrowing, equations 1.(9)–(10) define the equations of motion of private and government capital formation,

$$\dot{k}_p = s z_s(y + f_p d) - b - \gamma k_p, \tag{1}$$

$$\dot{k}_g = [sx_s + (1 - s)x_c](y + f_p d) + b - f_p d - \gamma k_g, \tag{2}$$

while

$$c = (1 - s)z_c(y + f_p d). \tag{3}$$

As before, for any feasible policy, it suffices that the instruments, $x_s$, $x_c$, $b$, be such that two of the above equations hold; the third will hold necessarily. Since there are three instruments, there are many ways of solving the two equations, unless other conditions are imposed. We then wish to study the stability of the instruments and, in particular, the behavior of the public debt, governed by 1.(8),

$$\dot{d} = b - \gamma d. \tag{4}$$

We shall now consider several cases in which various restrictions are placed on the taxes. First, suppose the only tax is an income tax—i.e., $x_c = x_s = x$, say—and let $z = 1 - x$ (for an earlier analysis, see Arrow 1966, section 6). Clearly, one can solve for $z$ from (3) and then for $b$ from (1) or (2). Hence, any feasible policy is certainly controllable. Since $z_s = z_c = z$, we can eliminate $z(y + f_p d)$ from (1) and (3), solve for $b$, and then substitute into (4).

$$\dot{d} = [sc/(1 - s)] - (\dot{k}_p + \gamma k_p) - \gamma d. \tag{5}$$

Here, $c$ and $k_p$ (and consequently $\dot{k}_p$) are taken as known functions of time, since they are given by the allocation policy to be controlled. Suppose that this policy is such that $k_p$ and $k_g$ converge to some limits and $\dot{k}_p$ and $\dot{k}_g$ converge to 0; in particular, the publicly optimal policy satisfies these conditions. Then, (5) is a differential equation to be satisfied by $d(t)$ with some given initial condition. The terms $[sc/(1 - s)] - (\dot{k}_p + \gamma k_p)$ converge to a finite limit. Since $\gamma > 0$, any solution is clearly stable.

Now consider the case where the only tax falls on consumption; $z_s = 1$. Again $z_c$ is determined by (3), and $b$ by (1), so that any feasible policy is controllable. If we substitute for $b$ in (4), we now have

$$\dot{d} = sy - (\dot{k}_p + \gamma k_p) + (sf_p - \gamma)d. \tag{6}$$

Again, the first two terms converge to a finite limit if $k_p$ and $k_g$ converge and $\dot{k}_p$, $\dot{k}_g$ converge to 0 in the policy being controlled. The coefficient of $d$ converges to a limit, $sf_p^\infty - \gamma$, which may be positive or negative, depending upon the policy being controlled. Even for the publicly optimal policy, we cannot be sure of the sign; all we know is that $f_p^\infty = \omega$ in this case; by assumption, $\omega > \gamma$, but this assertion conveys no assurance about the sign of $s\omega - \gamma$. The solutions of (6) will be stable if $sf_p^\infty - \gamma < 0$ but unstable in the contrary case; if they are unstable, then the solution $d(t)$ approaches either $+\infty$ or $-\infty$, except for one initial value of $d$. Since $d(0)$ is determined by past history, the controlling choice of instruments will be stable only by accident when $sf_p^\infty > \gamma$.

Now consider the possibility of a tax on savings alone. Then $z_c = 1$. But from (3) it is clear that there is no way of adjusting consumption, $c$, to any desired level. One might, indeed, think of so choosing the public debt, $d$, as to make (3) hold; i.e., inducing the desired consumption through the volume of interest on the public debt. In general, since $d(0)$ is historically determined, control of consumption through the debt will require an appropriate jump at the origin in the debt. But, from (1) and (2), a jump in debt entails an equal jump in $k_g$ and a jump of equal magnitude but opposite sign in $k_p$. The policy being controlled specifies such jumps, and there is no reason why the jump needed in (3) should equal that required to make (2) hold. Thus a tax on savings alone, plus borrowing, cannot in general achieve control.

This last case shows that *merely counting instruments and targets is not adequate to determine the controllability of a system.*

Finally, we can reconsider the two-budget model of section 6, where public investment is financed by borrowing and interest payments by taxes; now we permit the use of both kinds of taxes.

$$[sx_s + (1 - s)x_c](y + f_p d) = f_p d. \tag{7}$$

As before, $z_c$, and therefore $x_c$, are determined by (3), so that $x_s$ can be found from (7). If (7) is substituted into (2), we can then solve for $b$; if we then substitute into (4), we have

$$\dot{d} = (\dot{k}_g + \gamma k_g) - \gamma d,$$

and, as before, $d$ converges to a stable value (in fact to $k_g^\infty$) provided $k_g$ converges and $\dot{k}_g$ converges to 0.

PROPOSITION 9. *Suppose that private savings constitute a fixed fraction of personal income. Then any feasible policy is controllable if the government finances its investment by (a) borrowing and an income tax, (b) borrowing and a tax on consumption, or (c) borrowing for the investment itself and taxes on consumption and savings to pay for the interest. In general, feasible policies are not controllable by borrowing and a tax on savings.*

*If the allocation policy being controlled is such that $k_p$ and $k_g$ converge and $\dot{k}_g$ and $\dot{k}_p$ approach 0, then the instruments are always stable in cases (a) and (c), while in (b) they are stable if $sf_p^\infty < \gamma$, but not if $sf_p^\infty > \gamma$.*

## 9. Appropriability of Return on Government Capital

We have worked so far with models in which it was assumed that all of the output due to the public sector is held by the private sector. Thus (normalized) personal income was

$$y_p = y + f_p d.$$

As already argued in section V.5, the government may be in a position to appropriate some part of the return to its capital, either through user charges or through retaining the savings in costs resulting from the use of capital in government operations. Let the charge for the use of a unit of government capital be $r_g$. We suppose that $r_g$ is some given continuous function of the state of the system, as determined by $k_p$ and $k_g$. Then personal income is reduced by the amount $r_g k_g$, while the receipts of the government available for its investment are increased by the same amount. Equations 8.(1)–(3) have as their analogs,

$$\dot{k}_p = s z_s (y + f_p d - r_g k_g) - b - \gamma k_p, \tag{1}$$

$$\dot{k}_g = [s x_s + (1 - s) x_c](y + f_p d - r_g k_g) + b + r_g k_g - f_p d - \gamma k_g, \tag{2}$$

$$c = (1 - s) z_c (y + f_p d - r_g k_g) ; \tag{3}$$

equation (8.4),

$$\dot{d} = b - \gamma d, \tag{4}$$

remains unchanged. Now define

$$z'_s = z_s (y + f_p d - r_g k_g)/(y + f_p d),$$
$$z'_c = z_c (y + f_p d - r_g k_g)/(y + f_p d),$$
$$x'_s = 1 - z'_s, \; x'_c = 1 - z'_c. \tag{5}$$

Then (1)–(3) becomes precisely the same as 8.(1)–(3), with $x'_s$, $x'_c$ replacing $x_s$, $x_c$, respectively. Since the transition equations of all the models in this chapter are special cases of (1)–(3), we see that the introduction of charges for the services of government capital does not change the nature of the analysis at all; if $x'_s$, $x'_c$ are the tax rates that would be chosen in the absence of user charges for government capital, the tax rates in their presence are determined by solving for them in (5). The tax rates are, of course, reduced by the presence of user charges.

PROPOSITION 10. *If the use of government capital is charged for at a rate $r_g$, a continuous function of the two stocks of capital (normalized for growth), then all the results of Propositions 1–9 remain valid.*

*Remark.* Proposition 10 *does not imply that user charges are unimportant.* What it does mean is that they serve no function in intertemporal allocation. The purpose of user charges is to improve the allocation of resources at any moment of time. If they do so operate, there would be an upward shift in the production function, $f(k_p, k_g)$. Proposition 10 really assures us that user charges will have no deleterious effect on intertemporal allocations, since they can always be offset by appropriate changes in tax rates.

# VII

## CONSUMER BEHAVIOR IN A PERFECT MARKET

### 0. Introduction

In the preceding chapter we discussed the controllability of the economy under the assumption that consumers behaved according to the simple rule of saving a fixed proportion of their income. In this and the following chapter we shall take up the opposite hypothesis: the representative consumer is assumed to behave with perfect rationality in all respects. He looks ahead infinitely far with perfect foresight, he faces a perfect capital market, and he chooses his consumption-savings program so as to maximize the integral of discounted utility for himself and his descendants. The basic conceptual framework for the analysis of consumer behavior under these assumptions (but with a finite horizon) is from Fisher (1930); a more modern treatment was given by Yaari (1964*a*), who studied the case of a finite horizon with a bequest motive.

The income of the individual at any moment is the sum of interest income, wages, and rents (the latter arise from imputation to the private sector of the unappropriated returns to government investment, as explained in V.5). Noninterest income and the rate of return on material assets are both regarded as functions of time exogenously given to the individual.

The income received is divided between consumption and the accumulation of assets; however, as discussed in chapter V, the government imposes several kinds of taxes on both savings and consumption. The felicity of the individual at any moment of time is a function of consumption and possibly of the stock of government capital (as in the perfect planning model of chapter IV); the latter is taken as a known exogenous function of time by the individual.

The nature of the budget constraint in an infinite-horizon context needs some comment. An individual with anticipated future wages and rentals is, with respect to command over alternative possible consumption streams, in exactly the same situation as another individual with no anticipations of future noninterest income but instead with an initial stock of material assets equal to the integral of the first individual's future noninterest income discounted back to the present. The rate used in discounting is the (in general time-varying) post-tax rate of return on private capital. Then the budget constraint over infinite time requires that assets do not eventually become and remain negative. This will easily be seen to be equivalent to the statement that total assets are never negative.

This chapter is not designed as a complete analysis of the theory of consumer choice over time, even under the restrictive assumptions made. It is intended as a basis for the discussion in chapter VIII of the possibilities of controlling the private sector through government policy instruments—taxes, borrowing, and government investment—so as to achieve the same optimal program as would be achieved under perfect planning (as set forth in chapter IV). For the purpose of the present chapter, only a few qualitative characteristics of the optimal policies to be achieved are needed. First, it is assumed that the variables exogenous to the individual—the rate of return, noninterest income, and government capital—converge to balanced growth values with sufficient regularity. Second, it is assumed that, given these exogenous variables, the tax rates are such that the optimal consumption policy chosen by the individual converges to a balanced growth solution. Clearly, if the economy is in fact controllable, the optimal consumption policy will satisfy this condition.

The main conclusion we seek is on the asymptotic behavior of the stock of material assets held by the consumer in pursuit of his optimizing policy. For most, though not all, cases it will be shown that the desired stock of material assets converges to a balanced growth solution; i.e., the desired stock of material assets per effective worker converges to a finite nonzero limit. In the following chapter this will be shown to have important negative implications for the controllability of the economy by means that use only one form of taxation and therefore place a heavy reliance on borrowing. For in general, as will be shown, such policies will require the volume of debt (possibly negative) to grow more rapidly than the natural rate of growth; but if the desired stock of material assets grows at only the natural rate, the government cannot in fact place the debt.

## 1. The Consumer's Feasibility Condition

Before discussing the optimal behavior of the consumer, we have first to formulate precisely the conditions under which a given consumption policy is to be regarded as feasible. Suppose first that there are no taxes. Then, from Proposition V.1.(c), or V.5.(8), the stock of material assets evolves according to the equation

$$\dot{A}^M = rA^M + W - C. \tag{1}$$

For a finite-horizon optimization, the feasibility criterion is clearly that $A^M(T) \geqq 0$, where $T$ is the horizon. It might seem natural to extend this to the infinite-horizon case by stating the condition as

$$\liminf_{t\to\infty} A^M(t) \geqq 0 \;; \tag{2}$$

but we shall show by consideration of a special case that this condition is unsatisfactory.

Suppose the individual is maximizing

$$\int_0^\infty e^{-\rho t} U(C_t)\,dt,$$

subject to the constraints (1) and (2), where $r$ and $W$ are assumed constant. The Hamiltonian is

$$H = U(C) + p(rA^M + W - C),$$

and the necessary conditions of the Pontryagin principle are

$$U'(C) = p,$$
$$\dot{p}/p = \rho - r.$$

Assume further that $U'(C) = C^{-\sigma}$ and $r < \rho$. Then $p(t) = p_0 e^{(\rho-r)t}$, and therefore $C(t) = C_0 e^{-\alpha t}$, where $C_0 = p_0^{-1/\sigma}$ and $\alpha = (\rho - r)/\sigma > 0$. It remains only to determine the value of $C_0$. If we solve (1) for this consumption policy, we find

$$A^M(t) = \{A^M(0) + (W/r) - [C_0/(\alpha + r)]\}e^{rt} - (W/r) + C_0 e^{-\alpha t}/(\alpha + r). \tag{3}$$

If $A^M(0) + (W/r) - [C_0/(\alpha + r)] < 0$, then the dominant term approaches $-\infty$, and the feasibility condition (2) is certainly not satisfied. If $A^M(0) + (W/r) - [C_0/(\alpha + r)] > 0$, then the dominant term approaches $+\infty$ and certainly satisfies (2); but the expression would still be positive if $C_0$ were increased by a sufficiently small amount. Hence, the new consumption policy would still be feasible, and it would yield higher consumption at every moment of time. Hence, a necessary condition for optimality is that $A^M(0) + (W/r) - [C_0/(\alpha + r)] = 0$. But if this holds, the first term in (3) vanishes, and the second term, which is negative, becomes the dominant term so that (2) is not satisfied. Thus, if (2) is the definition of feasibility, there would be no optimal policy.

This is an unreasonable conclusion in such a simple situation. What happens is that material assets, $A^M(t)$, converge to $-W/r$ so that the individual builds up his debt in such a way that it converges to the capitalized value of his wage income. If we define *total assets*, $A(t)$, to be the sum of material assets and the discounted value of wage income,

$$A(t) = A^M(t) + (W/r),$$

(3) can be rewritten

$$A(t) = \{A(0) - [C_0/(\alpha + r)]\}e^{rt} + C_0e^{-\alpha t}/(\alpha + r). \tag{4}$$

Then if we write a new feasibility condition,

$$\liminf_{t\to\infty} A(t) \geqq 0, \tag{5}$$

all difficulties disappear; as before, a necessary condition for optimality is that $A(0) - [C_0/(\alpha + r)] = 0$, but when this holds, $A(t)$ is nonnegative and approaching zero.

(The reader may want to check that if $r \geqq \rho$, then the two feasibility conditions in fact come to the same thing. Also, it may be noted that if $r + \alpha < 0$, there is no optimal policy by either definition of feasibility.)

The general approach to the definition of discounted wage income (or, more generally, wage and rental income) will now be outlined; we shall term this value "human assets," though this may be something of a misnomer if rentals are included.

First, suppose there is no exogenous income; if this is so, (1) reduces to

$$\dot{A}^M = r(t)A^M - C(t). \tag{6}$$

In this case, something like the feasibility condition (2) certainly is appropriate. However, as shown in the appendix to this chapter (Corollary 1 to Lemma 1), if $A^M(t) \leqq 0$ for some $t$, $\limsup_{t\to\infty} A^M(t) < 0$. Hence, an alternative and possibly weaker requirement for feasibility is that

$$A^M(t) > 0, \text{ all } t. \tag{7}$$

Now let us compare two individuals, one of whom has exogenous income and no initial stock of material assets, while the other has a stock of material assets and no exogenous income. Under what conditions are the two equivalent in the sense of having command over the same set of consumption streams? The first individual can certainly have a consumption stream, $C(t) = W(t)$, for all $t$, and he certainly cannot have a consumption stream $C(t) > W(t)$ for all $t$. Consider the second individual, with initial stock $A^M(0)$. For the consumption stream $W(t)$ to be feasible, it is necessary, from (6) and (7), that the solution to the differential equation

$$\dot{A}^M(t) = r(t)A^M(t) - W(t), \tag{8}$$

with the given initial condition, $A^M(0)$, satisfy (7). It is demonstrated in the appendix (Theorem 2 under the assumption $r(t) \to r^\infty > 0$) that if (7) is satisfied for some solution, then it is satisfied for a solution with any larger initial value, $A^M(0)$, and in fact there is a least value, $\bar{A}^M$, such that $A^M(t) > 0$ for all $t$ if $A^M(0) \geqq \bar{A}^M$. Then an individual with an initial capital stock, $A^M(0) \geqq \bar{A}^M$, and no exogenous income can certainly consume according to the policy $C(t) = W(t)$; if, however, $A^M(0) > \bar{A}^M$, then the individual could follow the uniformly better policy, $C(t) = [A^M(0)/\bar{A}^M]W(t)$ and would be better off than his wage-earning counterpart.

We are therefore led to the following definition: $A^H(t)$, the *human assets* corresponding to an exogenous income stream $W(t)$, is that solution of the differential equation

$$\dot{A}^H(t) = r(t)A^H(t) - W(t), \tag{9}$$

which has the smallest initial value, $A^H(0)$, among all solutions for which $A^H(t) > 0$ for all $t$. In the notation introduced in the appendix (15),

$$A^H(0) = \Delta\{W; r\}. \tag{10}$$

Here, $\Delta\{W; r\}$ is the stream of wages discounted to time zero at the (variable) rate of interest $r(t)$. This notation will be used for this and parallel purposes henceforth.

In general, of course, an individual will possess both human and material assets; in their command over consumption streams the two types of assets are additive. *Total assets*, $A(t)$, can now be defined by

$$A(t) = A^M(t) + A^H(t). \tag{11}$$

If (9) is added to (1), it follows from (11) that

$$\dot{A}(t) = r(t)A(t) - C(t). \tag{12}$$

Since we have assumed that $C(t) \geqq 0$ and $C(t) > 0$ for large $t$, it follows from Lemma 1 and its corollary in the appendix that either $A(t) > 0$ for all $t$ or $\limsup_{t\to\infty} A(t) < 0$. Thus, the natural feasibility condition is that $A(t) > 0$ for all $t \geqq 0$.

It has not been shown that human capital is necessarily well defined.

If equation (9) has any nonnegative solution, then indeed it has one with smallest initial value (see Theorem 2 in the appendix). But it is conceivable that (9) has no nonnegative solution—for example, if $r$ is a negative constant. It can, however, be shown that if an optimal consumption policy exists which is bounded away from zero, where optimality is understood to be relative to some reasonable definition of feasibility, then human capital is always defined. The precise statement and proof appear in the next section.

Against the background of a growing economy it is, as usual, convenient to deflate all extensive magnitudes by a measure of growth, say $e^{\gamma t}$. Let

$$a^M(t) = e^{-\gamma t}A^M(t),\ a^H(t) = e^{-\gamma t}A^H(t),\ a(t) = e^{-\gamma t}A(t),$$
$$w(t) = e^{-\gamma t}W(t),\ c(t) = e^{-\gamma t}C(t).$$

Then essentially everything goes through as before, with uppercase magnitudes being replaced throughout by their lowercase equivalents, and $r(t)$ being replaced by $r(t) - \gamma$. The conditions $A^H(t) > 0$, $A(t) > 0$, are of course logically equivalent to the conditions $a^H(t) > 0$, $a(t) > 0$, respectively. Note that $a^M(0) = A^M(0)$; also that $\Delta\{W; r\} = \Delta\{w; r - \gamma\}$, by Lemma 5 in the appendix.

It is important to note that the definition of feasibility is not only a fine mathematical problem but, indeed, it reflects an assumption about the institutional framework in which the optimization takes place. If financial institutions follow the rule of not lending any funds to a family with nonpositive material assets, then the feasibility condition, $A^M(t) \geqq 0$, is imposed. We have seen that this restricts the class of cases for which an optimal solution exists. The definition of feasibility calling for $A(t) > 0$ removes the various paradoxes that can arise in a perfectly competitive capital market where individuals can increase their consumption without limit simply by following an ever-rising borrowing policy. It is clear that the definition of "perfect capital markets" is unreasonable if it allows the various borrowing paradoxes to arise. The feasibility condition, $A(t) > 0$, allows the family to borrow for consumption purposes against its human capital, but not to exceed it. In this sense it is assumed that there is an institutional rule that is sufficient to allow the existence of optimal solutions to most relevant optimization problems without giving rise to "borrowing paradoxes."

We turn now to a more detailed study of the question of feasibility. We shall specify three definitions of feasibility. These will be applicable to different economies, depending on the existence of money in the system and alternative fiscal systems. The first condition follows directly from our preceding discussion.

CONSUMER FEASIBILITY CONDITION I: ONE COMMODITY, NO TAXES.

*Let*

(a) $$\bar{r}(t) = r(t) - \gamma,$$

*and* $a(t)$ *be the solution of differential equation*

(b) $$\dot{a} = \bar{r}a - c(t),$$

*with* $a(0) = A^M(0) + \Delta\{w;\ \bar{r}\}$. *Then* $c(t)$ *is feasible if and only if* $a(t) > 0$, *all* $t$:

Before considering the role of taxes the discussion will be clarified by considering the case in which both a consumption good and money exist, and the money price of the consumption good may vary over time; assets and wages are measured in money. Let $p_c$ = price of the consumption good. Then the accumulation equation, (1) is generalized to

$$\dot{A}^M = r(t)A^M + W(t) - p_c(t)C(t). \tag{13}$$

The logic of the subsequent discussion of feasibility conditions remains unchanged, provided $p_cC$ is substituted for $C$ throughout; it is assumed that $p_c > 0$ (see remark below). It will now be convenient to deflate assets and wages not only for growth but also for changes in the price of the consumption good; the latter is taken as numeraire. Let

$$a^{*M} = A^M/p_ce^{\gamma t}, \qquad a^{*H} = A^H/p_ce^{\gamma t},$$
$$a^* = A/p_ce^{\gamma t}, \qquad w^* = W/p_ce^{\gamma t}. \tag{14}$$

Note that $a^{*M}(0) = A^M(0)/p_c(0)$. The accumulation equation becomes

$$\dot{a}^{*M} = [r - \gamma - (\dot{p}_c/p_c)]a^{*M} + w^* - c.$$

CONSUMER FEASIBILITY CONDITION II: ONE COMMODITY AND MONEY, NO TAXES.

*Let*

(a) $$\bar{r} = r - \gamma - (\dot{p}_c/p_c),$$

*and* $a^*(t)$ *be the solution of the differential equation*

(b) $$\dot{a}^* = \bar{r}a^* - c,$$

*with* $a^*(0) = [A^M(0)/p_c(0)] + \Delta\{w^*;\ \bar{r}\}$. *Then* $c(t)$ *is feasible if and only if* $a^*(t) > 0$, *all* $t$.

*Remark.* This feasibility condition makes sense only if $p_c > 0$. If, for any $t$, $p_c(t) \leqq 0$, then clearly any consumption rate is feasible, which is no constraint at all.

Now introduce taxes, but drop the possibility that the price of the consumption good may vary.

From Proposition V.1.(c),

$$\dot{A}^M = z_{sr}rA^M + z_{sw}W - vC. \tag{15}$$

Equation (15) is of the form of (13), with $z_{sr}r$ and $z_{sw}W$ replacing $r$ and $W$, respectively, and $v$ replacing $p_c$. The definitions (14) become

$$a^{*M} = A^M/ve^{\gamma t}, \qquad a^{*H} = A^H/ve^{\gamma t}, \qquad a^* = A/ve^{\gamma t} \tag{16}$$

and

$$w^* = z_{sw}W/ve^{\gamma t} = z_{cw}w, \tag{17}$$

since, from the definitions in Proposition V.1, $z_{sw}/v = z_s z_w/(z_s/z_c) = z_c z_w = z_{cw}$, and $w = We^{-\gamma t}$.

Consumer Feasibility Condition III: One Commodity and Taxes. *Let*

(a) $$\bar{r} = z_{sr}r - \gamma - (\dot{v}/v),$$

*and* $a^*(t)$ *be the solution of the differential equation*

(b) $$\dot{a}^* = \bar{r}a^* - c,$$

*with* $a^*(0) = [A^M(0)/v(0)] + \Delta\{z_{cw}w;\ \bar{r}\}$. *Then* $c(t)$ *is feasible if and only if* $a^*(t) > 0$, *all* $t$.

*Remark.* Parallel to the remark to Consumer Feasibility Condition II, we must assume $v(t) > 0$, all $t$, for there to be an effective constraint on consumption.

## 2. Some Boundedness Assumptions

The factors external to the private sector that govern its feasibility conditions, apart from taxes, are $r(t)$, the rate of return, and $w(t)$, the exogenous income normalized by growth of the economy. We will be concerned with situations where these two magnitudes tend to converge to stationary values. In the present context this proposition follows from the basic assumption that the economy is being controlled in a way that will achieve the same optimal policy that would be achieved if it were centrally controlled. In other contexts, this assumption might still be reasonable simply because the long-run general equilibrium of the economy requires a balance among the different kinds of income.

The stock of government capital is also exogenous to the individual. It does not affect the feasibility conditions. If, however, the utility of the private sector depends on government capital, the marginal rate of substitution between consumptions at different time points will, in general, be affected, and the optimal consumption policy for the private sector will depend on the time path of the stock of government capital. It will be assumed that $k_g(t)$, the normalized stock of government capital, approaches a stationary value.

Actually, as seen in section IV.4, the approach of these magnitudes to their stationary values is essentially exponential, so that we may assert something more about the regularity of the convergence.

BOUNDEDNESS ASSUMPTION I. *The magnitudes $r(t)$ and $k_g(t)$ converge to positive finite limits, $r^\infty$ and $k^\infty$, respectively. Further,*

$$\left| \int_0^{+\infty} [r(t) - r^\infty] dt \right| < +\infty ,$$

*and $\dot{k}_g(t)$ approaches zero.*

BOUNDEDNESS ASSUMPTION II. *The magnitude $w(t)$ converges to a positive finite limit, $w^\infty$.*

In this chapter we are investigating the implications of controllability. If the economy is controllable, then $c(t)$, the optimal consumption policy for the private sector, will in fact be the same as that which would be chosen by centralized planning.

BOUNDEDNESS ASSUMPTION III. *The optimal consumption policy for the private sector, $c(t)$, converges to a positive finite limit, $c^\infty$, and $\dot{c}(t)$ approaches zero.*

This assumption, like the first, is also a natural implication of many general equilibrium models of the infinite-horizon economy.

*Remark.* Under Boundedness Assumptions I and III, $U_c$ converges to a finite positive limit, and $d(\log U_c)/dt$ approaches zero.

*Proof:* Since $c$ and $k_g$ approach finite nonzero limits, $U_c$, $U_{cc}$, and $U_{cg}$ approach finite nonzero limits. But

$$d(\log U_c)/dt = (U_{cc}\dot{c} + U_{cg}\dot{k}_g)/U_c ,$$

which approaches zero since $\dot{c}$ and $\dot{k}_g$ approach zero.

These assumptions will be shown to have strong implications for possible tax policies, since only a limited range will lead to consumption policies satisfying Boundedness Assumption III when Boundedness Assumptions I and II are made. In this chapter no further use will be made of the fact that the economy is being controlled to achieve the aims set forth in chapter IV. The results will be valid for an attempt to realize any policies satisfying the three boundedness assumptions.

## 3. Private Sector Optimization and Some Implications

It is assumed that the motivation of the private sector has the same form as that of the public sector, though we do not assume that the utility functions and utility discount rates are the same. In the present chapter we will use the same notation as that used for the public sector; there should be no confusion since the optimizing behavior of only the private sector is considered. In the next chapter we will use special subscripts and superscripts to distinguish the utility functions and utility discount rates of the two sectors.

The representative individual in the private sector is assumed to consider the welfare of each descendant equally with himself (except for time discounting), and of course all individuals are considered to be alike. Then the private sector seeks to maximize

$$\int_0^\infty e^{-\rho t} P(t) U(C/P, K_g/P) dt,$$

where the symbols have the same meaning as in chapters III and IV. By the boundedness assumptions, the economy is growing in the limit at a rate $\gamma$. Then the rate of growth of per capita consumption or income is $\tau = \gamma - \pi$, where $\pi$ is the rate of population growth. Assume further, as in chapters III and IV, that the utility function is homogeneous of degree $1 - \sigma$. Then the maximand can be rewritten in terms of magnitudes deflated by growth.

Consumer Behavior. *The private sector acts to maximize*

(a) $$\int_0^\infty e^{-\lambda t} U(c, k_g) dt,$$

*where $U$ is concave and homogeneous of degree $1 - \sigma$,*

(b) $$\lambda = \omega - \gamma > 0, \quad \textit{and} \quad \omega = \rho + \sigma\tau,$$

*subject to the appropriate consumer feasibility condition, section 1.*

Before deriving the necessary conditions for an optimal policy we will demonstrate, as promised in section 1, that if an optimal policy exists for any reasonable definition of feasibility and if it is bounded, then human capital is well defined.

For simplicity of notation we state the proposition for a situation with one commodity and no taxes, as in Consumer Feasibility Condition I.

PROPOSITION 1. *For any given consumption policy, $c(t)$, let $a^M(t)$ be the solution of the differential equation*

(a) $$\dot{a}^M = \bar{r}(t)a^M + w(t) - c(t)\,,$$

*with $a^M(0)$ given. Suppose we have some definition of feasibility for consumption paths satisfying the following two conditions:*

(b) *If $a^M(t) \geqq 0$ for all $t$ sufficiently large, then $c$ is feasible;*

(c) *If $c$, $\underline{c}$ are two consumption policies and $a^M$, $\underline{a}^M$ the corresponding solutions of* (a), *$c$ is feasible, and $\underline{a}^M(t) \geqq a^M(t)$ for all $t$ sufficiently large, then $\underline{c}$ is feasible.*

*Finally, suppose that $w(t) \geqq 0$ for all $t$, $w(t) > 0$ for $t$ sufficiently large, $k_g(t)$ converges to a finite nonzero limit, and that $c^*$ maximizes*

(d) $$\int_0^{\infty} e^{-\lambda t} U(c, k_g)dt$$

*among all feasible policies and converges to a finite nonzero limit. Then the differential equation*

(e) $$\dot{a}^H = \bar{r}a^H - w\,,$$

*has a nonnegative solution.*

*Proof:* Suppose every solution of (e) were negative for some $t$. Since $w(t) \geqq 0$ for all $t$, and $w(t) > 0$ for large $t$, it follows from Lemma 1 (appendix) that, for any solution of (e), $a^H(t) < 0$ for $t$ sufficiently large. Since $c^*(t) \geqq 0$ and $c^*(t) > 0$ for large $t$, Theorem 1 (appendix) is applicable when $A(t)$ is replaced by $\bar{r}(t)$, $B(t)$ by $w(t)$, and $C(t)$ by $c^*(t)$. In the interval, $0 \leqq t \leqq 1$, choose $c^{**}(t) > c^*(t)$, and define

$$c(t, \epsilon) = \begin{cases} c^{**}(t), \; 0 \leqq t \leqq 1\,, \\ (1 - \epsilon)c^*(t), \; t > 1\,. \end{cases}$$

Finally, let $a^M(t, \epsilon)$ be the solution of (a) with $c(t) = c(t, \epsilon)$. Then, from Theorem 1 (appendix), it follows that for $\epsilon$ small, either $a^M(t, \epsilon) > 0$, all $t$ sufficiently large, or $a^M(t, \epsilon) > a^M(t)$, all $t$ sufficiently large, where $a^M(t)$ is the solution of (a) with $c(t) = c^*(t)$. Then by (b) and (c), $c(t, \epsilon)$ is certainly feasible. It remains to prove that $c(t, \epsilon)$ is preferred to $c^*(t)$, a contradiction to the assumed optimality of $c^*$.

$$\int_0^{\infty} e^{-\lambda t} U[c(t, \epsilon), k_g(t)]dt - \int_0^{\infty} e^{-\lambda t} U[c^*(t), k_g(t)]dt$$

$$= \int_0^{1} e^{-\lambda t}\{U[c^{**}(t), k_g(t)] - U[c^*(t), k_g(t)]\}dt$$

$$- \int_1^{\infty} e^{-\lambda t}\{U[c^*(t), k_g(t)] - U[(1 - \epsilon)c^*(t), k_g(t)]\}dt.$$

The first integral is positive and independent of $\epsilon$. It then suffices to show that the second integral can be made arbitrarily small. Since $U$ is concave, it follows by a well-known inequality that, for $t > 1$,

$$\begin{aligned} U[c^*(t), k_g(t)] &- U[(1-\epsilon)c^*(t), k_g(t)] \\ &\leqq U_c[(1-\epsilon)c^*(t), k_g(t)][c^*(t) - (1-\epsilon)c^*(t)] \\ &= \epsilon U_c[(1-\epsilon)c^*(t), k_g(t)]c^*(t) = \epsilon F(t, \epsilon), \qquad (1) \end{aligned}$$

say.

Since $c^*(t)$ and $k_g(t)$ converge to finite nonzero limits, say $c^{*\infty}$ and $k_g^\infty$, it follows that for $\epsilon$ small and $t$ large, $F(t, \epsilon)$ is arbitrarily close to the positive constant, $U_c(c^{*\infty}, k_g^\infty)c^{*\infty}$. Since $\lambda > 0$, there is a constant $M$ for which

$$\int_1^\infty e^{-\lambda t} F(t, \epsilon) dt < M,$$

for $\epsilon$ small. Then, from (1),

$$\int_1^\infty e^{-\lambda t}\{U[c^*(t), k_g(t)] - U[(1-\epsilon)c^*(t), k_g(t)]\}dt < \epsilon M,$$

and can be made arbitrarily small by suitable choice of $\epsilon$.

Although Proposition 1 has been stated for a world of one commodity and no taxes, one need only reinterpret the symbols in order to apply the results to the cases for which Consumer Feasibility Conditions II or III are applicable. Since no assumption is made about $\bar{r}$, the various redefinitions of $\bar{r}$ do not affect the validity of the proposition. Similarly, since all that is assumed about $w$ is that it is positive, it can be replaced by $w^*$ in Condition II or by $z_{cw}w$ in Condition III.

COROLLARY. *Proposition 1 remains valid if $w$ is replaced by $w^*$ (as in Consumer Feasibility Condition II) or by $z_{cw}w$ (as in Consumer Feasibility Condition III).*

Proposition 1 can undoubtedly be extended to a wide variety of multi-commodity general equilibrium models in which there is ultimately a state of balanced growth.

The necessary conditions for the optimal solution to the problem of consumer behavior, assuming Boundedness Conditions I and III, will now be derived. Let $p$ be the dual variable associated with the equation of motion of the system, equation (b), in the appropriate consumer feasibility condition. We start by assuming the simplest case of one commodity so that Consumer Feasibility Condition I is appropriate. As before, the extension to the other cases will be immediate.

Then the current-value Hamiltonian is

$$H = U(c, k_g) + p(\bar{r}a - c). \tag{2}$$

Since $k_g$ is given to the individual, his only instrument is $c$. Then the necessary conditions are

$$U_c = p \tag{3}$$

and

$$\dot{p}/p = \lambda - \bar{r}. \tag{4}$$

Substitution from (3) into (4) yields

$$\bar{r}(t) = \lambda - d(\log U_c)/dt = r_c - \gamma, \tag{5}$$

where $r_c$ is the consumption rate of interest, $\omega - d(\log U_c)/dt$, as introduced in III.1. Note that, in view of our earlier remark, if Boundedness Assumptions I and III are satisfied, then $\bar{r}(t)$ must approach $\lambda$ as $t$ approaches infinity. This is a condition for the long-run general equilibrium of the economy.

The equation of motion, Consumer Feasibility Condition I(b), is

$$\dot{a} = \bar{r}a - c. \tag{6}$$

Substitute (5) into (6):

$$\dot{a} = (r_c - \gamma)a - c. \tag{7}$$

The expression in parentheses approaches a positive limit, as does $c$ under Boundedness Assumption III. Hence, by Lemmas 2 and 3 (appendix),

$$a(t) \to \begin{cases} c^{\infty}/\lambda & \text{if} \quad a(0) = \\ +\infty & \text{if} \quad a(0) > \\ -\infty & \text{if} \quad a(0) < \end{cases} \Delta\{c; r_c - \gamma\}. \tag{8}$$

Further, $a(t) > 0$, all $t$, in the first two cases [Corollary 2 to Lemma 1 (appendix)]. In the last case, the feasibility condition is certainly violated, and $c$ cannot be optimal. Suppose now that $a(0) \geqq \alpha = \Delta\{c; r_c - \gamma\}$. Let $a'$ be the solution of

$$\dot{a}' = \bar{r}a' - [a(0)/\alpha]c,$$

with $a'(0) = a(0)$. If we define $a''(t) = [\alpha/a(0)]a'(t)$, then $a''$ satisfies (6), $a''(0) = \alpha$, so that $a''(t) > 0$, all $t$, and therefore $a'(t) > 0$, all $t$. Hence, $[a(0)/\alpha]c$ would be a feasible solution; but if $a(0) > \alpha$, then $[a(0)/\alpha]c$ would be better than $c$, contradicting the optimality of the latter. Hence, a necessary condition for $c$ to be optimal is that

$$a(0) = \Delta\{c; r_c - \gamma\}. \tag{9}$$

Two alternative forms of (9) will be useful in interpreting its meaning. Both follow from Lemma 5 (appendix). First,

$$\Delta\{c; r_c - \gamma\} = \Delta\{ce^{\gamma t}; r_c\} = \Delta\{C; r_c\}. \tag{10}$$

Second, from (5),

$$\Delta\{c; r_c - \gamma\} = \Delta\{c; \omega - \gamma - d(\log U_c)/dt\} = \Delta\{(U_c/U_c^0)C; \omega\}, \tag{11}$$

where $U_c^0 = U_c[c(0), k_g(0)]$, the marginal utility of consumption at time 0. From (9) and (11), $a(0)$ is the value of consumption discounted to the present both for subjective utility discount and for variations in the marginal utility of consumption.

From Proposition 1, another necessary condition is that human capital be well defined. The equation of motion of human capital is

$$\dot{a}^H = \bar{r}a^H - w. \tag{12}$$

Then, from Theorem 2 and (15) (appendix), the value of human capital at time 0 is

$$a^H(0) = \Delta\{w; r_c - \gamma\} = \Delta\{W; r_c\}, \tag{13}$$

by the same argument as the preceding. The condition that human capital be well defined is simply that

$$\Delta\{W; r_c\} < +\infty. \tag{14}$$

From Consumer Feasibility Condition I, $a(0) = A^M(0) + a^H(0)$; since $A^M(0)$ is a datum of the problem, we use (10) and (13) to rewrite (9):

$$A^M(0) = \Delta\{C - W; r_c\}. \tag{15}$$

A given consumption policy will be optimal only for one particular initial position of material assets.

We have thus derived three necessary conditions: (5), (14), and (15). But now it is easy to see that they are sufficient if Boundedness Assumptions I and III hold. For the given consumption pattern, define $p$ by (3); then, from (5), (4) holds. It is then sufficient, by Proposition II.8, to show that the transversality condition

$$e^{-\lambda t}p(t)a(t) \to 0 \tag{16}$$

is satisfied. But from our earlier remark, $U_c$, and therefore $p$, converges to a finite limit; from the argument leading to (15) we see that if (15) holds, then $a(t)$ approaches the finite limit, $c^\infty/\lambda$, so that (16) certainly holds. If we now substitute in (5) the definition of $\bar{r}$ given in Consumer Feasibility Condition I(a), we can state:

PROPOSITION 2. *If Boundedness Conditions I and III hold, then in a system with one commodity the policy $c(t)$ is optimal consumer behavior if and only if the following three conditions are satisfied:*

(a) $$r(t) = r_c(t);$$

(b) $$\Delta\{W; r_c\} < +\infty;$$

(c) $$A^M(0) = \Delta\{C - W; r_c\}.$$

*If Boundedness Condition II holds also, then $A^M(t)/e^{\gamma t}$ approaches $(c^\infty - w^\infty)/\lambda$, and condition* (b) *is automatically satisfied.*

The last can be seen as follows: If $w(t)$ converges, then the analysis of the differential equation (12) is parallel to that of (6), so that $a^H(t)$ approaches $w^\infty/\lambda$; then simply note that $A^M/e^{\gamma t} = a^M = a - a^H$. Also, of course, if $w$ is bounded, then by Lemma 3 (appendix), (b) must hold.

If there is one commodity and money (but no taxes), the whole argument remains valid exactly as before, with some obvious substitutions. In particular, the definition of $\bar{r}$ changes, and

$$A^M(0)/p_c(0) = a^{*M}(0) = \Delta\{c - w^*; r_c - \gamma\}.$$

Also note that, by definition, $w^* = w/p_c$.

PROPOSITION 3. *If Boundedness Assumptions I and III hold, then in a system with one commodity and money, the policy $c(t)$ is optimal consumer behavior if and only if the following three conditions are satisfied:*

(a) $$r(t) - (\dot{p}_c/p_c) = r_c(t);$$

(b) $$\Delta\{w^*; r_c - \gamma\} < +\infty;$$

(c) $$A^M(0) - p_c(0)\Delta\{c - w^*; r_c - \gamma\}.$$

*Further, $a^{*M} + a^{*H}$ approaches the finite positive limit $c^\infty/\lambda$, where $a^{*M}$ and $a^{*H}$ are defined by 1.(14).*

The last statement can be seen as follows: by definition, $a^{*M} + a^{*H} = a^*$, and $a^*$ approaches $c^\infty/\lambda$ by the proof of Proposition 2 suitably modified.

With these two propositions as background, it will now be easy to understand the basic proposition for the optimality (from the individual's point of view) of a bounded consumption policy in the presence of taxes.

PROPOSITION 4. *If Boundedness Assumptions I and III hold, then in a system with one commodity and taxes, the policy $c(t)$ is optimal consumer behavior if and only if the following three conditions are satisfied:*

(a) $$z_{sr}r - (\dot{v}/v) = r_c(t);$$

(b) $$\Delta\{z_{cw}W\,;\, r_c\} < +\infty\,;$$

(c) $$A^M(0) = v(0)\Delta\{C - z_{cw}W\,;\, r_c\}\,.$$

*Further,* $a^{*M} + a^{*H}$ *approaches the finite positive limit,* $c^\infty/\lambda$, *where* $a^{*M}$ *and* $a^{*H}$ *are defined by 1.(16). If* $z_{cw}$ *converges to a finite positive limit* $z_{cw}^\infty$, *and Boundedness Assumption II holds, then* (b) *holds automatically, and* $a^{*M} \to (c^\infty - z_{cw}^\infty w^\infty)/\lambda$.

For proof of the last sentence, note that the analog of 1.(9) for the case of one commodity and taxes is

$$\dot{a}^{*H} = \bar{r}a^{*H} - z_{cw}w\,.$$

By Lemma 2, Theorem 2 and (15) of the appendix, $a^{*H}(t) \to z_{cw}^\infty w^\infty/\lambda$, since $\bar{r} = r_c(t) - \gamma \to \omega - \gamma = \lambda$, if $a^{*H}(0) = \Delta\{z_{cw}w; r_c - \gamma\}$. Since $a^{*M} + a^{*H} \to c^\infty/\lambda$, $a^{*M} \to (c^\infty - z_{cw}^\infty w^\infty)/\lambda$.

The implications for controllability of Proposition 4, the basic proposition, will be developed in the next chapter.

# MATHEMATICAL APPENDIX

In this appendix some of the mathematical properties of the differential equations that appear in the text are analyzed. These are of two types:

$$\dot{x} = A(t)x - B(t), \tag{1}$$

$$\dot{x} = A(t)x + B(t) - C(t), \tag{2}$$

where all functions $A(t)$, $B(t)$, and $C(t)$ are usually assumed to be nonnegative. In some instances we shall assume that these functions converge, and if such limits exist we shall use our standard notation:

$$\lim_{t \to \infty} A(t) = A^{\infty};$$

$$\lim_{t \to \infty} B(t) = B^{\infty};$$

$$\lim_{t \to \infty} x(t) = x^{\infty}.$$

Also, we shall denote by $x(t|x_0)$ the solution of the differential equation that satisfies $x(t_0) = x_0$. For these linear equations the solution $x(t|x_0)$ is unique and continuous in the initial condition.

LEMMA 1: *Let $x(t)$ satisfy the differential equation*

$$\dot{x} = A(t)x - B(t). \tag{3}$$

*Suppose $B(t) \geqq 0$ for all $t$, and $B(t) > 0$ for $t > \bar{t}$ for some $\bar{t} < \infty$. If $x(t_0) \leqq 0$ for some $t_0$, then $x(t) \leqq 0$ for all $t > t_0$, and $x(t) < 0$ for $t >$* max $[t_0, \bar{t}]$.

*Proof:* Suppose first that $t_0 > \bar{t}$, thus $B(t) > 0$, all $t \geqq t_0$. Now suppose the conclusion is false; then the set $M = \{t \mid t > t_0, x(t) \geqq 0\}$ would be non-null. Let $t_1 = \inf M$. Clearly, $t_1 \geqq t_0$, while by continuity $x(t_1) \geqq 0$. Now if $t_1 = t_0$, then $x(t_1) = 0$; but $x(t) \geqq 0$ for values of $t > t_1$ and arbitrarily close so that $\dot{x}(t_1) \geqq 0$. But $\dot{x}(t_1) = A(t_1)x(t_1) - B(t_1) = -B(t_1) < 0$, which is a contradiction.

If, on the other hand, $t_1 > t_0$, then $x(t) < 0$ for $t_0 < t < t_1$ while $x(t_1) \geqq 0$. Hence, $\dot{x}(t_1) \geqq 0$, while by continuity $x(t_1) = 0$. This involves again the same contradiction as above.

Now suppose that $t_0 \leqq \bar{t}$. Suppose we can prove that $x(t) \leqq 0$ for all $t > t_0$. Then, for any $t > \bar{t}$, choose $t_0'$, $\bar{t} < t_0' < t$; since $x(t_0') \leqq 0$, it follows from the first result that $x(t) < 0$.

Let $x(t, \epsilon)$ satisfy the differential equation

$$\dot{x}(t, \epsilon) = A(t)x(t, \epsilon) - [B(t) + \epsilon],$$

with $x(t_0, \epsilon) = x(t_0)$. For $\epsilon > 0$, $B(t) + \epsilon > 0$ for all $t$; hence, by the first result, $x(t, \epsilon) < 0$ for all $t > t_0$. For any fixed $t$, $x(t, \epsilon)$ is a continuous function of $\epsilon$; hence, $x(t, 0) = x(t) \leqq 0$, all $t > t_0$, as was to be proved.

COROLLARY 1. *Under the conditions of the Lemma, if $A(t) > 0$, then $x(t_0) \leqq 0$ for some $t_0$ implies $\limsup_{t\to\infty} x(t) < 0$.*

*Proof:* From Lemma 1 it follows that for all $t > \max\,[t_0, \bar{t}]$ we must have $x(t) < 0$. But at $t$ we also have

$$\dot{x}(t) = A(t)x(t) - B(t) \leqq -B(t) < 0.$$

Thus, for all $t > \max\,[t_0, \bar{t}]$, $x(t) < 0$ and is monotonically decreasing. Thus, $\limsup_{t\to\infty} x(t) < 0$.

COROLLARY 2. *Suppose $A(t) > 0$, $B(t) \geqq 0$ for all $t$, $B(t) > 0$ for $t > \bar{t}$. If $x(t)$ satisfies*

(a) $$\dot{x}(t) = A(t)x - B(t),$$

*and $\liminf_{t\to\infty} x(t) \geqq 0$, then $x(t) > 0$, all $t$.*

*Proof:* Suppose not. Then there exists a $t_0$ such that $x(t_0) \leqq 0$. Then it follows from Corollary 1 that $\liminf_{t\to\infty} x(t) \leqq \limsup_{t\to\infty} x(t) < 0$, which contradicts the hypothesis.

LEMMA 2. *Suppose $\lim_{t\to\infty} A(t) = A^\infty > 0$, and $\lim_{t\to\infty} B(t) = B^\infty$, both finite. Then there exists $\xi$ such that every solution of the differential equation*

(a) $$\dot{x} = A(t)x - B(t)$$

*for which* $x(0) > \xi$ *approaches* $+\infty$, *every solution for which* $x(0) < \xi$ *approaches* $-\infty$, *while the solution for which* $x(0) = \xi$ *approaches* $B^\infty/A^\infty$.

*Proof:* If $\dot{x}$ converges to a nonzero limit, then for $t$ sufficiently large, $x(t)$ would be bounded either above or below by a linear function with a nonzero slope, and therefore approaches either $+\infty$ or $-\infty$. If $x(t)$ converges to a finite limit, $\dot{x}$ would have to converge to a limit. Together, these remarks show that

$$\text{if } x(t) \text{ converges at all, } x^\infty = B^\infty/A^\infty. \tag{4}$$

Choose now $t_0$ so that $A(t) > 0$ for $t \geqq t_0$. Let $x(t|x_0)$ be that unique solution of (a) for which $x(t_0) = x_0$. Suppose $x_0' > x_0$ and let $y(t) = x(t|x_0') - x(t|x_0)$. Then

$$\dot{y} = A(t)y, \qquad y(t_0) > 0, \tag{5}$$

so that

$$y(t) = y(t_0)e^{\int_{t_0}^{t} A(u)du}$$

which approaches $+\infty$. Therefore,

$$\text{if } x(t|x_0) \text{ is bounded below, then } x(t|x_0') \to +\infty \text{ if } x_0' > x_0; \tag{6}$$

$$\text{if } x(t|x_0) \text{ is bounded above, then } x(t|x_0') \to -\infty \text{ if } x_0' < x_0. \tag{7}$$

Now let $\bar{x}(t) = \sup_{\tau \geqq t} [B(\tau)/A(\tau)]$, $\underline{x}(t) = \inf_{\tau \geqq t} [B(\tau)/A(\tau)]$.

The functions $\bar{x}(t)$, $\underline{x}(t)$ are well defined for $t \geqq t_0$; $\bar{x}$ is monotone decreasing, $\underline{x}$ monotone increasing.

$$\lim_{t\to\infty} \bar{x}(t) = \lim_{t\to\infty} \underline{x}(t) = B^\infty/A^\infty. \tag{8}$$

Next we show that if $x(t_1) > \bar{x}(t_1)$ for some $t_1 \geqq t_0$, then $\dot{x}(t) > 0$ for all $t \geqq t_1$, for then certainly $x(t_1) > B(t_1)/A(t_1)$, and

$$\dot{x}(t_1) = A(t_1)x(t_1) - B(t_1) > A(t_1)[B(t_1)/A(t_1)] - B(t_1) = 0.$$

Suppose $\dot{x}(t) \leq 0$ for some $t > t_1$; let

$$t_2 = \inf \{t | t > t_1, \dot{x}(t) \leq 0\}. \tag{9}$$

Then, by definition, $\dot{x}(t) > 0$, $t_1 \leqq t < t_2$ so that, by continuity, $\dot{x}(t_2) = 0$; also $x(t_2) > x(t_1)$, and therefore

$$x(t_2) > \bar{x}(t_1) \geqq B(t_2)/A(t_2),$$

from which it follows as before that $\dot{x}(t_2) > 0$, a contradiction. Hence, $\dot{x}(t) > 0$ for all $t \geqq t_1$, and $x(t)$ is strictly increasing; since $\bar{x}(t)$ is monotone decreasing, $x(t) - \bar{x}(t)$ is strictly increasing. Since $x(t_1) - \bar{x}(t_1) > 0$, $x(t) - \bar{x}(t)$, for $t > t_1$, is positive and strictly increasing. Hence, it approaches either $+\infty$ or a positive finite limit. But $\bar{x}(t) \to B^\infty/A^\infty$ so that if $x(t)$ converges to a finite limit we would have $x^\infty > B^\infty/A^\infty$, a contradiction to (4).

We have thus proved:

$$\text{If } x(t_1) > \bar{x}(t_1) \text{ for some } t_1 \geqq t_0, \text{ then } x^\infty = +\infty\ ; \tag{10}$$

$$\text{if } x(t_1) < \underline{x}(t_1) \text{ for some } t_1 \geqq t_0, \text{ then } x^\infty = -\infty\,. \tag{11}$$

The only remaining possibility is that $\underline{x}(t) \leqq x(t) \leqq \bar{x}(t)$ for all $t \geqq t_0$, in which case $x^\infty = B^\infty/A^\infty$, by (8). Thus, for any solution $x(t)$ of (a), either $x(t) \to +\infty$ or $x(t) \to B^\infty/A^\infty$ or $x(t) \to -\infty$.

Finally we turn to the proof of the existence of a unique $\xi$ as stated in the lemma.

Let

$$\begin{aligned} U &= \{x_0 \,|\, x(t\,|\,x_0) \to +\infty\}\,, \\ M &= \{x_0 \,|\, x(t\,|\,x_0) \to B^\infty/A^\infty\}\,, \\ L &= \{x_0 \,|\, x(t\,|\,x_0) \to -\infty\}\,. \end{aligned}$$

If $x_0 \in U$, $x(t|x_0)$ is bounded from below; hence, if $x_0' > x_0$, $x_0' \in U$ by (6). Also, $\bar{x}(t_0)$ is finite; if $x_0 > \bar{x}(t_0)$, then by (10) $x_0 \in U$. Thus, $U$ is non-null and, if it contains any number, it contains all larger ones. Similarly, $L$ is non-null and, if it contains any number, it contains all smaller ones. Finally, if $x_0 \in M$, then $x(t|x_0)$ is certainly bounded below; hence, if $x_0 \in M$ and $x_0' > x_0$, $x(t|x_0') \to +\infty$ and $x_0' \notin M$. Thus, $M$ can have at most one element.

From these remarks it follows that $U$ is bounded below and $L$ bounded above, and indeed

$$\inf U = \sup L\,.$$

Let $\xi'$ be the common value. We seek to show that $\xi'$ is the unique element of $M$. If $\xi'$ belonged to $U$, then $x(t_1|\xi') > \bar{x}(t_1)$, some $t_1 \geqq t_0$. For fixed $t_1$, $x(t_1|x_0)$ is a continuous function of $x_0$; hence, we can choose $x_0 < \xi'$ so that $x(t_1|x_0) > \bar{x}(t_1)$. Then $x_0 \in U$, a contradiction to the definition of $\xi'$. Similarly, $\xi'$ cannot belong to $L$. Hence, $\xi' \in M$.

Since $x(0|x_0)$ is easily seen to be a strictly increasing function of $x_0$, let $\xi = x(0|\xi')$. Then the lemma is established.

THEOREM 1. *Let $x(t)$ satisfy the differential equation:*

(a) $$\dot{x} = A(t)x + B(t) - C(t)\,,$$

*where* $B(t) \geqq 0$, *all* $t$, *and* $B(t) > 0$ *for* $t > \bar{t}$; $C(t) \geqq 0$, *all* $t$, $C(t) > 0$ *for large* $t$. *Suppose that for every solution of the differential equation*

(b) $$\dot{y} = A(t)y - B(t),$$

$y(t) < 0$ *for* $t$ *sufficiently large. Let* $C^*(t) > C(t)$, $0 \leqq t \leqq 1$, *and let*

(c) $$C(t, \epsilon) = \begin{cases} C^*(t) \text{ for } 0 \leqq t \leqq 1 \\ (1 - \epsilon)C(t) \text{ for } t > 1, \end{cases}$$

*and* $x(t, \epsilon)$ *satisfy the differential equation*

(d) $$\dot{x} = A(t)x + B(t) - C(t, \epsilon),$$

*with the initial condition* $x(0, \epsilon) = x(0)$. *Then either, for all* $\epsilon$, $x(t, \epsilon) > x(t)$ *for* $t$ *sufficiently large or for all* $\epsilon$ *sufficiently small*, $x(t, \epsilon) > 0$ *for all* $t$ *sufficiently large.*

*Proof:* Let $z(t, \epsilon) = x(t) - x(t, \epsilon)$. If (d) is subtracted from (a), we see that

$$\dot{z} = A(t)z + C(t, \epsilon) - C(t), z(0, \epsilon) = 0.$$

For $0 \leqq t \leqq 1$, $C(t, \epsilon) - C(t) = C^*(t) - C(t) > 0$ and independent of $\epsilon$. Hence, $z(t, \epsilon) = z(t)$ independent of $\epsilon$ for $0 \leqq t \leqq 1$. Further, $z(0) = 0$, $\dot{z}(0) > 0$, so that $z(t) > 0$ in a right-hand neighborhood of 0. Let $t_1$ be the smallest value of $t$ for which $z(t) \leqq 0$. By continuity, $z(t_1) = 0$; but then $\dot{z}(t_1) = C^*(t_1) - C(t_1) > 0$, which implies $z(t) < 0$ in a left-hand neighborhood of $t_1$, contradicting its definition. Hence, $z(t) > 0$, $0 \leqq t \leqq 1$, and in particular $z(1) > 0$.

Now let $w(t, \epsilon) = z(t, \epsilon)/\epsilon$. Then

$$w(1, \epsilon) > 0, \lim_{\epsilon \to 0} w(1, \epsilon) = +\infty, \tag{12}$$

and

$$\dot{w} = A(t)w - C(t), \qquad t > 1. \tag{13}$$

There are two possibilities: (a) for any $w(t)$ satisfying (13), $w(t) \leqq 0$ for some $t$; or (b) for some solution of (13), $w(t) > 0$, all $t$. If (a) holds, then, since $C(t) \geqq 0$ and $C(t) > 0$ for large $t$, it follows from Lemma 1 that $w(t) < 0$ for all large $t$. But this means that $x(t, \epsilon) > x(t)$ for all $t$ sufficiently large.

Now suppose (b) holds. Since two solutions of (13) cannot cross anywhere (otherwise the solution would not be unique), $w(t)$ is a strictly increasing function of $w(1)$ for any fixed $t > 1$. Hence, there is a number $\bar{w}$ such that if $w(1) > \bar{w}$, then $w(t) > 0$, all $t$. But by (12), then,

$$\text{for all } \epsilon \text{ sufficiently small, } w(t, \epsilon) > 0 \text{ for all } t. \tag{14}$$

Let $y(t, \epsilon) = w(t, \epsilon) - x(t)$. Then, from (13) and (a), $y(t, \epsilon)$ satisfies (b) for $t > 1$. From the definitions of $z(t, \epsilon)$ and $w(t, \epsilon)$, $x(t) = x(t, \epsilon) + \epsilon w(t, \epsilon)$, from which we see that

$$x(t, \epsilon) = (1 - \epsilon)w(t,\epsilon) - y(t, \epsilon).$$

But from (14), for $\epsilon$ sufficiently small, $w(t, \epsilon) > 0$ for all $t$, while, by hypothesis, $y(t, \epsilon) < 0$ for $t$ sufficiently large. Hence, $x(t, \epsilon) > 0$ for $t$ sufficiently large.

THEOREM 2. *Suppose* $\int_0^\infty A(t)dt = +\infty$ *and* $B(t) \geqq 0$, *all* $t$, *while* $B(t) > 0$ *for large* $t$. *If, for some solution* $x(t)$ *of*

(a) $$\dot{x} = A(t)x - B(t),$$

$x(t) > 0$, *all* $t$, *then there exists* $\xi$ *such that* $x(t) > 0$, *all* $t$, *if and only if* $x(0) \geqq \xi$, *and*

(b) $$\xi = \int_0^\infty e^{-\int_0^t A(u)du} B(t)dt.$$

*Conversely, if the integral in* (b) *converges, then indeed* $\xi$ *is the smallest initial value for which* $x(t) > 0$, *all* $t$.

*Proof:* Let $x(t|x_0)$ be the solution of (a) with $x(0) = x_0$, $U = \{x_0 | x(t|x_0) > 0, \text{ all } t\}$, $L = \{x_0 | x(t|x_0) < 0 \text{ for all } t \text{ sufficiently large}\}$. It is implied by Lemma 1 that $U$ and $L$ exhaust all real numbers since $B(t) \geqq 0$ and $B(t) > 0$ for large $t$. By hypothesis, $U$ is non-null; since $x(t|x_0)$ is a strictly increasing function of $x_0$, if $x_0 \in U$ and $x_0' > x_0$, then $x_0' \in U$. Similarly, $0 \in L$ by Lemma 1, and $x_0 \in L$, $x_0' < x_0$, imply that $x_0' \in L$. Let

$$\xi = \sup L = \inf U.$$

We shall now show that $\xi \in U$. Suppose not; then $\xi \in L$ and $x(t|\xi) < 0$ for $t$ large. Then $x(t_1|\xi) < 0$, some $t_1$; by continuity, $x(t_1|x_0) < 0$ for some $x_0 > \xi$. But then $x_0 \in L$, contrary to the definition of $\xi$. Hence, $\xi \in U$, as was to be shown.

The explicit solution of (a) is

$$x(t|x_0) = e^{\bar{A}(t)}\left[x_0 - \int_0^t e^{-\bar{A}(u)}B(u)du\right],$$

where $\bar{A}(t) = \int_0^t A(u)du$. If $x_0$ is greater than the integral in (b), then the bracket is positive and bounded away from 0 as $t$ approaches infinity; since the first factor approaches infinity by hypothesis, $x(t|x_0)$

approaches infinity and therefore is positive for all $t$. But then we could choose $x_0'$ slightly smaller than $x_0$ for which the same would hold, so that $x_0 > \xi$. Similarly, if $x_0$ is less than the integral in (b), then $x(t|x_0)$ approaches $-\infty$, and $x_0 < \xi$. Hence, (b) is proved.

Conversely, suppose the integral in (b) is finite. Since

$$\int_0^t e^{-\bar{A}(u)} B(u) du$$

has a positive integrand and, hence, is an increasing function of $t$, $x(t|x_0) \geqq 0$ if $x_0 \geqq \xi$. On the other hand, if $x_0 < \xi$, it follows as before that $x(t|x_0)$ approaches $-\infty$.

Theorem 2, and particularly statement (b) of the theorem, motivates our introduction of the notion of the "discount operator" which is denoted $\Delta\{B; A\}$. This operator is defined by

$$\Delta\{B; A\} = \int_0^\infty e^{-\int_0^t A(u)du} B(t) dt. \tag{15}$$

It follows, however, from Theorem 2 and Lemma 2 that if $B(t) > 0$, all $t$, and we define

$$x(0) = \Delta\{B; A\}, \tag{16}$$

then $x(0)$ is the smallest initial value such that the differential equation $\dot{x} = A(t)x - B(t)$ has the solution $x[t|x(0)] > 0$, all $t \geqq t_0$. In the following discussion we shall refer to $x(0)$ with the above property as the "critical value."

Although the discount operator is defined for $B(t) > 0$, it can be defined for more general cases; in fact, it suffices for our purposes to consider $B(t)$ bounded. Choose $\underline{B} < 0$ so that $B(t) - \underline{B} > 0$, all $t$. Consider the differential equations:

$$\dot{x}_1 = A(t)x_1 - [B(t) - \underline{B}], \tag{17}$$

$$\dot{x}_2 = A(t)x_2 - (-\underline{B}), \tag{18}$$

$$\dot{x} = A(t)x - B(t). \tag{19}$$

By Theorem 1,

$$\left.\begin{aligned} x_1(t) &\to +\infty \text{ if } x_1(0) > \Delta\{B - \underline{B}; A\} \\ x_2(t) &\to -\infty \text{ if } x_2(0) < \Delta\{-\underline{B}; A\} \end{aligned}\right\}. \tag{20}$$

Now suppose $x(0) > \Delta\{B; A\} = \Delta\{B - \underline{B}; A\} - \Delta\{-\underline{B}; A\}$, by (20). Then choose $x_1(0)$, $x_2(0)$ so that

$$x_1(0) > \Delta\{B - \underline{B}; A\},\ x_2(0) < \Delta\{-\underline{B}; A\},\ x_1(0) - x_2(0) = x(0).$$

From (17)–(19), $x(t) = x_1(t) - x_2(t)$ is a solution of (19); but $x(t) \to +\infty$ by (20). Similarly, $x(0) < \Delta\{B; A\}$ implies $x(t) \to -\infty$.

LEMMA 3. *If* $\int_0^\infty A(t)dt = +\infty$ *and* $B(t)$ *is bounded, then* $\Delta\{B; A\}$ *is finite. The solution,* $x(t)$, *of the differential equation,*

$$\dot{x} = A(t)x - B(t),$$

*approaches* $+\infty$ *if* $x(0) > \Delta\{B; A\}$, $-\infty$ *if* $x(0) < \Delta\{B; A\}$.

The linear operator $\Delta\{B; A\}$ has a few important properties which are used repeatedly in chapters VII and VIII. These will be presented here.

LEMMA 4. *Let* $F(t)$ *be a differentiable function,* $\dot{F}$ *bounded,* $F(\infty) < \infty$ *and* $\int_0^\infty g(t)dt = +\infty$. *Then*

$$\Delta\{\dot{F}; g\} = -F(0) + \Delta\{Fg; g\}.$$

*Proof:* By our earlier notation and Lemma 3, a critical value, $x(0) = \Delta\{\dot{F}; g\}$, exists for the differential equation $\dot{x} = g(t)x - \dot{F}(t)$. From theorems 1 and 2 it follows that the conditions of the lemma are sufficient to ensure $x(0) < +\infty$.

Now let

$$y(t) = x(t) + F(t)\,; \tag{21}$$

thus,

$$\begin{aligned}\dot{y}(t) &= \dot{x}(t) + \dot{F}(t)\\ &= [g(t)x - \dot{F}(t)] + \dot{F}(t)\\ &= g(t)x\\ &= g(t)[y(t) - F(t)],\end{aligned}$$

which means

$$\dot{y}(t) = g(t)y(t) - F(t)g(t). \tag{22}$$

Thus there exists a critical value $y(0)$ of (22) such that

$$y(0) = \Delta\{Fg; g\}.$$

But since

$$y(0) = x(0) + F(0)$$

we have

$$\Delta\{\dot{F}; g\} = x(0) = y(0) - F(0) = -F(0) + \Delta\{Fg; g\}.$$

LEMMA 5. *Let $F(t)$ be a differentiable function. Assume* $\int_0^{\infty} A(t)dt = +\infty$ *and $B(t)$ bounded. Then* $\Delta\{B; A - \dot{F}\} = \Delta\{Be^{F(t)-F(0)}; A\}$.

*Proof:* $x(0) = \Delta\{B; A - \dot{F}\}$ is the critical value of the differential equation $\dot{x} = (A - \dot{F})x - B$.

Now consider the change of variables

$$y(t) = x(t)e^{F(t)-F(0)} ;$$

thus

$$\begin{aligned}\dot{y}(t) &= \dot{x}(t)e^{F(t)-F(0)} + \dot{F}(t)x(t)e^{F(t)-F(0)} \\ &= \{(A - \dot{F})x - B\}e^{F(t)-F(0)} + \dot{F}xe^{F(t)-F(0)} \\ &= Axe^{F(t)-F(0)} - Be^{F(t)-F(0)} \\ &= Ay - Be^{F(t)-F(0)} .\end{aligned}$$

This means that

$$y(0) = \Delta\{Be^{F(t)-F(0)}; A\} .$$

But $y(0) = x(0)$; thus,

$$\Delta\{B; A - \dot{F}\} = \Delta\{Be^{F(t)-F(0)}; A\} .$$

LEMMA 6. $\Delta\{A; A\} = 1$ *if* $\int_0^{\infty} A(t)dt = +\infty$.

*Proof:* $x(0) = \Delta\{A; A\}$ is the critical value of $\dot{x} = A(t)x - A(t)$. Since $x(t) = 1$ all $t$ is a solution it must also be the unique critical value.

# VIII

# CONTROLLABILITY OF PUBLIC POLICY IN PERFECT CAPITAL MARKETS

## 0. Introduction

In this chapter, as in chapter VI, we shall consider the problem of achieving through limited government instruments a desired allocation of resources among consumption, private investment, and public investment; in short, the problem of controllability. The problem differs from that of chapter VI in only one respect, but that is crucial: the savings policy of the private sector is governed not by a fixed savings ratio but by completely competitive behavior. Specifically, consumers are assumed to behave in accordance with the model studied in the last chapter; they maximize the sum of discounted utilities over an infinite horizon, with perfect foresight of future rates of return on assets, non-interest income (referred to for convenience as wages), and tax rates.

The government can directly choose only the rate of public capital formation, tax rates, and the rate of borrowing; these decisions are subject to a budget limitation: that public capital formation equals the sum of tax collections, borrowing, and returns on public capital to the extent collected, less interest on the accumulated debt. For given tax rates (possibly varying over time), the private sector directly chooses the rate of consumption and savings. Finally, the volume of private capital formation is determined as the difference between private savings and government borrowing.

As discussed in chapter V, the fundamental question of controllability, then, is whether the government, by choice of admissible values for the instruments at its disposal, can achieve a desired allocation of resources over time. Even if the economy is controllable, we can also ask if the instruments show stable or unstable behavior over time.

The controllability of the economy is, of course, examined in relation to the range of instruments available. By the same argument that was used in chapter VI, it is clear that an income tax, without borrowing, is not sufficient for control. We shall therefore study the control of the economy through a combination of borrowing and a tax (income tax, consumption tax, and so forth). Unlike the situation in which there is a fixed savings ratio, controllability of the economy is not necessarily ensured by a single tax, and even when it is, instability is possible. We shall also study some examples of the use of two taxes and show that in these cases the debt may also be made the object of policy; for example, an initial debt can be extinguished, if desired.

As a matter of notation, we now attach a subscript, or superscript, $p$, to any magnitudes indicating valuation by the private sector. Thus, the felicity function of the private sector will be denoted by $U^p(\tilde{c}, \tilde{k}_g)$. Its elasticity with respect to scale changes in both variables, assumed constant, will be denoted by $\sigma_p$; the rate at which the individual discounts future utilities is then $\rho_p$. The asymptotic rate of *per capita* growth of the economy, $\tau$, is of course the same for both public and private sectors, as is the rate of growth of population, $\pi$. Then we define

$$\omega_p = \rho_p + \sigma_p \tau, \qquad \lambda_p = \omega_p - (\pi + \tau). \tag{1}$$

Similarly, the consumption rate of interest will be given a superscript $p$;

$$r_c^p = \omega_p - d(\log U_c^p)/dt. \tag{2}$$

In all the results of chapter VII, the subscript $p$ should be inserted as just indicated.

The intent of this study is to show how the publicly optimal plans developed in chapter IV can be implemented. Therefore we will also have occasion to refer to public values; the government's felicity function will be given a superscript $g$, while scalar-valued magnitudes will be given a subscript $g$.

Most of the results to be obtained are valid for any set of policies that the government may desire for any reason, provided only that the boundedness assumptions of VII.2 are satisfied; the policies need not, in fact, be derived from a full optimization. But it is especially interesting to discuss controllability in the case of no divergence between public and private values; i.e., where $U^p(\tilde{c}, \tilde{k}_g) = U^g(\tilde{c}, \tilde{k}_g)$ for all $\tilde{c}$ and $\tilde{k}_g$, and $\rho_p = \rho_g$. From these assumptions it follows that $\sigma_p = \sigma_g$, $\omega_p = \omega_g$, and $\lambda_p = \lambda_g$. Also, in the general case where there is divergence between public and private values, it will be seen that the asymptotic (steady-state) behavior of the instruments will in most cases be qualitatively determined by the relation between the rates of discount of private utilities, $\omega_p$, and the discount of the future implicit in the desired policy, as expressed by $f_p^\infty$, the asymptotic value of the marginal productivity of capital.

In section 1 we show that Proposition VII.4 yields general characterizations of controllability and stability and examine the particular form that the characterization takes in the case of no divergence. In section 2 we examine the possibilities of controllability without any taxes. This exercise is designed simply to show that even without divergence of values, fiscal policy is still needed for two reasons: the failure of the government to recover the market return on its investment and the existence of a historically given public debt at the initial moment of planning.

In subsequent sections we consider in turn different possible taxes and combinations of taxes; for each we examine controllability, stability, and the special nature of the tax policy for the case of no divergence. Results of the chapter are summarized in section 10.

Some of the topics in this chapter have been studied by Phelps (1965, section 2.1.6 and 2.2.3) from a viewpoint basically similar to ours, though couched in different language. His specific results are different and non-overlapping; his positive analysis assumes lump-sum taxes, while his discussion of the difficulties of controllability with income or consumption taxes emphasizes the labor-leisure margin, which we ignore, rather than the savings-consumption margin, which we stress.

## 1. Some General Characterizations of Controllability and Stability

In a perfect capital market, the rate of return to the private sector before taxes is the marginal productivity of private capital. Suppose now that the government has a desired *allocation policy*, $C(t)$, $K_p(t)$, $K_g(t)$. Then, by definition of controllability, the taxes must be such that $C(t)$ is optimal consumer behavior when $K_p(t)$ and $K_g(t)$ are the actual paths of private and government capital formation, respectively. (Note that $K_p$ affects consumer behavior only through its effect on the marginal productivity of private capital, $f_p = r$; $K_g$ may affect consumer behavior both by its influence on $f_p$ if the two types of capital are complements or substitutes in production, and by its influence on $U_c^p$, the private marginal utility of consumption, if public capital and consumption are complements or substitutes in utility.) Hence, conditions (a)–(c) of Proposition VII.4 must hold (with the subscript or superscript $p$ added as appropriate).

Conversely, suppose the conditions (a)–(c) of Proposition VII.4 are satisfied, with $r = f_p$. Then we note that, by Walras's Law, the demand for government debt by the private sector is exactly sufficient to enable the government to finance its desired public capital formation. For this purpose, let $X$ represent tax collections plus payments to the government for the use of public capital ($r_g K_g$ in the notation introduced in V.5), less interest on the government debt. Then private disposable income is $Y - X$, where $Y$ is total national income. The private sector allocates its disposable income between consumption and accumulation of material assets: $Y - X = C + \dot{A}^M$. On the other hand, the government has to borrow (increase its debt) by the difference between its desired program of public capital formation and $X$; $\dot{D} = \dot{K}_g - X$. Finally, feasibility for the desired program means that $Y = C + \dot{K}_p + \dot{K}_g$; from these budget and feasibility conditions, we deduce immediately that $\dot{A}^M = \dot{K}_p + \dot{D}$; i.e., private savings will automatically just balance the needs for private capital formation and government borrowing.

Proposition VII.4 will be used to give a general characterization of controllability. This proposition states necessary and sufficient conditions to achieve consistency between private optimization and the values of the variables which are exogenously given to the individual optimizer. Thus, a discussion of controllability actually amounts to analyzing whether, given bounded targets of public policy, it is feasible to choose values for public instruments so that conditions (a)–(c) of Proposition VII.4 are satisfied.

It will be illuminating to rewrite Proposition VII.4(c):

$$A^M(0) = v(0)\Delta\{C - z_{cw}W; r_c^p\}, \tag{1}$$

where

$$r_c^p = \lambda_p + \gamma - d(\log U_c^p)/dt = \omega_p - d(\log U_c^p)/dt.$$

First, write total income as a sum of incomes and of outputs, as usual in national income accounting:

$$Y = C + I_p + I_g = W + f_p K_p + r_g K_g, \tag{2}$$

where $I_p$ and $I_g$ are the rates of investment in private and government capital, respectively, and $r_g$ is the rental charged for the use of government capital [see IV.1.(3) and V.5.(4)]. Normalize for growth by multiplying through by $e^{-\gamma t}$, and note

$$I_p e^{-\gamma t} = \dot{k}_p + \gamma k_p, \qquad I_g e^{-\gamma t} = \dot{k}_g + \gamma k_g. \tag{3}$$

From (2) and (3),

$$c - w = (f_p - \gamma)k_p + (r_g - \gamma)k_g - \dot{k}_p - \dot{k}_g. \tag{4}$$

Since $r_c^p$ converges to $\omega_p > \gamma$,

$$\int_0^\infty (r_c^p - \gamma)dt = +\infty$$

and, by Lemma VII.4 (appendix to chapter VII),

$$\Delta\{\dot{k}_p; r_c^p - \gamma\} = -k_p(0) + \Delta\{(r_c^p - \gamma)k_p; r_c^p - \gamma\},$$
$$\Delta\{\dot{k}_g; r_c^p - \gamma\} = -k_g(0) + \Delta\{(r_c^p - \gamma)k_g; r_c^p - \gamma\}. \tag{5}$$

The discount operator, $\Delta$, is linear, by which is meant that

$$\Delta\{B_1 + B_2; A\} = \Delta\{B_1; A\} + \Delta\{B_2; A\}.$$

Then, from (4) and (5),

$$\Delta\{c - w; r_c^p - \gamma\} = \Delta\{(f_p - \gamma)k_p + (r_g - \gamma)k_g; r_c^p - \gamma\}$$
$$+ k_p(0) + k_g(0) - \Delta\{(r_c^p - \gamma)k_p + (r_c^p - \gamma)k_g; r_c^p - \gamma\},$$

or, equivalently, by Lemma VII.5 (appendix),

$$\Delta\{C - W; r_c^p\} = K_p(0) + K_g(0) + \Delta\{(f_p - r_c^p)K_p$$
$$+ (r_g - r_c^p)K_g; r_c^p\}, \tag{6}$$

where use is made of the definitional relations, $K_p(0) = k_p(0)$, $K_g(0) = k_g(0)$, $K_p(t) = k_p(t)e^{\gamma t}$, $K_g(t) = k_g(t)e^{\gamma t}$. Note now that $A^M(0) = K_p(0) + D(0)$ and that $C - z_{cw}W = (C - W) + (1 - z_{cw})W$. Then, from (6), (1) can be written

$$D(0) = K_g(0) + [v(0) - 1]K(0)$$
$$+ v(0)\Delta\{(f_p - r_c^p)K_p + (r_g - r_c^p)K_g + (1 - z_{cw})W; r_c^p\}, \tag{7}$$

where $K(0) = K_p(0) + K_g(0)$, the total amount of capital in the economy.

An alternative rewriting of (1) will also be useful in some contexts. Note that from Proposition VII.4(a), with $r = f_p$,

$$v(0)\Delta\{z_{cw}W; r_c^p\} = v(0)\Delta\{z_{cw}W; z_{sr}f_p - (\dot{v}/v)\} \quad \text{(by Lemma VII.5, appendix)}$$
$$= v(0)\Delta\{z_{cw}W[v/v(0)]; z_{sr}f_p\}$$
$$= \Delta\{z_{sw}W; z_{sr}f_p\}, \tag{8}$$

where use is made of the definitional identity $z_{sw} = z_{cw}v$.

Substituting in (1) and solving for $v(0)$ yields

$$v(0) = \frac{A^M(0) + \Delta\{z_{sw}W; z_{sr}f_p\}}{\Delta\{C; r_c^p\}}.$$

On the basis of Proposition VII.4 and the analysis leading to (7) above, we can now state a general proposition:

Proposition 1. *If Boundedness Assumptions I and III hold, then a proposed policy is controllable by a given set of instruments if and only if the following three conditions are satisfied:*

(a) $$z_{sr}f_p - (\dot{v}/v) = r_c^p;$$

(b) $$\Delta\{z_{cw}W;\, r_c^p\} < +\infty;$$

(c) $$D(0) = K_g(0) + [v(0) - 1]K(0) + v(0)\Delta\{(f_p - r_c^p)K_p + (r_g - r_c^p)K_g + (1 - z_{cw})W;\, r_c^p\}.$$

*Equation* (c) *is equivalent to*

(c′) $$v(0) = \frac{A^M(0) + \Delta\{z_{sw}W;\, z_{sr}f_p\}}{\Delta\{C;\, r_c^p\}}.$$

*For such a policy,* $a^{*M} + a^{*H}$ *approaches the finite positive limit,* $c^\infty/\lambda_p$, *where* $a^{*M}$ *and* $a^{*H}$ *are defined by VII.1.(16). If* $z_{cw}$ *converges to a finite limit,* $z_{cw}^\infty$, *and Boundedness Assumption II holds, then* (b) *is automatically satisfied and*

(d) $a^{*M}$ *converges to* $[(f_p^\infty - \gamma)k_p^\infty + (r_g^\infty - \gamma)k_g^\infty + (1 - z_{cw}^\infty)w^\infty]/\lambda_p$.

To prove the last statement, we need the following lemma:

LEMMA 1. *Under Boundedness Assumptions I–III,* $k_p$ *approaches a limit* $k_p^\infty$, *and* $\dot{k}_p$ *approaches* 0.

*Proof:* By Boundedness Assumption I, $f_p[k_p(t), k_g(t)]$ and $k_g(t)$ approach limits $f_p^\infty$ and $k_g^\infty$, respectively. Since $f$ is strictly concave, $f_p$ is a strictly decreasing function of $k_p$ for fixed $k_g$, so that the equation $f_p(k_p, k_g^\infty) = f_p^\infty$ has a unique solution in $k_p$. Therefore, $k_p$ must converge to this solution, say $k_p^\infty$. From the Boundedness Assumptions I–III, every term in (4) other than $\dot{k}_p$ must converge to a finite limit; hence, $\dot{k}_p$ converges. It cannot converge to a nonzero limit since if it did $k_p$ would not converge to a finite limit.

Then Proposition 1(d) follows from the corresponding statement of Proposition VII.4 when one notices that

$$\begin{aligned} c^\infty - z_{cw}^\infty w^\infty &= (c^\infty - w^\infty) + (1 - z_{cw}^\infty)w^\infty \\ &= (f_p^\infty - \gamma)k_p^\infty + (r_g^\infty - \gamma)k_g^\infty + (1 - z_{cw}^\infty)w^\infty, \end{aligned}$$

where use is made of (4), Boundedness Assumptions I–III, and Lemma 1.

*Remark.* Equation (c) relates the initial debt level that will just permit the desired policy to be controlled by the given instruments to the different sources of imperfection in the market system.

For the publicly optimal policy we have the following necessary conditions (by Proposition IV.1):

$$U_c^g = p, \qquad \dot{p}/p = \omega_g - f_p,$$

or

$$f_p = \omega_g - d(\log U_c^g)/dt = r_c^g,$$

the consumption rate of interest from the public point of view. If there is no divergence between public and private values, $r_c^g = r_c^p$. Hence, Proposition 1(a) can be written

$$(z_{sr} - 1)f_p = \dot{v}/v.$$

The boundedness assumptions hold necessarily for publicly optimal policies.

COROLLARY. *If there is no divergence between public and private values, a publicly optimal policy is controllable if and only if Proposition 1(b)–(c) and the following condition are satisfied:*

(a) $$(z_{sr} - 1)f_p = \dot{v}/v.$$

We shall now restate the conditions for the special case where the policy is controllable with stable instruments (see Definition V.2). The consumption rate of interest, $r_c^p$, approaches $\omega_p$ by its definition, 0.(2) and the remark in VII.2. By definition of stability, $z_{sr}$ approaches some constant, and by Boundedness Assumption I, $f_p$ approaches a constant, $f_p^\infty$, since $r = f_p$. From Proposition 1(a), then, $\dot{v}/v$ approaches a limit; if this limit is not zero, then $v$ approaches infinity or zero. But since $v$ is the ratio of two instruments, stability requires it to converge to a non-zero finite limit. Hence, $\dot{v}/v$ must approach zero. In this case, $z_{cw}$ converges to a finite limit; by Proposition 1, condition (b) holds if Boundedness Assumption II holds, and $a^{*M}$ approaches a finite limit, $a^{*M\infty}$. Since $a^{*M}(t) = a^M(t)/v(t)$, and $v(t)$ approaches a positive finite limit, $a^M(t)$ approaches the finite limit, $v^\infty a^{*M\infty}$. Finally, since $a^M(t) = d(t) + k_p(t)$ and $k_p(t)$ approaches $k_p^\infty$, by Lemma 1, the government debt, normalized for growth, approaches a finite limit (which may, of course, be negative).

PROPOSITION 2. *If Boundedness Assumptions I–III hold, then a proposed policy is controllable by a given set of stable instruments if and only if Propositions 1(a) and (c) hold. Further, the following conditions are all necessary:*

(a) $\dot{v}/v$ *approaches zero;*

(b) $z_{sr}f_p$ *approaches* $\omega_p$*;*

(c) $d(t)$ *approaches* $$d^\infty = v^\infty[(f_p^\infty - \gamma)k_p^\infty + (r_g^\infty - \gamma)k_g^\infty + (1 - z_{cw}^\infty)w^\infty]/\lambda_p - k_p^\infty.$$

If $f_p^\infty \neq \omega_p$, then the desired public policy is not compatible with the private sector's attitudes toward the future; we refer to this case as *futurity divergence*. In this case, (b) tells us that $z_{sr}$ has to approach a limit different from 1, and therefore must differ from 1 for large $t$. Therefore, either $z_s$ or $z_r$ must differ from 1 for large $t$; i.e., $x_s \neq 0$ or $x_r \neq 0$.

*Remark* 1. If the proposed policy exhibits futurity divergence, then controllability with stable instruments requires a tax either on savings or on interest income.

*Remark* 2. If a policy is controllable with stable instruments, then the ratio of debt to national income approaches a finite limit. Thus, the stability of this ratio is not an additional requirement that one might consider imposing on the instruments.

COROLLARY. *If there is no divergence between public and private values, then the publicly optimal policy is controllable with stable instruments if and only if condition (a) of the Corollary to Proposition 1 and Proposition 1(c) hold. In addition to Proposition 2(a)–(c) it is also necessary that* $z_{sr}$ *approach 1.*

As a preliminary to a deeper study of controllability, we shall show that, with all the instruments available, any policy satisfying the boundedness assumptions is controllable and indeed can be controlled with stable instruments by a variety of choices of tax parameters.

Substitution of (8) into Proposition 1(b) yields

$$[1/v(0)]\Delta\{z_{sw}w;\, z_{sr}f_p - \gamma\} < +\infty\,. \tag{9}$$

To ensure that $v(0)$ is finite, it is necessary and sufficient from Proposition 1(c′) that

$$\Delta\{z_{sw}W;\, z_{sr}f_p\} < +\infty\,, \tag{10}$$

while to ensure that $v(0) > 0$, it is sufficient that

$$A^M(0) > 0 \text{ and } z_{sw} > 0, \text{ all } t, \tag{11}$$

for all the other factors in the integrals in the numerator and denominator of (c′) are certainly positive. If (10) holds and $v(0) > 0$, then certainly (9) holds. There are a variety of conditions sufficient to ensure that (10) holds; we simply note here one simple pair of conditions:

$$z_{sw} \text{ bounded, } \lim_{t\to\infty} (z_{sr}f_p - \gamma) > 0. \tag{12}$$

For if these assumptions are fulfilled, then, with the aid of Boundedness Assumption II, $z_{sw}w$ is bounded and positive; then by (12) and Lemma VII.3 (appendix to chapter VII),

$$\Delta\{z_{sw}w;\, z_{sr}f_p - \gamma\} < +\infty\,,$$

while

$$\Delta\{z_{sw}W; z_{sr}f_p\} = \Delta\{z_{sw}w; z_{sr}f_p - \gamma\},$$

by Lemma VII.5 (appendix to chapter VII).

Note that the assumption $A^M(0) > 0$ is equivalent to $D(0) + K_p(0) > 0$; since $K_p(0) > 0$ necessarily, we note that a failure of the assumption to hold means that the government is the net creditor of the economy to an extent at least equal to the volume of private capital.

To sum up, suppose $A^M(0) > 0$ and policies $z_s$, $z_r$, and $z_w$ are chosen to satisfy (11) and (12). Then $v(t)$ is determined by integration of Proposition 1(a) with initial condition (c′); since $v = z_s/z_c$, and $z_s$ has already been chosen, $z_c$ is determined.

PROPOSITION 3. *Suppose $A^M(0) > 0$. Then any policy satisfying the boundedness assumptions is controllable by any set of instruments, $z_s(t)$, $z_c(t)$, $z_w(t)$, and $z_r(t)$ satisfying the following conditions:*

(a) $z_{sw}(t)$ *is bounded and positive;*

(b) $$\lim_{t\to\infty} z_{sr}(t) > \gamma/f_p^\infty;$$

(c) $$z_s(t)/z_c(t) = v(0)e^{\int_0^t (z_{sr}f_p - r_c^p)du},$$

*where*

(d) $$v(0) = \frac{A^M(0) + \Delta\{z_{sw}W; z_{sr}f_p\}}{\Delta\{C; r_c^p\}}.$$

Actually, it is easy to see that we can even demand that the controllability be achieved with stable instruments. By definition of stability, the four tax parameters are so chosen as to converge to positive finite limits so that $z_{sw}$ will necessarily be bounded. Further, by Proposition 2(b), $z_{sr}$ must converge to $\omega_p/f_p^\infty$, which is necessarily greater than $\gamma/f_p^\infty$, so that (b) holds. It is necessary for stability that $v(t)$ converge to a positive finite limit; and, from the previous remarks, if it does then controllability obtains. Since $r_c^p = \omega_p - d(\log U_c^p)/dt$,

$$\int_0^t (z_{sr}f_p - r_c^p)dt = \int_0^t (z_{sr}f_p - \omega_p)dt + \log(U_c^p/U_c^{p0}).$$

The last term certainly converges along any bounded policy. From (c), then, a necessary and sufficient condition that $v(t)$ converge to a finite positive limit is that

$$\left|\int_0^\infty (z_{sr}f_p - \omega_p)dt\right| < +\infty. \tag{13}$$

Since $f_p$ converges by Boundedness Assumption I and $z_{sr}$ converges by the definition of stability, $z_{sr}f_p$ converges; (13) implies the condition that $z_{sr}f_p$ must converge to $\omega_p$, or $z_{sr}$ to $\omega_p/f_p^{\infty}$.

COROLLARY. *Suppose $A^M(0) > 0$. Then any policy satisfying the Boundedness Assumptions I–III is controllable with stable instruments by any tax parameters, $z_s(t)$, $z_c(t)$, $z_w(t)$, and $z_r(t)$, which converge to positive finite limits and satisfy the following conditions:*

(a) $$z_{sw}(t) > 0, \text{ all } t;$$

(b) $$\left| \int_0^{\infty} (z_{sr}f_p - \omega_p)dt \right| < +\infty;$$

*and (c) and (d) of Proposition 3.*

*Remark.* If there are no taxes on wages or interest as such, then $z_w = z_r = 1$. It is clearly still possible to satisfy (a) and (b), and indeed in many ways (e.g., let $z_s$ be the constant $\omega_p/f_p^{\infty}$; then (b) holds by Boundedness Assumption I). Hence, controllability with stable instruments can be achieved with only consumption and savings taxes (and borrowing). Alternatively, savings taxes can be replaced by taxes on interest; simply set $z_s$ and $z_w$ equal to 1.

In the methods of controllability suggested in Proposition 3 and corollary, it is essential that the government should be free to choose $v(t)$; i.e., that the government, through its tax powers, should be able to vary the exchange ratio between savings and consumption. Since only sufficient conditions have been developed, it is not excluded that tax systems in which $v$ is not variable may still yield controllability. We turn to this question in the next two sections.

## 2. Controllability Without Taxes

It will be enlightening to examine the possibility of control with no taxes at all. This will give us some perspective on the several reasons that enter into the need for taxes in achieving optimal allocation over time. In the analysis below we use Proposition 1.

By "no taxes" we mean that $z_s$, $z_c$, $z_w$, and $z_r$ are all equal to 1, and therefore so are $z_{sr}$, $z_{cw}$, and $v$. Proposition 1(a) becomes

$$f_p = r_c^p, \tag{1}$$

which is a necessary condition that the policy be optimal if private values are used as the criterion. Since the policy is bounded, it is easy to see that the transversality conditions are satisfied. Thus, if in fact it is controllable without taxes, the policy must be judged optimal on the basis of private values. This means that we have to restrict ourselves to the case of no divergence between public and private values.

To calculate the initial debt $D(0)$ set in Proposition 1(c): $v(0) = 1$, $z_{cw} = 1$ for all $t$, and use (1) above. We thus have:

PROPOSITION 4. *If there is no divergence between public and private values, then the publicly optimal policy is controllable without taxes if and only if*

(a) $$D(0) = K_g(0) - \Delta\{(f_p - r_g)K_g;\, r_c^p\}.$$

*If the policy is controllable, then*

(b) $$d(t) \rightarrow d^\infty = [(r_g^\infty - \gamma)/\lambda_p]k_g^\infty.$$

To derive (b), note that with no taxes, $v^\infty = 1$ and $z_{cw}^\infty = 1$; and also that $a^M(t) = k_p(t) + d(t) = a^{*M}(t)$. Therefore,

$$d^\infty = [(f_p^\infty - \gamma)k_p^\infty + (r_g^\infty - \gamma)k_g^\infty]/\lambda_p - k_p^\infty,$$

and (b) follows since, in this case, $f_p^\infty - \gamma = \omega_p - \gamma = \lambda_p$.

If the government were able to charge for the use of its capital in an economic manner, the charge would be $f_p$, the same as that for private capital. If this charge were in fact levied, then the condition reduces to the interesting one that $D(0) = K_g(0)$; i.e., that the present situation is as if in the past the government had borrowed solely for government investment and had never paid for government investment out of taxes.

COROLLARY. *If there is no divergence between public and private values and if the charge for the use of government capital is the same as that for private capital, then the publicly optimal policy is controllable without taxes if and only if* $D(0) = K_g(0)$.

This argument was designed to show that the government must engage in taxation if there is a violation of any one of the following conditions: no divergence between private and public values, full economic pricing of the use of government capital, and an initial debt equal to the stock of government capital (strictly speaking, there can be offsetting deviations in the last two conditions, but this would require a remarkable historical coincidence). Further, in an increasing returns model it is, of course, impossible that the government be paid the marginal value of its capital if private capital and labor are paid theirs.

## 3. The Income Tax

The previous section has shown that, in the no-divergence case, the optimal policy would be controllable if there were any way of changing the initial level of debt to the critical magnitude given in Proposition 4.

Suppose now that the government is authorized to collect an income tax of any magnitude. As a limiting version, it might collect a once-for-all levy, a transfer of wealth rather than income to the government. This could be regarded as a limiting case of an income tax at a very high rate for a very short period. With such a levy, the debt can be reduced to any desired figure; the individuals will be willing to sell the debt to pay for the tax, and the government will have the finances to buy the debt back. Of course, it might be the case that the critical debt level is greater than the existing debt; in that case, the government will pay out a once-for-all wealth transfer to the private sector, and thereby increase the debt.

The income of the private sector is determined by the state variables (amount of private capital, government capital, and government debt); hence, a tax or subsidy imposed on income at the initial moment of time has no incentive effects.

Observe that an income tax means that the tax on savings and consumption is the same and that there is no tax on wages or profits as such (equivalently, there is an equal tax on wages and profits and no tax on savings or consumption). Let $x$ be the rate of income tax, $z = 1 - x$. Then $v$ is identically constant at $v = 1$; also $z_s = z_{cw} = z$. Then, in the case of no divergence, it follows from the corollary to Proposition 1 that $z = 1$ for all $t$, since $\dot{v}/v = 0$. Hence, in fact, no income tax can be imposed except for the first instant (where incentive effects are absent). The fact that income taxes cannot be used to achieve an optimal program is nothing but the classical conclusion that the income tax is not neutral but constitutes a "double tax on savings"; see Kaldor (1955, chapter II) and the references to earlier work, particularly that of John Stuart Mill and Irving Fisher.

PROPOSITION 5. *If there is no divergence between public and private values, then the optimal policy is controllable by transferring wealth at the initial moment to change the government debt to the level prescribed in Proposition 4, and then continuing with no taxes.*

In the case of divergence, Proposition 1(a), applied to the case where the government has available an income tax but no other tax instruments, states that

$$z f_p = r_c^p , \tag{1}$$

since $z_{sr} = z$ and $\dot{v}/v = 0$. There will in general be a nonzero income tax, but now it is completely determined by (1). Note that $z$ converges to $\omega_p/f_p^\infty$, so that $z$ is bounded and therefore Proposition 1(b) is automatically satisfied if Boundedness Assumption II holds, since $z_{cw} = z$.

But in Proposition 1(c) we note that $v(0) = 1$ and $z$ is already determined by (1). Hence, the equality can hold only by accident. As in the case of divergence, this difficulty can be resolved by the use of the income tax at the initial moment of time as a wealth tax to change the government debt, and therefore $A^M(0)$, to the level necessary to satisfy Proposition 1(c). Setting $v(0) = 1$, $r_c^p = zf_p$ [from (1)], and $z_{cw} = z$ in Proposition 1(c) yields

$$D(0) = K_g(0) + \Delta\{(1 - z)f_pK_p + (r_g - zf_p)K_g + (1 - z)W;\, r_c^p\}. \qquad (2)$$

Let $x = 1 - z$ be the income tax rate, and note that $r_g - zf_p = xr_g - z(f_p - r_g)$, and that $f_pK_p + r_gK_g + W = Y$, the total output.

Proposition 6. *Any policy satisfying the Boundedness Assumptions I–III is controllable with stable instruments by an income tax and borrowing as follows: after the initial moment, choose the tax rate*

(a) $$x(t) = 1 - (r_c^p/f_p)\,;$$

*at the initial moment, use the income tax in an extreme form as a wealth transfer to change the initial level of debt to*

(b) $$D(0) = K_g(0) + \Delta\{xY - z(f_p - r_g)K_g;\, r_c^p\}\,.$$

*As t approaches infinity, the income tax rate converges,*

(c) $$x(t) \to x^\infty = 1 - (\omega_p/f_p^\infty)\,,$$

*and the debt, normalized by growth, also converges,*

(d) $$d(t) \to d^\infty = k_g^\infty + (1/f_p^\infty\lambda_p)[\omega_p(r_g^\infty - f_p^\infty)k_g^\infty + (f_p^\infty - \omega_p)y^\infty]\,.$$

To see the last statement, note that $v(t)$ is identically 1, so that $a^{*M}(t) = a^M(t) = d(t) + k_p(t)$. Then substitute from Proposition 6(c) into Proposition 1(d), let $a^{M\infty} = d^\infty + k_p^\infty$, and simplify.

The interpretation of Proposition 6(a) and (b) is straightforward. The purpose of the income tax is to make the post-tax marginal productivity of capital equal to the consumption rate of interest of the private sector (along the path). The critical debt level that must be achieved by the initial wealth transfer to permit the rest of the policy to be carried out is the sum of the initial stock of government capital and the discounted difference between future tax collections (other than those on government interest payments) and future underpricing of the services of government capital (reckoned post-tax, since the tax enables the government to recover part of the underpricing).

In the case of no futurity divergence—i.e., $f_p^\infty = \omega_p$—the steady-state behavior of the system assumes a simpler form.

COROLLARY. *If there is no futurity divergence and control is achieved as in Proposition 6, then the income tax rate approaches zero, and the debt (normalized for growth) approaches* $[(r_g^\infty - \gamma)/\lambda_p]k_g^\infty$, *which in turn equals* $k_g^\infty$ *if there is full economic pricing for the services of government capital.*

One further remark may be needed to clarify the applicability of Proposition 6. Suppose that the policy under consideration is a publicly optimal one, with $f_p^\infty = \omega_g$. It is usually assumed that if there is any divergence between public and private values, it is because the government values the future more highly than does the private sector; i.e., that $\omega_g < \omega_p$. But then, from Proposition 6(c), the income tax rate is eventually negative; the government wishes in effect to subsidize savings, and the nonneutrality of the income tax means that a negative income tax accomplishes this (this is not a "negative income tax" in the current popular usage, which is approximately a proportional income tax with a lump-sum transfer, but rather a tax with a negative marginal rate). The initial debt, then, has to be made small enough to compensate for its subsequent growth due to income subsidies.

The analysis of control by a single tax that falls only on interest income is almost identical to that of control by the income tax. At the initial moment, interest income is determined by the state variables; hence, as in the case of the income tax, an arbitrary tax can be imposed at the initial moment without incentive effect. Thus, Proposition 5 remains perfectly valid for a tax on interest income.

For a tax on interest income, $z_s = z_c = z_w = 1$; only $z_r$ is allowed to vary. Then $v(t)$ is identically 1. The analysis leading to Proposition 6 remains valid with only a few slight changes. Equation (1) now reads:

$$z_r f_p = r_c^p. \tag{3}$$

In the derivation of (2), the only change is that $z_{cw} = 1$ rather than $z$. Then (2) is replaced by

$$D(0) = K_g(0) + \Delta\{(1 - z_r)f_p K_p + (r_g - z_r f_p)K_g; r_c^p\}. \tag{4}$$

In the derivation of Proposition 6(d), again, we note now that $z_{cw}^\infty$ is now 1.

PROPOSITION 7. *Any policy satisfying the Boundedness Assumptions I–III is controllable with stable instruments by a tax on interest income and borrowing as follows: After the initial moment, choose the tax rate*

(a) $$x_r(t) = 1 - (r_c^p/f_p);$$

*at the initial moment, use the tax on interest income in an extreme form as a wealth transfer to change the initial level of debt to*

(b) $D(0) = K_g(0) + \Delta\{x_r(Y - W) - z_r(f_p - r_g)K_g; r_c^p\}$.

*As t approaches infinity, the tax rate on interest income converges,*

(c) $$x_r(t) \to x^\infty = 1 - (\omega_p/f_p^\infty),$$

*and the debt, normalized by growth, also converges,*

(d) $$d(t) \to d^\infty = k_g^\infty + (1/f_p^\infty\lambda_p)[\omega_p(r_g^\infty - f_p^\infty)k_g^\infty + (f_p^\infty - \omega_p)(y^\infty - w^\infty)].$$

COROLLARY. *If there is no futurity divergence and control is achieved as in Proposition 7, then the tax rate on interest income approaches zero, and the debt (normalized for growth) approaches* $[(r_g^\infty - \gamma)/\lambda_p]k_g^\infty$, *which in turn equals* $k_g^\infty$ *if there is full economic pricing for the services of government capital. If there is no divergence between public and private values at all, then the optimal policy is controllable by transferring wealth initially in proportion to interest income (or, equivalently, to material assets) to change the government debt to the level prescribed in Proposition 4 and then continuing with no taxes.*

## 4. The Consumption Tax

As might be expected in view of the standard arguments for the optimality and neutrality of the consumption tax in the static context (see Kaldor 1955, chapter II), the analysis of controllability through the consumption tax alone (but with borrowing allowed) is very straightforward. It has some distinctly satisfactory properties: it is always adequate for controllability, without special provisions for drastic initial steps, provided only that the desired rate of return on capital exceeds the rate of growth; it is, in addition, stable (and therefore the debt-income ratio is stable) if there is no futurity divergence; and it is actually constant over time if there is no divergence at all. We already know (Remark 1 to Proposition 2) that in the event of futurity divergence, stability is impossible with only the consumption tax available.

Most of the properties just stated are immediate consequences of Proposition 3 and its corollary. Assume now that $z_s$, $z_w$, and $z_r$ are identically 1; then $z_{sw}$ and $z_{sr}$ are identically 1, and $v(t) = 1/z_c(t)$. Then Proposition 3(a) holds trivially, and Proposition 3(b) holds if $f_p^\infty > \gamma$. Then controllability involves satisfaction of Proposition 3(c) and 3(d), with $z_{sr}$ and $z_{sw}$ both set equal to 1. This can of course always be done, but in only one way.

$$v(t) = 1/z_c(t) = v(0)e^{\int_0^t (f_p - r_g^p)du}, \tag{1}$$

$$v(0) = \frac{A^M(0) + \Delta\{W; f_p\}}{\Delta\{C; r_c^p\}}. \tag{2}$$

By the argument leading to (b) of the corollary to Proposition 3, stability holds if and only if

$$\left| \int_0^\infty (f_p - \omega_p)dt \right| < +\infty. \tag{3}$$

From Boundedness Assumption I,

$$\left| \int_0^\infty (f_p - f_p^\infty)dt \right| < +\infty$$

so that (3) holds if and only if $f_p^\infty = \omega_p$; i.e., there is no futurity divergence. By Proposition 2(c), $d(t)$ then approaches a finite limit. The asymptotic debt level is

$$d^\infty = (v^\infty - 1)[k_p^\infty + (w^\infty/\lambda_p)] + v^\infty(r_g^\infty - \gamma)k_g^\infty/\lambda_p,$$

which depends on the value of $v^\infty$ (finite in this case); but as can be seen from (2) and (1), $v(0)$ varies linearly with $D(0)$ and, for any $t$, $v(t)$ varies in the same proportion as $v(0)$; hence, $v^\infty$ is a linear strictly increasing function of $D(0)$. Thus, $d^\infty$ depends on $D(0)$: the initial value of debt has a permanent effect on debt and on the consumption tax rate.

If there is no divergence at all, then since $z_{sr} = 1$ always, the corollary to Proposition 1 assures us that $v$ is constant. This can also be seen from (1) since $f_p = r_c^p$ in the absence of divergence.

All that remains is to examine the behavior of tax rates and debt in the unstable situations. By Proposition 1(a), $\dot{v}/v \to f_p^\infty - \omega_p$ since $z_{sr} = 1$ and $r_c^p \to \omega_p$. It will be noted that $v(t)$ is the post-tax price of consumption goods. If $f_p^\infty > \omega_p$, the post-tax price rises to infinity; in effect there is a tax on postponement of consumption that approaches $f_p^\infty - \omega_p$, and therefore an incentive to bring savings and capital accumulation to a level below that which the private sector would seek spontaneously.

The opposite case is, as noted at the end of the previous section, the one usually thought to be most likely. Here, the post-tax price of the consumption good falls to zero; i.e., there is a subsidy on consumption approaching 100 per cent. The rate of increase of the subsidy is a subsidy to the postponement of consumption and therefore an encouragement to saving and capital accumulation in excess of the private sector's own desires.

To consider the asymptotic behavior of debt, first study that of human assets. Since $z_{sr} = 1$, $a^H(t)$ (human assets normalized by growth) is

by Lemma VII.6 (appendix). Subtract $K_p(0)$ from both sides of (6) and substitute (7).

$$-K_p(0) < D(0) \leqq \bar{D}, \tag{8}$$

where

$$\bar{D} = \frac{K_g(0) + \Delta\{(f_p - r_c^p)[K_p(t) - K_p(0)] + (r_g - r_c^p)K_g(t); r_c^p\}}{\Delta\{f_p; r_c^p\}}. \tag{9}$$

The lower bound in (8) derives from the assumption that $A^M(0) > 0$. In the unlikely case that $A^M(0) < 0$, the same reasoning leads to the reversal of the inequalities in (8):

$$-K_p(0) > D(0) \geqq \bar{D}.$$

[If $A^M(0) = 0$, then (2) can be solved for $z_s(0)$ only if the denominator of (5) also vanishes. In that case, any value of $z_s(0)$ is a solution, and it can also be concluded that $\bar{D} = -K_p(0)$.] Thus, a given policy is controllable by a savings tax which satisfies (1) with initial conditions (5) if and only if

$$D(0) \text{ lies between } -K_p(0) \text{ and } \bar{D}. \tag{10}$$

If $D(0) = \bar{D}$, then, by (4c), $z_s(t)$ approaches the finite limit, $\omega_p/f_p^\infty$, so that the control is stable in this case. If $D(0)$ satisfies (10) but $D(0) \neq \bar{D}$, then, by (4b), $z_s(t)$ approaches 0; i.e., the tax on savings approaches 100 per cent, a situation which might be described as "asymptotic socialism."

In the case where $D(0) = \bar{D}$, Proposition 2(c) is applicable, with $v^\infty = \omega_p/f_p^\infty$; after a little rewriting, we have

$$d^\infty = k_g^\infty + [\gamma(f_p^\infty - \omega_p)k^\infty + \omega_p(r_g^\infty - f_p^\infty)k_g^\infty]/f_p^\infty\lambda_p \text{ if } D(0) = \bar{D}. \tag{11}$$

In this case (i.e., $D(0) = \bar{D}$), if there is no futurity divergence, then $z_s$ approaches 1; i.e., there is no tax or subsidy on savings in the limit, and

$$d^\infty = k_g^\infty + [(r_g^\infty - \omega_p)k_g^\infty/\lambda_p].$$

If, in addition, there is full economic pricing for the services of government capital, then $d^\infty = k_g^\infty$.

If (10) holds but $D(0) \neq \bar{D}$, the asymptotic behavior of the debt is very different. By Proposition 1(d), $a^{*M}$ converges to a finite limit. Since $a^M = a^{*M}v$, and $v$ approaches zero, $a^M$ approaches 0. Since $a^M = k_p + d$,

$$d^\infty = -k_p^\infty \text{ if } D(0) \neq \bar{D}. \tag{12}$$

In this case, the government is asymptotically the creditor of the private sector to an amount equal to the holdings of private capital, a result which reinforces the intuitive idea of "asymptotic socialism."

In the case of no divergence, some of the formulas simplify. In this case, $f_p = r_c^p$ so that

$$\Delta\{f_p; r_c^p\} = 1,$$

by Lemma VII.6 (appendix). Then (5) and (9) take the forms:

$$z_s(0) = \frac{A^M(0)}{K(0) - \Delta\{(f_p - r_g)K_g; f_p\}}, \tag{13}$$

$$\bar{D} = K_g(0) - \Delta\{(f_p - r_g)K_g; f_p\}. \tag{14}$$

If, in addition, there is full economic pricing of the services of government capital, then

$$z_s(0) = A^M(0)/K(0) \text{ and } \bar{D} = K_g(0). \tag{15}$$

Incidentally, (14) demonstrates that the critical debt level, $\bar{D}$, may be rather small so that the range of initial debt values which permit controllability through the savings tax may be quite limited.

The possibility of altering the initial debt level through an infinitely high tax or subsidy on savings at the initial moment should also be considered. An initial $z_s$ of $-\infty$ is ineffective; the individual can always avoid the tax by increasing consumption so that savings are zero (indeed he would increase consumption to infinite levels so as to achieve a transfer of wealth to him). However, if $z_s(0)$ is set at $+\infty$, the individual's maximum possible response is to set consumption at the initial instant equal to zero. Since the response is only for an instant, neither capital accumulation nor the integral of discounted utility are affected. However, a transfer of wealth to the individual can be accomplished. Thus, it is possible to raise the initial debt to any desired level, but not to lower it. By increasing the debt level to $\bar{D}$, control with stable instruments is achieved.

In the following summary of these results, we assume $A^M(0) > 0$; the other cases are too farfetched.

Proposition 9. *Suppose $A^M(0) > 0$. A policy is controllable through a savings tax and borrowing if and only if*

(a) $$D(0) \leqq \bar{D},$$

*where*

(b) $$\bar{D} = \frac{K_g(0) + \Delta\{(f_p - r_c^p)[K_p(t) - K_p(0)] + (r_g - r_c^p)K_g(t); r_c^p\}}{\Delta\{f_p; r_c^p\}}.$$

*A control is achieved by increasing the initial debt level to any level, $D^+(0)$, $D(0) \leqq D^+(0) \leqq \bar{D}$, by an infinite subsidy to savings at the* *initial moment, and then choosing $z_s(t)$ to be the solution of the differential equation*

(c) $$z_s f_p - (\dot{z}_s/z_s) = r_c^p,$$

*with the initial value*

(d) $$z_s^+(0) = \frac{A^{M+}(0)}{K(0) + \Delta\{(f_p - r_c^p)K_p + (r_g - r_c^p)K_g;\, r_c^p\}}.$$

*If $D^+(0) = \bar{D}$, then*

(e) $$z_s \to \omega_p/f_p^\infty,$$

*and*

(f) $$d(t) \to d^\infty = k_g^\infty + [\gamma(f_p^\infty - \omega_p)k^\infty + \omega_p(r_g^\infty - f_p^\infty)k_g^\infty]/f_p^\infty\lambda_p.$$

*If $D^+(0) < \bar{D}$, then*

(g) $$z_s \to 0,$$

*and*

(h) $$d(t) \to d^\infty = -k_p^\infty.$$

*If there is no divergence between public and private values, then*

(i) $$z_s^+(0) = \frac{A^{M+}(0)}{K(0) - \Delta\{(f_p - r_g)K_g;\, f_p\}},$$

(j) $$\bar{D} = K_g(0) - \Delta\{(f_p - r_g)K_g;\, f_p\},$$

*and*

(k) $$z_s = 1 \textit{ for all } t \textit{ if } D^+(0) = \bar{D}.$$

*Remark.* It is perfectly possible either that $K_p(0) + \bar{D} > 0$ or that $K_p(0) + \bar{D} \leqq 0$; but in the latter case, control is impossible for any debt level for which $A^M(0) > 0$.

To understand the latter clause, note that $\bar{D} + K_p(0) \leqq 0$ implies that (8) can hold for no value of $D(0)$.

To prove the former clause, it suffices to exhibit examples of both cases. Assume no divergence, $r_g = 0$, and a state of balanced growth. Then

$$K_g(t) = k_g^\infty e^{\gamma t},\; K_p(0) = k_p^\infty, \qquad f_p = f_p^\infty = \omega_p.$$

From (j),

$$\begin{aligned} \bar{D} + K_p(0) &= k_p^\infty + k_g^\infty - \Delta\{\omega_p k_g^\infty e^{\gamma t};\, \omega_p\} \\ &= k^\infty - \omega_p k_g^\infty \Delta\{1;\, \omega_p - \gamma\} \\ &= k_g^\infty\{(k^\infty/k_g^\infty) - [\omega_p/(\omega_p - \gamma)]\}. \end{aligned}$$

Suppose now that $k_g$ does not enter the felicity function, so that optimality requires $f_p = f_g$, and that the production function is Cobb-Douglas:

$$f(k_p, k_g) = k_p^\alpha k_g^\beta .$$

Then

$$k_p^\infty / k_g^\infty = \alpha/\beta ,$$

or

$$k^\infty / k_g^\infty = (\alpha + \beta)/\beta .$$

Clearly, there is no a priori reason that $k^\infty/k_g^\infty$ should either exceed or fall short of $\omega_p/(\omega_p - \gamma)$.

## 6. The Wages Tax

In the present model the supply of labor is assumed to be exogenously given. Hence, a tax on wages is a lump-sum tax. As might be expected, it is only useful if there is no divergence between public and private values, but in that case a wide variety of time patterns of wages tax are equally suitable for control.

A wages tax means that $z_s = z_r = z_c = 1$, and hence that $v = 1$. Then Proposition 1(a) reduces to

$$f_p = r_c^p ,$$

which implies the absence of divergence between public and private values. If $x_w$ is the tax rate on wages, then $1 - z_{cw} = x_w$. With $v(0) = 1$, Proposition 1(c) can be written:

$$\Delta\{x_w W; f_p\} = D(0) - K_g(0) + \Delta\{(f_p - r_g)K_g; f_p\} . \tag{1}$$

Since $z_{cw} = z_w = 1 - x_w$,

$$\Delta\{z_{cw} W; f_p\} = \Delta\{W; f_p\} - \Delta\{x_w W; f_p\} ,$$

so that if (1) holds, Proposition 1(b) holds automatically.

Hence, control requires only the satisfaction of (1). If stability is also required, $x_w$ can be so chosen as to satisfy (1) and approach a limit, $x_w^\infty$. Since $v(t)$ is identically 1, $a^{*M} = a^M = k_p + d$, and $k_p \to k_p^\infty$. Then $d^\infty$ can be computed from Proposition 1(d), when use is being made of the condition of nondivergence.

Proposition 10. *If there is no divergence between public and private values, then the optimal policy is controllable by any tax on wages, $x_w(t)$, such that*

(a) $$\Delta\{x_w W; f_p\} = D(0) - K_g(0) + \Delta\{(f_p - r_g)K_g; f_p\} .$$

*If $x_w$ is chosen to converge to some limit, $x_w^\infty$, then*

(b) $$d^\infty = k_g^\infty + [x_w^\infty w^\infty - (\omega_p - r_g^\infty)k_g^\infty]/\lambda_p .$$

## 7. Controllability of Both Allocation and Debt with Two Taxes: General Considerations

Up to this point the possibilities of controllability have been severely limited by the assumption that only one tax can be used. It is already obvious from Proposition 3 that if two suitable taxes are used, controllability with stable instruments can be obtained and, indeed, in many ways (see the remark to the corollary to Proposition 3). The alternative tax structures yield the same allocation policy but different time paths of public borrowing and debt. This suggests that when two taxes are considered, the analysis of controllability can be extended to the case where the time path of public debt is part of the target policy. In other words, so far we have imposed the Boundedness Assumptions I–III on the target paths of consumption, private capital, and public capital; now, with two suitable taxes, we also include the time path of government debt as a target policy. Of course, the initial value of the debt policy must be the historically given debt. It will also be assumed that the ratio of debt to national income converges to a finite limit; it may be negative, but it is assumed that the material assets of the private sector (the sum of government debt and private capital) tends to a positive limit. Finally, the convergence is assumed sufficiently regular that $\dot{d}$ tends to zero.

It is more convenient to express the condition on government debt, $d$, as one on $a^M = d + k_p$. Because $k_p$ is already specified and satisfies Boundedness Assumption I, there is no loss of generality in this procedure.

Boundedness Assumption IV. *The magnitude $a^M(t)$ converges to a positive finite limit, $a^{M\infty}$. Further, $a^M(0) = A^M(0)$, as given historically, and $\dot{a}^M \to 0$.*

The magnitude $A^M(t)$ evolves according to the differential equation of capital accumulation:

$$\dot{A}^M = z_{sr} f_p A^M + z_{sw} W - vC ,$$

according to VII.1.(15), with $f_p = r$. Since $a^M = A^M e^{-\gamma t}$, this equation can be rewritten

$$\dot{a}^M + \gamma a^M = z_{sr} f_p a^M + z_{sw} w - vc. \tag{1}$$

If $a^M(t)$ is taken as given, then (1) constitutes an equation in the tax parameters $z_{sr}$, $z_{sw}$, and $v$. These parameters also satisfy the differential equation of Proposition 1(a):

$$z_{sr} f_p - (\dot{v}/v) = r_c^p. \tag{2}$$

Now consider any set of stable instruments which satisfy (1) and (2). It will be shown that Proposition 1(c) is necessarily satisfied; since Proposition 1(a) is satisfied by (2), it follows from Proposition 2 that the given policy is controllable by these instruments.

Proposition 1(c) is equivalent to Proposition VII.4(c). We can simply reverse the reasoning leading to the last. Let $a^{*M} = a^M/v$; with stable instruments, Boundedness Assumption IV implies that

$$\dot{a}^{*M} = [z_{sr}f_p - \gamma - (\dot{v}/v)]a^{*M} + z_{cw}w - c,$$

or, from (2),

$$\dot{a}^{*M} = (r_c^p - \gamma)a^{*M} + z_{cw}w - c. \quad (3)$$

But since $r_c^p - \gamma \rightarrow \omega_p - \gamma > 0$, Lemma VII.2 (appendix) tells us that (3) has only one solution converging to a finite positive limit; for it, by Theorem VII.2 (appendix),

$$a^{*M}(0) = \Delta\{c - z_{cw}w;\, r_c^p - \gamma\},$$

which is equivalent to Proposition VII.4(c).

PROPOSITION 11. *A given allocation and debt policy satisfying Boundedness Assumptions I–IV is controllable by stable instruments if and only if*

(a) $$(\dot{a}^M/a^M) + \gamma = z_{sr}f_p + z_{sw}(w/a^M) - v(c/a^M),$$

*and*

(b) $$d(1/v)/dt = (r_c^p - z_{sr}f_p)(1/v).$$

Formulas (a) and (b) are minor rewritings of (1) and (2) respectively.

We will now consider all six ways of using two of the four taxes being considered (consumption, savings, interest income, and wages).

## 8. Controllability with a Tax on Wages and One Other Tax

First, suppose that one of the taxes falls on wages. There are three possibilities for the other tax; in each case, the analysis of controllability by stable instruments depends primarily on an examination of Proposition 11(b) alone. The economic reason is that the tax on wages is a lump-sum tax without incentive effect; control over incentives is measured in Proposition 11(b), and then the tax on wages can be adjusted as needed to meet the debt requirement in Proposition 11(a).

If the second tax falls on savings, then $z_{sr} = z_s = v$. Equation (b) becomes

$$d(1/v)dt = r_c^p(1/v) - f_p. \quad (1)$$

This equation has a positive, bounded solution, which is unique, with

$$1/v(0) = \Delta\{f_p; r_c^p\},\ 1/v^\infty = f_p^\infty/\omega_p\ ;$$

i.e.,

$$z_s(0) = 1/\Delta\{f_p; r_c^p\},\ z_s^\infty = \omega_p/f_p^\infty .$$

If there is no divergence between public and private values, the unique stable solution of (1) is $1/v = 1$ for all $t$; i.e., no tax on savings. Once $v(t)$ is determined, substitute $z_{sr} = v$, $z_{sw} = z_w v$ in Proposition 11(a):

$$z_w = [\dot{a}^M - (vf_p - \gamma)a^M + cv]/wv. \tag{2}$$

If the second tax falls on consumption, then $z_{sr} = 1$. Equation (b) in Proposition 11 becomes

$$d(1/v)dt = (r_c^p - f_p)(1/v).$$

But then, if there is futurity divergence, any solution $1/v(t)$ tends to zero or infinity, and hence is not stable. If there is no futurity divergence, then indeed any solution tends to a finite limit; for each such solution we can solve for $z_w = z_{sw}$ from Proposition 11(a):

$$z_w = [\dot{a}^M - (f_p - \gamma)a^M + cv]/w.$$

In particular, if there is no divergence at all between public and private values, $v$ must be constant. Note that $v = 1/z_c$ in this case.

If the second tax falls on interest income, then $v = 1$ identically and $z_{sr} = z_r$. Thus, $z_r = r_c^p/f_p$. If we substitute in Proposition 11(a) and let $v = 1$, we have

$$z_w = [\dot{a}^M - (r_c^p - \gamma)a^M + c]/w.$$

If there is no divergence between public and private values, then $z_r = 1$, all $t$; the tax falls solely on wages, as in Proposition 10, but the tax is now adjusted to meet the new requirement of a given debt policy.

PROPOSITION 12. *A given allocation and debt policy satisfying Boundedness Assumptions I–IV is controllable by stable instruments either by taxes on wages and savings or by taxes on wages and interest income. In the first case, the tax on savings is defined by the unique positive stable solution of the differential equation*

(a) $$d(1/z_s)/dt = r_c^p(1/z_s) - f_p;$$

*the initial and asymptotic values of the tax on savings are*

(b) $$z_s(0) = 1/\Delta\{f_p; r_c^p\}, \qquad z_s = \omega_p/f_p^\infty .$$

*The tax on wages is then given by*

(c) $$z_w = [\dot{a}^M - (z_s f_p - \gamma)a^M + z_s c]/wz_s .$$

*If there is no divergence between public and private values, then* $z_s = 1$, *all* $t$.

*In the second case, the taxes on interest income and wages are given by*

(d) $$z_r = r_c^p/f_p, \qquad z_w = [\dot{a}^M - (r_c^p - \gamma)a^M + c]/w.$$

*The given policy is controllable with stable instruments by taxes on consumption and wages if and only if there is no futurity divergence. The tax on consumption is then*

(e) $$z_c(t) = z_c(0)e^{\int_0^t (r_c^p - f_p)du},$$

*where* $z_c(0)$ *is an arbitrary positive number; the tax on wages is then*

(f) $$z_w = [\dot{a}^M - (f_p - \gamma)a^M + (c/z_c)]/w.$$

## 9. Controllability with Two Taxes, Neither on Wages

We now consider the three cases where the taxes fall on two of the three flows: consumption, savings, and interest income; $z_w = 1$ throughout. A simple notational device will enable us to treat the three cases simultaneously. Let $\delta_c = 1$ if consumption is not taxed (so that the taxes fall on savings and interest income), and 0 otherwise; similarly, let $\delta_s = 1$ if savings are not taxed, and 0 if they are; $\delta_r = 1$ or 0 according to whether interest income is untaxed or taxed. Since wages are untaxed, there is precisely one other untaxed flow; hence, one and only one of the three numbers—$\delta_c$, $\delta_s$, and $\delta_r$—equals 1.

Note that $z_{sw} = z_s$. If consumption is untaxed, then $z_s = v$; if savings are untaxed, then $z_s = 1$; and if interest income is untaxed, then $z_s = z_{sr}$. These statements may be summarized compactly as

$$z_{sw} = \delta_c v + \delta_s + \delta_r z_{sr}. \tag{1}$$

Substitute in Proposition 11(a) and solve for $z_{sr}$;

$$z_{sr} = \frac{(\dot{a}^M + \gamma a^M - \delta_s w) + (c - \delta_c w)v}{f_p a^M + \delta_r w}. \tag{2}$$

Substitute (2) in Proposition 11(b):

$$d(1/v)/dt = A(t)(1/v) - B(t), \tag{3}$$

where

$$A(t) = [(r_c^p - \gamma)f_p a^M - f_p \dot{a}^M + (\delta_r r_c^p + \delta_s f_p)w]/(f_p a^M + \delta_r w), \tag{4}$$

and

$$B(t) = (c - \delta_c w)f_p/(f_p a^M + \delta_r w). \tag{5}$$

Since $r_c^p \to \omega_p$ and $\dot{a}^M \to 0$, we can calculate that

$$A^\infty = [\lambda_p(f_p^\infty a^{M\infty} + \delta_r w^\infty) + (\delta_r\gamma + \delta_s f_p^\infty)w^\infty]/(f_p^\infty a^{M\infty} + \delta_r w^\infty) \geqq \lambda_p > 0 \tag{6}$$

and

$$B^\infty = (c^\infty - \delta_c w^\infty)f_p^\infty/(f_p^\infty a^{M\infty} + \delta_r w^\infty). \tag{7}$$

From Lemma VII.2 (appendix), (6) implies that there is a unique stable solution to (3); by Lemma VII.1 (appendix), the solution is everywhere positive if $B(t) \geqq 0$ everywhere, $B(t) > 0$ for $t$ large, but not necessarily if $B(t) < 0$ somewhere. From (5), then, there is an everywhere positive solution provided that

$$c - \delta_c w \geqq 0, \text{ all } t,\ c - \delta_c w > 0 \text{ for large } t. \tag{8}$$

If $\delta_c = 0$, (8) will certainly hold; by construction this means that consumption is taxed. If consumption is not taxed, then $\delta_c = 1$.

> The policy is controllable with stable instruments by taxes on consumption and either savings or interest income. (9)

> The policy is controllable with stable instruments by taxes on savings and interest income if $c - w \geqq 0$, all $t$, $c - w > 0$, for large $t$. (10)

For the stable policy,

$$1/v(0) = \Delta\{B; A\},\ 1/v^\infty = B^\infty/A^\infty. \tag{11}$$

For each of the three possible cases of taxes on a pair from among the three flows (consumption, savings, and interest income), a corresponding one of the three numbers, $\delta_c$, $\delta_r$, and $\delta_s$, is 1 and the other two are 0. Then $A^\infty$, $B^\infty$, and $\Delta\{B; A\}$ can be calculated for each case, and initial and final values for one of the taxes (or a ratio of two of them) computed from (11); then $z_{sr}$ can be calculated from (2). Note that, by Proposition 2(b), $z_{sr}^\infty = \omega_p/f_p^\infty$.

To illustrate the calculation, consider the most complicated case: that of taxes on savings and consumption. In this case, $\delta_s = 0$, $\delta_c = 0$, and $\delta_r = 1$; also, $v = z_s/z_c$, $z_{sr} = z_s$. Then $z_c/z_s = 1/v$ is the stable solution of the differential equation

$$d(z_c/z_s)/dt = \frac{[(r_c^p - \gamma)f_p a^M - f_p\dot{a}^M + r_c^p w](z_c/z_s) - cf_p}{f_p a^M + w}; \tag{12}$$

$$z_c(0)/z_s(0) = \Delta\{cf_p/(f_p a^M + w); [(r_c^p - \gamma)f_p a^M - f_p\dot{a}^M + r_c^p w]/(f_p a^M + w)\}; \tag{13}$$

$$z_c^\infty/z_s^\infty = c^\infty f_p^\infty/(\lambda_p f_p^\infty a^{M\infty} + \omega_p w^\infty). \tag{14}$$

Since $z_s^\infty = z_{sr}^\infty = \omega_p/f_p^\infty$,

$$z_c^\infty = \omega_p c^\infty/(\lambda_p f_p^\infty a^{M\infty} + \omega_p w^\infty). \tag{15}$$

We can make similar calculations for the other two cases.

PROPOSITION 13. *A given allocation and debt policy satisfying Boundedness Assumptions I–IV is controllable by stable instruments either by taxes on consumption and savings or on consumption and interest income. It is also controllable with stable instruments by taxes on savings and interest income if $c(t) \geqq w(t)$, all $t$, with the strict inequality holding for large $t$.*

*If the policy is controlled by taxes on consumption and savings, then:*

(a) $z_c z_s$ *is the stable solution of the differential equation*

$$d(z_c/z_s)/dt = \frac{[(r_c^p - \gamma)f_p a^M - f_p \dot{a}^M + r_c^p w](z_c/z_s) - cf_p}{f_p a^M + w};$$

(b) $$z_s = \frac{(\dot{a}^M + \gamma a^M) + c(z_s/z_c)}{f_p a^M + w};$$

(c) $$z_c^\infty = \omega_p c^\infty/(\lambda_p f_p^\infty a^{M\infty} + \omega_p w^\infty).$$

*If the policy is controlled by taxes on consumption and interest income, then*

(d) $z_c$ *is the stable solution of the differential equation*

$$dz_c/dt = \frac{[(r_c^p - \gamma)a^M - \dot{a}^M + w]z_c - c}{a^M};$$

(e) $$z_r = [\dot{a}^M + \gamma a^M - w + (c/z_c)]/f_p a^M;$$

(f) $$z_c^\infty = c^\infty/(\lambda_p a^{M\infty} + w^\infty).$$

*If the policy is controlled by taxes on savings and interest income, then*

(g) $1/z_s$ *is the stable solution of the differential equation*

$$d(1/z_s)/dt = [r_c^p - \gamma - (\dot{a}^M/a^M)](1/z_s) - [(c - w)/a^M];$$

(h) $$z_r = [\dot{a}^M + \gamma a^M + (c - w)z_s]f_p a^M z_s;$$

(i) $$z_s^\infty = \lambda_p a^{M\infty}/(c^\infty - w^\infty);$$

(j) $$z_r^\infty = [\omega_p(c^\infty - w^\infty)]/\lambda_p f_p^\infty a^{M\infty}.$$

It is worth remarking that the assumption of no divergence between public and private values does not, in these cases, lead to any significant simplification of the formulas.

## 10. Summary

In this chapter we assume that consumers are behaving rationally and facing perfect capital markets; however, their values may or may not be the ones which guide the government. The government then seeks to have its policy realized by a suitable choice of tax policies and borrowing. By an *allocation policy* we mean a choice of feasible time paths for consumption, private capital, and government capital. The government may also seek to control the volume of its public debt over time; in that case, we speak of an *allocation and debt policy*.

Although it is pointless to repeat all the results of this chapter here, the leading ideas can be restated. It is always assumed that the policies the government wishes to control are bounded, as defined by Boundedness Assumptions I–IV (see section VII.2 and section 7 above).

a) The need for taxes to enable controllability by the government can arise from any one of three causes: divergence between public and private values; the pricing of the services of government capital at a level different from the marginal productivity of private capital; and the historically conditioned initial volume of debt unless it happens to have one special critical value which depends on the future desired policy (see section 2).

b) Suppose that the government is restricted to one tax and borrowing as its instruments, but that there is no divergence between public and private values. Then the optimal policy can be controlled with stable instruments in any of the following ways: (1) an initial wealth transfer (in either direction) between the government and the private sector in proportion to income or to material assets to adjust the government debt to a certain level, after which all government investment and payment of interest on debt is financed solely by borrowing (Proposition 5; corollary to Proposition 7); (2) an initial wealth transfer from the government to the private sector in proportion to savings to raise the government debt to a certain critical level, after which all government investment and payment of interest on debt is financed solely by borrowing (Proposition 9); (3) a constant tax on consumption, the rate of which depends on the initial debt level among other factors, together with borrowing (Proposition 8); or (4) any of a wide variety of time paths of taxes on wages (Proposition 10).

c) Suppose that the government is restricted to one tax and borrowing as its instruments, but that there is a possible divergence between public and private values. Then the desired government policy can be controlled with stable instruments in any of the following ways: (1) an initial wealth transfer (in either direction) between the government and the private sector in proportion to income or to material assets to adjust the government debt to a certain critical level, followed by a tax on income or on interest income that exactly compensates for the difference between the consumption rate of interest in the private sector and the marginal productivity of private capital along the desired path (Propositions 6, 7); or (2) an initial wealth transfer from the government to the private sector in proportion to savings to raise the government debt to a certain critical level, after which the savings tax and borrowing follow a prescribed path (Proposition 9).

d) Suppose that the government is restricted to one tax and borrowing as its instruments. There is a possible divergence between public and private values at any instant of time, but the marginal productivity of private capital planned by the government approaches as a limit the rate at which the private sector discounts future utilities (no *futurity divergence*). Then, in addition to the controls specified in paragraph c, the desired policy can be controlled with stable instruments by a properly chosen consumption tax and borrowing (Proposition 8).

e) With one tax and borrowing, there are also possibilities for control with unstable instruments by taxes on consumption or savings (Propositions 8 and 9).

f) If the government can tax two of the four flows (consumption, savings, interest income, and wages) as well as borrow, then an allocation policy can be controlled with stable instruments in a variety of ways, though either savings or interest income must be included if there is futurity divergence (see corollary to Proposition 3, Remark 1 to Proposition 2).

g) Any given allocation and debt policy (including, for example, a policy of no borrowing) can be controlled by stable instruments by a tax on either wages or consumption plus a tax on either savings or interest income (Propositions 12, 13).

# BIBLIOGRAPHY

ABADIE, J. 1967. On the Kuhn-Tucker theorem. In *Nonlinear programming*, ed. J. Abadie, pp. 21–36. Amsterdam: North-Holland.

ALLAIS, M. 1947. *Economie et intérêt*. Paris: Imprimerie Nationale.

ARROW, K. J. 1962. The economic implications of learning by doing. *Review of Economic Studies* 29:155–73.

———. 1964*a*. The role of securities in the optimal allocation of risk-bearing. *Review of Economic Studies* 31:91–96.

———. 1964*b*. Optimal capital policy, the cost of capital, and myopic decision rules. *Annals of the Institute of Statistical Mathematics* 16:21–30.

———. 1966. Discounting and public investment criteria. In *Water research*, ed. A. V. Kneese and S. C. Smith, pp. 13–32. Baltimore: The Johns Hopkins Press for Resources for the Future.

———. 1968. Optimal capital policy with irreversible investment. In *Value, Capital and Growth*, ed. J. N. Wolfe, pp. 1–20. Edinburgh: Edinburgh University Press.

ARROW, K. J.; HURWICZ, L.; and UZAWA, H. 1961. Constraint qualifications in nonlinear programming. *Naval Research Logiotics Quarterly* 8:175–91.

ARROW, K. J., and KURZ, M. 1969. Optimal public investment policy and controllability with fixed private savings ration. *Journal of Economic Theory* 1:141–77.

———. 1970. Optimal growth with irreversible investment in a Ramsey model. *Econometrica* 38:333–46.

ARROW, K. J. and LIND, R. C. 1970. Uncertainty and the evaluation of public investment decisions. *American Economic Review* 60.

BECKER, G. 1965. *Human capital: A theoretical and empirical inquiry*. New York: National Bureau of Economic Research, Inc.

BELLMAN, R. 1953. *Stability theory of differential equations*. New York, Toronto, and London: McGraw-Hill.

———. 1957. *Dynamic programming.* Princeton, N. J.: Princeton University Press.

BELLMAN, R., and DREYFUS, S. 1962. *Applied dynamic programming.* Princeton, N. J.: Princeton University Press.

DEBREU, G. 1959. *Theory of value.* New York: Wiley and Sons.

DESROUSSEAUX, J. 1961. Expansion stable et taux d'intérêt optimal. *Annales des Mines*, pp. 829–44.

DOMAR, E. D. 1946. Capital expansion, rate of growth, and employment. *Econometrica* 14:137–47.

DREYFUS, S. 1965. *Dynamic programming and the calculus of variations.* New York and London: Academic Press.

DURAND, D. 1957. Growth stocks and the St. Petersburg paradox. *Journal of Finance* 12:348–63.

ECKSTEIN, O. 1957. Investment criteria for economic development and the theory of intertemporal welfare economics. *Quarterly Journal of Economics* 71:56–85.

———. 1958. *Water resource development.* Cambridge, Mass.: Harvard University Press.

EVANS, G. C. 1930. *Mathematical introduction to economics.* New York: McGraw-Hill.

FISHER, I. 1930. *The theory of interest.* New Haven, Conn.: Yale University Press.

FRIEDMAN, M. 1957. *A theory of the consumption function.* New York: National Bureau of Economic Research, Inc.

———. 1963. Windfalls, the "horizon," and related concepts in the permanent-income hypothesis. In *Measurement in economics,* by C. Christ and others, pp. 3-28. Stanford, Calif.: Stanford University Press.

FRISCH, R. 1964. Dynamic utility. *Econometrica* 32:418–24.

GALE, D. 1967. Optimal development in a multi-sector economy. *Review of Economic Studies* 34:1–18.

GALE D., and NIKAIDÔ, H. 1965. The Jacobian matrix and global univalence of mappings. *Mathematische Annalen* 159:81–93.

GORMAN, W. M. 1957. Convex indifference curves and diminishing marginal utility. *Journal of Political Economy* 65:40–50.

HAAVELMO, T. 1960. *A study in the theory of investment.* Chicago: University of Chicago Press.

HAHN, F. H., and MATTHEWS, R. C. O. 1964. The theory of economic growth: a survey. *Economic Journal* 74:779–902.

HALKIN, H. 1964. On the necessary conditions for optimal control of nonlinear systems. *Journal d'analyse mathématique* 12:1–82.

Hamburger, W. 1955. The relation of consumption to wealth and the wage rate. *Econometrica* 23:1–17.

Harrod, R. F. 1937. Review of Joan Robinson's *Essays in the theory of employment*. *Economic Journal* 47:326–30.

———. 1939. An essay in dynamic theory. *Economic Journal* 49:14–33.

Hicks, J. R. 1932. *The theory of wages*. London: Macmillan, 1932.

———. 1946. *Value and capital*. 2nd ed. Oxford: Clarendon Press.

Hirshleifer, J. 1964. Efficient allocation of capital in an uncertain world. *American Economic Review Papers and Proceedings* 54:77–85.

Hirshleifer, J.; De Haven, J. C.; and Milliman, J. W. 1960. *Water supply: economics, technology, and policy*. Chicago: University of Chicago Press.

Hotelling, H. 1931. The economics of exhaustible resources. *Journal of Political Economy* 39:137–75.

Kaldor, N. 1955. *An expenditure tax*. London: George Allen and Unwin.

Kalman, R. 1963. The theory of optimal control and the calculus of variations. In *Mathematical optimization techniques,* ed. R. Bellman, pp. 309–31. Berkeley and Los Angeles: University of California Press.

Keynes, J. M. 1936. *The general theory of employment, interest, and money*. New York: Harcourt, Brace.

Koopmans, T. C. 1960. Stationary ordinal utility and impatience. *Econometrica* 28:287–309.

———. 1965. On the concept of optimal economic growth. In Study Week on *The econometric approach to development planning,* pp. 225–87. Amsterdam: North-Holland.

———. 1968. Representation of preference orderings over time. In "Structure of preference over time," by T. C. Koopmans. Cowles Foundation Discussion Paper No. 206-Revised, Cowles Foundation for Research in Economics at Yale University. To appear as Chapter 4 in *Decision and organization,* ed. C. B. McGuire and R. Radner.

Koopmans, T. C.; Diamond, P. A; and Williamson, R. E. 1964. Stationary utility and time perspective. *Econometrica* 32:82–100.

Kuhn, H. W., and Tucker, A. W. 1951. Non-linear programming. In *Proceedings of the second Berkeley symposium on mathematical statistics and probability,* ed. J. Neyman, pp. 481–92. Berkeley and Los Angeles: University of California Press.

Kurz, M. 1963. Substitution vs. fixed production coefficients: A comment. *Econometrica* 31:209–17.

———. 1968*a*. Optimal economic growth and wealth effects. *International Economic Review* 9:348–57.

———. 1968*b*. The general instability of a class of competitive growth processes. *Review of Economic Studies* 35(2):155–74.

Levhari, D. 1966. Extensions of Arrow's "Learning by doing." *Review of Economic Studies* 29:155–73.

LEVHARI, D., and SHESHINSKI, E. 1969. A theorem on returns to scale and steady state growth. *Journal of Political Economy* 77:60–65.

LIND, R. C. 1964. The social rate of discount and the optimal rate of investment: Further comment. *Quarterly Journal of Economics* 78:336–45.

MANGASARIAN, O. L. 1966. Sufficient conditions for the optimal control of nonlinear systems. *SIAM Journal on Control* 4:139–52.

MARGLIN, S. A. 1963*a*. *Approaches to dynamic investment planning*. Amsterdam, North-Holland.

———. 1963*b*. The social rate of discount and the optimal rate of investment. *Quarterly Journal of Economics* 77:95–111.

———. 1963*c*. The opportunity costs of public investment. *Quarterly Journal of Economics* 77:275–89.

MASSÉ, P. 1946. *Les réserves et la régulation de l'avenir*. Paris: Herman.

MEADE, J. E. 1955. *Trade and welfare: The theory of international economic policy*. London, New York, and Toronto: Oxford University Press.

MIRRLEES, J. 1967. Optimum growth when technology is changing. *Review of Economic Studies* 34:95–124.

MODIGLIANI, F., and BRUMBERG, R. 1954. Utility analysis and the consumption function: An interpretation of cross-section data. Chapter 15 in *Post-Keynesian economics,* ed. K. K. Kurihara, pp. 388–436. New Brunswick, N. J.: Rutgers University Press.

OKAMOTO, T., and INADA, K. 1962. A note on the theory of economic growth. *Quarterly Journal of Economics* 76:503–7.

PHELPS, E. S. 1961. The golden rule of accumulation: A fable for growthmen. *American Economic Review* 51:638–43.

———. 1965. *Fiscal neutrality toward economic growth.* New York: McGraw-Hill.

PIGOU, A. C. 1952. *The economics of welfare.* 4th ed. London: Macmillan.

PONTRYAGIN, L. S.; BOLTYANSKII, V. G.; GAMKRELIDZE, R. V.; and MISCHENKO, E. F. 1962. *The mathematical theory of optimal processes.* New York and London: Interscience.

RAMSEY, F. P. 1928. A mathematical theory of saving. *Economic Journal* 38: 543–59.

———. 1931. *The foundations of mathematics and other logical essays.* London: Routledge and Kegan Paul.

RISHEL, R. W. 1965. An extended Pontryagin principle for control systems whose control laws contain measures. *Journal of the Society for Industrial and Applied Mathematics on Control* 3:191–205.

ROBINSON, J. 1937–38. The classification of inventions. *Review of Economic Studies* 5:139–42.

———. 1962. A neo-classical theorem. *Review of Economic Studies* 29:219–26.

SAMUELSON, P. A. 1947. *The foundations of economic analysis*. Cambridge, Mass.: Harvard University Press.

SEN, A. K. 1961. On optimizing the rate of saving. *Economic Journal* 71:479–96.

SOLOW, R. M. 1956. A contribution to the theory of economic growth. *Quarterly Journal of Economics* 70:65–94.

———. 1963. *Capital theory and the rate of return*. Amsterdam: North-Holland.

STEINER, P. 1959. Choosing among alternative public investments. *American Economic Review* 49:893–916.

SWAN, T. 1956. Economic growth and capital accumulation. *Economic Record* 32:334-61.

———. 1964. Growth models: Of golden ages and production functions. In *Economic development with special reference to East Asia,* ed. K. Berrill, pp. 3–16. London and New York: Macmillan and St. Martin's Press.

TINBERGEN, J. 1952. *On the theory of economic policy*. Amsterdam: North-Holland.

TULLOCK, G. 1964. The social rate of discount and the optimal rate of investment: Comment. *Quarterly Journal of Economics* 78:331–36.

UZAWA, H. 1961. Neutral inventions and the stability of growth equilibrium. *Review of Economic Studies* 28:117–24.

———. 1966. An optimum fiscal policy in an aggregate model of economic growth. In *The theory and design of economic development,* ed. I. Adelman and E. Thorbecke, pp. 113–39. Baltimore: The Johns Hopkins Press.

VIND, K. 1967. Control systems with jumps in the state variables. *Econometrica* 35:273–77.

VON WEIZSÄCKER, C. C. 1962. *Wachstum, Zins und optimale Investitionsquote*. Basel and Tübingen: Kyklos-Verlag, Basel; J. C. B. Mohn (Paul Siebeck), Tübingen.

WARGA, J. 1966. Variational problems with unbounded controls. *Journal of the Society for Industrial and Applied Mathematics on Control* 3:424–38.

YAARI, M. E. 1964*a*. On the consumer's lifetime allocation process. *International Economic Review* 5:304–17.

———. 1964*b*. On the existence of an optimal plan in a continuous-time allocation process. *Econometrica* 32:576–90.

# INDEX